MASQUERADE
AND
GENDER

MASQUERADE AND GENDER

Disguise and Female Identity in Eighteenth-Century Fictions by Women

Catherine Craft-Fairchild

THE PENNSYLVANIA STATE UNIVERSITY PRESS
University Park, Pennsylvania

Library of Congress Cataloging-in-Publication Data

Craft-Fairchild, Catherine.
Masquerade and gender : disguise and female identity in eighteenth-century fictions by women / Catherine Craft-Fairchild.
p. cm.
Includes bibliographical references and index.
ISBN 0-271-00918-7 — ISBN 0-271-00919-5 (pbk.)
1. English fiction—Women authors—History and criticism.
2. Women and literature—Great Britain—History—18th century.
3. English fiction—18th century—History and criticism.
4. Femininity (Psychology) in literature. 5. Identity (Psychology) in literature. 6. Sex role in literature. 7. Disguise in literature. I. Title.
PR858.W6C73 1993
823′.5099287—dc20 92-30851
CIP

Published by The Pennsylvania State University Press,
Barbara Building, Suite C, University Park, PA 16802-1003

It is the policy of The Pennsylvania State University Press to use acid-free paper for the first printing of all clothbound books. Publications on uncoated stock satisfy the minimum requirements of American National Standard for Information Sciences—Permanence of Paper for Printed Library Materials, ANSI Z39.48–1984.

To Daniel,
my heart's home

Contents

Acknowledgments ix

1 Introduction 1

2 Aphra Behn's *The Dumb Virgin* and Mary Davys's *The Accomplished Rake:* The Darker Side of Masquerade 23

3 Eliza Haywood and the Masquerade of Femininity 51

4 Elizabeth Inchbald's Not So Simple Story 75

5 Feminine Excess: Frances Burney's *The Wanderer* 123

Conclusion 163

Bibliography 175

Index 185

Acknowledgments

I wish to express my gratitude to the many friends and colleagues who helped make this book a reality. I have profited greatly from the scholarly expertise of Paula Backscheider, who asked me provocative questions that enabled me to rethink and reformulate my critical positions on women's writing. Bette London's extensive commentaries on and warm supportiveness of my early work spurred much of the rewriting.

The early mentorship of three beloved friends has influenced and will continue to shape what I write, how I teach, and who I am. Warmest thanks to Paul Dowling, Ben Fiore, and Frank Riga.

A Bucknell University Summer Research Grant and a Rotary International Foundation Fellowship offered financial support for this work. The latter enabled me to study, teach, and conduct research in England for a semester. The University of St. Thomas allowed me that semester of leave time and has also been liberal in its support of my conference travel, seminar attendance, and ongoing research. A course release from the Department of English helped me to see the book through production.

I am continually grateful to the dedicated faculty at St. Thomas for demonstrating and encouraging good teaching and scholarship. The following colleagues, in particular, have been wonderfully generous in their willingness to read and discuss my work: Michael Bellamy, Luann Dummer, Michael Jordan, Kelli Larson, Michael Mikolajczak, Brenda Powell, Thomas Redshaw, Don Rignalda, Robert Wellisch, and Gale Yee. Kelli Larson and Michael Mikolajczak deserve special thanks for bringing to my life their own endearing eccentricities and deep joyfulness.

Finally, I thank my husband, Daniel Fairchild, to whom this book is dedicated. His steady love and unflinching support may help me someday to become the person he already believes me to be.

Chapter One

Introduction

I

In *The Masquerade, A Poem. Inscribed to C—T H—D—G—R.* (1728), Henry Fielding rehearses the several dangers of the eighteenth-century diversion known as the masked assembly. His poem illustrates how the adoption of disguises allows those in attendance freedoms and excesses of behavior that they would not customarily enjoy. For example, costumes hide the anatomical distinctions that permit guests to be categorized as males and females; Fielding asks, "For when men women turn—why then / May women not be chang'd to men?" (ll. 131–32).[1] Even more urgently, Fielding wonders, "how from another woman / Do you [a] strumpet masqu'd distinguish?" (ll. 198–99)—masquerade disguise obliterates the marks of dress that separate virgin from whore. The consequences to be feared from such promiscuous blending, Fielding insists, are dire; venereal disease, for example, is the contagion obtained from illicit sexual liaison:

> The lover, who has now possess'd,
> From unknown Flora, his request;
> (Who with a pretty, modest grace,
> Discover'd all things but her face:)
> Pulls off her masque in am'rous fury,

1. Henry Fielding, *The Masquerade, A Poem. Inscribed to C—T H—D—G—R.* (London: J. Roberts and A. Dodd, 1728), n.p.

And finds a gentle nymph of Drury,
Curses his lust—laments his fate,
And kicks her out of bed too late.
(ll. 375–82)

In the world of Fielding's poem, upper-class men suffer the ill effects of the mingling of classes and sexes. In the absence of the markers that divide human beings into categories, the privileged class and gender lose their customary prerogatives.

Terry Castle's study *Masquerade and Civilization: The Carnivalesque in Eighteenth-Century English Culture and Fiction* (1986) traces the history of the masked assembly and explores the function of masquerade scenes in several novels of the period. Castle views as positive those very elements of the masquerade that Fielding abhorred. Working in part from Mikhail Bakhtin's discussion of the carnivalesque in *Rabelais and His World,* Castle celebrates eighteenth-century masquerade as "a World Upside-Down" and insists that "the masquerade threatens patriarchal structures. . . . 'for a brief moment,' perhaps no longer than its own duration, the masquerade effected an ecstatic liberation from the burdens of structure and hierarchy."[2] In writing about this "highly visible public institution," Castle emphasizes its power to disrupt but neglects to stress that, to the extent that masquerade assemblies were tolerated, they had to conform in some ways to the dominant culture.[3] Castle's bias colors her readings both of historical detail and of fiction: for instance, Castle writes that the dragoons who lined the walls of Heidegger's assemblies "marked off . . . a physical and symbolic boundary. They represented a self-conscious attempt on Heidegger's part to maintain a separation—between inside and outside, between paying customers and riffraff, and between the space of privileged license and the surrounding inchoate, potentially disruptive urban scene."[4] Castle reads the dragoons as preventing those "outside" from coming "inside"; the line of soldiers, however, equally prevented the excesses

2. Terry Castle, *Masquerade and Civilization: The Carnivalesque in Eighteenth-Century English Culture and Fiction* (Stanford, Calif.: Stanford University Press, 1986), 125, 88.

3. Ibid., 2. In *Rabelais and His World,* trans. Helene Iswolsky (Bloomington: Indiana University Press, 1984), Bakhtin acknowledges that the carnival was "tolerated and even legalized. . . . All of it was consecrated by tradition and, to a certain extent, tolerated by the Church" (9, 14).

4. Castle, *Masquerade and Civilization,* 27–28.

allowed inside from spilling over and infecting the outside community. While Castle does admit the possibility that masquerades could function "as safety valves that reaffirm the status quo by exorcising social tensions," her interpretation of the event as subversive continually negates this point of view.[5]

I certainly do not wish to dismiss Castle's important work. *Masquerade and Civilization* offers ground-breaking, careful scholarly research of a fascinating subject and insightful analysis of both canonical and noncanonical texts. I would assert, however, that Castle's efforts to interpret the masquerade as "a feminocracy . . . a gynesium—a realm pervaded by female desire, authority, and influence"[6] are problematical. While antimasquerade writers like Fielding feared that the entertainment encouraged the development of an "Amazonian race" (l. 130) and attacked it for allowing too much power and freedom to women, female authors often mistrusted such claims. Women perceived the ways in which the masquerade conformed to patriarchal structures; in their writing, they attempted to outline how its apparent freedoms were frequently nothing more than sophisticated forms of oppression. Again, Castle admits complexity: "women novelists of the eighteenth century do not necessarily render this feminine utopia [offered by the masquerade] in an unconflicted way."[7] In her discussion of Frances Burney's *Cecilia,* however, Castle elides the difficulties and writes that the masked assembly is for the heroine a "masquerade triumph":

> The utopian aspect of the [masquerade] scene is revealed most strikingly in its obsessive spectacles of homage. For Cecilia the Harrels' party is a festival of celebration, in which she is at the center of an effusive and ever-growing throng of sycophants. . . .
>
> . . . Though Cecilia feels self-conscious, her situation is unmistakably similar to that of narcissistic fantasy. . . .
>
> . . . The heroine's admirers perform a kind of ritual theater of submission in her presence. . . .
>
> . . . She seems passive, "imprisoned" by her admirers, but they are in fact her slaves.[8]

5. Ibid., 88.
6. Ibid., 254.
7. Ibid., 258.
8. Ibid., 270, 271, 273, 274, 282.

In the masquerade scene of Burney's novel, Cecilia does not merely *seem* imprisoned by her admirers—she actually is confined as she submits to "the torment of *three guardians*" (112).[9] The "devil," Monckton, for example, places her in "captivity" while retaining "all authority in his own hands" (103–4). Cecilia enters without a disguise and is "far more conspicuous in being almost the only female in a common dress, than any masquerade habit could have made her" (102). The masquerade, rather than a narcissistic fantasy, seems a painful submission of the woman to male scopophilia: "Cecilia now became seriously uneasy; for she was made an object of general attention, yet could neither speak nor be spoken to" (107). Objectified and mute, the "truth" or reality against which the male masqueraders define themselves, Cecilia is spectacle rather than spectator. When rescued by the white domino, Cecilia insists, "I was so tired of confinement, that my mind seemed almost as little at liberty as my person" (108). The masquerade in Burney's text, contrary to Castle's interpretation, denies Cecilia the power of choice and offers her as the one who is chosen and made compliant to the desires of the men who surround her; her masquerade is submission to, not subversion of, the dominant economy.

Female masquerade, I would argue, must be theorized differently from male masquerade. Mary Anne Schofield's *Masking and Unmasking the Female Mind: Disguising Romances in Feminine Fiction, 1713–1799* (1990) attempts to do this: it specifically addresses the subject of masquerade in eighteenth-century narratives by women. Schofield's study suffers, however, from her essentialist approach; she writes, for example,

> Feminine stories and masculine plots do, indeed, exist. . . .
>
> It is my purpose here to uncover the "two plots" of the minor fiction of the eighteenth century by examining the disguises the female romancers-novelists employ. . . .
>
> . . . As her heroines put on a different self and reveal other selves heretofore hidden from public view, so the novelist herself can express her own anger and frustration at the female condition through her adoption of the disguising romance. Barker, Davys, Haywood, Fielding, Smith, Inchbald, and the others engage in a process of double writing. Not content merely to adopt a masquerade technique in terms of their female protagonists, these

9. Frances Burney, *Cecilia; or, Memoirs of an Heiress* (1782), introd. Judy Simons (New York: Penguin Books, 1986).

> novelists use the cover story of their romance plots to mask their own feminist, aggressive intentions and to unmask the facile and fatuous fictions they are supposed to be writing as members of the weaker sex. Thus, the novelist appears to be telling a fashionable tale of love and romance but is actually presenting a vivid picture of the exploitation and frustration of her sex in the eighteenth century.[10]

Schofield's attempt to separate strands of narrative into "male" and "female" plots assumes the existence of universal, transhistorical sexual identities. It is not at all clear on what basis Schofield decides that women would read these texts one way, men another. Furthermore, while Schofield usefully resurrects many largely neglected works, her uncovering of subversive counterplots in women's fictions fails to produce readings that challenge the underlying terms of representation itself or question essentialist notions of gender. To offer counterideology is not to subvert ideology; simple role reversals that do not question the roles themselves cannot finally produce lasting change. Moreover, by ignoring the ways in which writing by women often upheld or promoted ideologies of female inferiority and subservience, Schofield misses the opportunity of examining women's complicity in the construction of eighteenth-century femininity. Instead, Schofield assumes that each woman writer wished to be as feminist as she possibly could, self-censoring her radical views only to allow her works to gain public acceptance.

In the chapters that follow, I reconsider the masquerade as it appears in the fictions of a selection of Restoration and eighteenth-century women writers. The texts that I have chosen—Aphra Behn's *The Dumb Virgin; or, The Force of Imagination* (1700), Mary Davys's *The Accomplished Rake; or, Modern Fine Gentleman* (1727), Eliza Haywood's *The Masqueraders: or, Fatal Curiosity* (I, 1724; II, 1725), *Fantomina: or, Love in a Maze* (1724), and *The City Jilt; or, The Alderman Turn'd Beau* (1726), Elizabeth Inchbald's *A Simple Story* (1791), and Frances Burney's *The Wanderer; or, Female Difficulties* (1814)—are similar only in that each contains a masquerade scene or a significant instance of disguise. I have made no effort to be exhaustive—have not, in other words, attempted to provide a comprehensive assess-

10. Mary Anne Schofield, *Masking and Unmasking the Female Mind: Disguising Romances in Feminine Fiction, 1713–1799* (Newark: University of Delaware Press, 1990), 9–10, 24.

ment of the subject of masquerade in eighteenth-century women's writing. Although I do reread several texts discussed by Schofield and Castle, I am not, like them, writing literary history or reconstructing the cultural history of masquerade. My purpose is more limited in scope: I wish to analyze the relationship of masquerade to the construction of femininity in eighteenth-century fiction by women and have selected texts for extended discussion that most effectively and efficiently exemplify my central arguments. Three of the narratives, for example, trace gender formation during childhood: Behn's *The Dumb Virgin* and Davys's *The Accomplished Rake* examine the construction of masculinity through mother/son relationships, while Inchbald's *A Simple Story* treats the formation of femininity within father/daughter unions. Haywood's three fictions and Burney's *The Wanderer* posit a psychological double-sidedness to masquerade; readings of these works counter any straightforward celebration of masquerade as a female-dominated sphere. Inchbald's *A Simple Story* explores female masquerade through an art of compression, a speaking through the blanks and gaps of discourse, while Burney's *The Wanderer* develops through excess, overwriting, and mimicry. Similar concerns are addressed in each chapter as they are refracted by varied textual prisms; my effort throughout is to balance one reading with another, one text with another, to avoid oversimplifications and to allow female masquerade to remain problematic.

In exploring the constructedness of gender identity, I have had recourse throughout to psychoanalytic theories. In their introductory essay to *The New Eighteenth Century: Theory, Politics, English Literature,* Felicity Nussbaum and Laura Brown discuss "the resistance to contemporary theory that has largely characterized the study of eighteenth-century English literature."[11] Psychoanalysis, in particular, has been perceived by scholars as ahistorical and anachronistic. The difficulties of combining transhistorical theory with historical contextualization—what Nussbaum and Brown refer to as "an historicized psychoanalysis"[12]—are undeniable; carefully and intelligently applied, however, psychoanalytic theories offer what are perhaps the most useful conceptual models for an analysis of sexual difference and, in particular, for an understanding of the precariousness

11. Felicity Nussbaum and Laura Brown, "Revising Critical Practices: An Introductory Essay," in *The New Eighteenth Century: Theory, Politics, English Literature* (New York: Methuen, 1987), 1.

12. Ibid., 18.

of female sexual and social identity. Psychoanalysis posits "feminine" and "masculine" as psychical rather than biological categories, cultural constructions rather than essential oppositions. The questions addressed by psychoanalytic theories—those of representation, subjectivity, spectatorship, and gender identity—are the same questions raised by masquerade. My effort is to trace the points of intersection, to regard masquerade as the creation of an image or spectacle for the benefit of a spectator, and to explore the distance or proximity between the representation and the self beneath in order to determine the significance of the masked moment in fiction.

II

The women's fictions I have chosen to examine group themselves into two chronological clusters: the first five works come from the late Restoration and early eighteenth century, while the last two were published in the late eighteenth and early nineteenth centuries, respectively. Several critics, in studies of the early novel, have drawn attention to a shift in women's fiction that takes place around the middle of the eighteenth century. What this shift is and what it might mean to the study of gender construction must be explored; the sustained readings of masquerade texts in the chapters that follow should be set within the context of recent scholarship on women's writing.

In *The Rise of the Woman Novelist,* Jane Spencer describes a contrast between the earlier women writers, such as Aphra Behn, Mary Davys, and Eliza Haywood, who saw themselves as men's antagonists and who insisted on explicit treatment of the subject of female sexual desire, and later women writers, including Elizabeth Inchbald and Frances Burney, who earned respectability by promulgating a new ideology of modest femininity. Spencer writes of a "change in the literary market," saying that "as the eighteenth century advanced the 'feminine' qualities of delicacy and propriety became more generally important to bourgeois society. Women writers, because they could be taken as representatives of these central values, became more acceptable, but also more restricted."[13] Spencer

13. Jane Spencer, *The Rise of the Woman Novelist: From Aphra Behn to Jane Austen* (Oxford: Basil Blackwell, 1986), 76, 75.

traces the importance of Samuel Richardson in helping "to create the climate in which they [women novelists] would be accepted"—only, however, if they conformed to Richardson's "exemplary morality."[14] J. Paul Hunter insists that "the new species" of writing, the novel, "had established . . . a distinctive character . . . by the 1750s in the wake of Fielding and Richardson,"[15] while Patricia Meyer Spacks, in her most recent book, *Desire and Truth,* implies a division of the period by beginning her study of "the working out of sexual assumptions in novelistic plots" at 1740.[16] Janet Todd, in *The Sign of Angellica,* is most explicit:

> Because of my view of the development of women's fiction I have divided my study into three parts, the first dealing with the Restoration and early eighteenth century, a period of considerable frankness in writing when the status of female fiction remained dubious; the second dealing with the mid-eighteenth century, when sentimentalism and the cult of sensibility flourished, giving a new respectable image and restricted subject matter to the woman writer; and thirdly the last two decades, in which there is in part a reaction to this restriction and in part a conscious and public embracing of it.[17]

As the literary climate changed from the Restoration to the beginning of the nineteenth century, so did women's fictional portrayals of female and male sexual relationships. In a brief overview of several female fictions created during this period, I will attempt to trace some of those transformations in the representation of sexuality that form the background to my study of masquerade and gender.

In many works that grew under their pens, the earlier women writers seemed to equate the two halves of their love plots. The male half was portrayed as undeniably predatory, rapaciously desiring, and endlessly erect. Aphra Behn insists that "it is now too much the Nature of that inconstant Sex, to cease to love as soon as they are sure of the Conquest"

14. Ibid., 89–90.

15. J. Paul Hunter, *Before Novels: The Cultural Contexts of Eighteenth-Century English Fiction* (New York: W. W. Norton, 1990), 22.

16. Patricia Meyer Spacks, *Desire and Truth: Functions of Plot in Eighteenth-Century English Novels* (Chicago: University of Chicago Press, 1990), 6.

17. Janet Todd, *The Sign of Angellica: Women, Writing and Fiction, 1660–1800* (New York: Columbia University Press, 1989), 3.

(370).[18] She shows this borne out by several of her heroes, such as Don Henrique of *The Nun; or, The Perjur'd Beauty* (1698), who betrays both his former mistress and his best friend to obtain the faithless Ardelia. Eliza Haywood's "charming Rover" Dorimenus, in *The Masqueraders: or, Fatal Curiosity* (I, 1724; II, 1725), is "a passionate Lover of Intrigue" (I.5) who manages to obtain and discard four women in succession in the course of the narrative.[19] "Few Men," insists Haywood, "how dull and stupid soever they appear in other things, but have Artifice enough this way" (I.9). Her "*Courtal* . . . *Lysander* . . . [or] the too lovely, faithless, *Bellamy*" (135) in *The British Recluse* (1722) has more artifice than most.[20] Amazingly amorous, "inconstant, changing, and hunting after Pleasure in every Shape" (13) and "too *Base* not to make use of any means, which might give him the gratification of his Wishes" (129), Bellamy, in his various personas, seduces one mistress and drives her to attempt suicide by his inconstancy (85); entices another woman away from her betrothed (113); obtains a wife and then presses her to attend a play with him in company with his latest conquest (123); with yet another woman "seek[s] by *Force,* to obtain what, he was now convinc'd, Entreaties wou'd for-ever fail to give him" (133); and finally is the cause for which two of his jilted lovers take "Resolutions of abandoning the World" (137) and living in seclusion. In Mary Davys's *The Accomplished Rake; or, Modern Fine Gentleman* (1727), Galliard is also quite "accomplished" in this way—his "darling diversion was intriguing, which he carried on with so much address that he had a mistress in almost every street in town" (304).[21] Galliard's desires, like that of most early heroes, "were always too sharp set to want a poignant sauce" (289).

If they depicted men as predatory and aggressive, the early women

18. Aphra Behn, *The Lucky Mistake* (1689), in *Oroonoko and Other Prose Narratives,* ed. Montague Summers (New York: Benjamin Blom, 1967). All references to Behn's fictions are to this edition.

19. Eliza Haywood, *The Masqueraders: or, Fatal Curiosity* (I, 1724; II, 1725), in *Masquerade Novels of Eliza Haywood,* ed. Mary Anne Schofield (Delmar, N.Y.: Scholars' Facsimiles & Reprints, 1986).

20. Eliza Haywood, *The British Recluse: or, The Secret History of Cleomira, Suppos'd Dead* (London: D. Browne, W. Chetwood, and S. Chapman, 1722). Spencer writes, "Lysander/Courtal/Bellamy . . . [is] the seducer of practically every women [*sic*] he meets . . . " (*Rise of the Woman Novelist,* 117).

21. Mary Davys, *The Accomplished Rake; or, Modern Fine Gentleman* (1727), in *Four Before Richardson: Selected English Novels, 1720–1727,* ed. William H. McBurney (Lincoln: University of Nebraska Press, 1963).

writers often compensated by creating "female rakes" who were equally amorous and belligerent. Miranda's high level of aggression causes Behn's *The Fair Jilt* (1688) to proceed by role-reversal—it is she who snatches a young friar who "could not defend himself from receiving a thousand Kisses from the lovely Mouth of the charming Wanton" (93). Behn's Isabella in *The History of the Nun; or, The Fair Vow-Breaker* (1689) obtains two husbands, then uses her skill in sewing to rid herself of both: she stitches the bag containing the husband she has already murdered to the collar of the husband she hopes to murder, thereby disposing of the two when the second attempts to throw the first into a swift-moving river (319). In *The Masqueraders,* Eliza Haywood equates male and female sexuality by calling her lovers "An amorous Pair with mutual Warmth inspir'd, / Alike desiring, and alike desir'd" (I.10). She shows this also to be the case in *Fantomina: or, Love in a Maze* (1724): her Fair Incognita is a clever match for the "all-conquering" Beauplaisir. By disguising and remaking herself into another woman every time her inconstant lover becomes satiated with his latest conquest, Fantomina "had all the Sweets of Love, but as yet had tasted none of the Gall" (277).[22] She thinks, "I have outwitted even the most Subtle of the deceiving Kind" (277), and "she could not forbear . . . applauding her own Strength of Genius, and Force of Resolution, which by such unthought-of Ways could triumph over her Lover's Inconstancy, and render that very Temper, which to other Women is the greatest Curse, a Means to make herself more bless'd" (283).

Female characters whose lovers' infidelity *was* a curse responded actively rather than passively to the injury. For the abandoned Glicera in Haywood's *The City Jilt; or, The Alderman Turn'd Beau* (1726), the "Memory of her Wrongs . . . left her not a Moment, and by degrees settled so implacable a hatred in her Nature, not only to *Melladore* [her faithless lover], but to that whole undoing Sex" (20).[23] Glicera "seem'd born only to give Torment to the whole Race of Man" (29), but she gives more torment to

22. Eliza Haywood, *Fantomina: or, Love in a Maze,* 2d ed. (1725), in *Masquerade Novels of Eliza Haywood.* In her article "Preparatives to Love: Seduction as Fiction in the Works of Eliza Haywood," Ros Ballaster notes that "Fantomina is the female equivalent to Haywood's male rakes, who assume a series of different identities to court their mistresses and avert the possibility of discovery" (in *Living by the Pen: Early British Women Writers,* ed. Dale Spender [New York: Teachers College Press, 1992], 60).

23. Eliza Haywood, *The City Jilt; or, The Alderman Turn'd Beau,* 2d ed. (London: J. Roberts, 1726).

Melladore than to others, for she manages to get his mortgage into her hands and thereby triumphs "in the ruin of his Fortune" (41). Even the comparatively shy Galesia in Jane Barker's *Love Intrigues: Or, The History of the Amours of Bosvil and Galesia* (1713) sends "a pretty Pair of Horns" (67)[24] to the lover who has deserted her to marry another.

The sexual freedom offered to women in these early works is in some ways illusory, however. The very term "female rake" privileges man as the norm, making woman a variation of that norm. The female protagonists in these texts effect role reversals, a sort of transvestism that leaves the foundational terms of representation intact. Furthermore, the woman's transgressiveness is usually contained and controlled at the end of the narrative through her confinement, exile, or death. Miranda in Behn's *Fair Jilt* is sent to Holland, where she remains "very penitent for her Life past" (124), while Isabella, *The Fair Vow-Breaker,* is condemned to destruction: "the Executioner, at one Blow, sever'd her Beautiful Head from her Delicate Body" (324). Haywood's Fantomina is sent to a French convent and Glicera remains a spinster, as does Barker's Galesia (although the extent to which these are "punishments" is certainly debatable). The female rake of *The British Recluse,* Melissa, a woman "the most intreaguing upon Earth" who "cou'd not hear of a Man fam'd for any Perfection, without desiring to engage him" (55), experiences a fate far more miserable than the exile chosen by the more modest seduced heroines: " . . . her Husband . . . as a just Reward for her Infidelity, entirely cast her off . . . she was now reduc'd to . . . wretched Circumstances . . . she was become one of the most expos'd and unpitied Women in the World . . . [left] to all the Miseries which attend a common Prostitution" (68).

The explicit sexuality that Behn, Haywood, Davys, and other early women writers built their romantic fictions upon was no longer possible later in the eighteenth century, as the growing emphasis on moral instruction and sentimentality banished licentiousness and ribaldry from the novel. Heroines in particular had to be chaste and pure. At the end of the century, Mary Wollstonecraft would complain that "heroines . . . are to be born immaculate, and to act like goddesses of wisdom, just come forth highly finished Minervas from the head of Jove" (21).[25] Such a one, for

24. Jane Barker, *Love Intrigues: Or, The History of the Amours of Bosvil and Galesia* (London: E. Curll and C. Crownfield, 1713).

25. Mary Wollstonecraft, *Maria, or The Wrongs of Woman* (1798), ed. Moira Ferguson (New York: W. W. Norton, 1975).

example, is Charlotte Smith's Monimia in *The Old Manor House* (1794): described repeatedly as an "angel," Monimia is banished, for much of the text, to an "apartment . . . in the turret that terminated one wing of the house . . . [and] had only one high long window in a very thick wall. . . . narrow as it was, the small square of the casement that opened was secured by iron bars" (25–26).[26] Needless to say, it is the hero Orlando, not the confined damsel, who engages in the adventures that make up the bulk of this novel.

If heroines were to be perfectly virtuous, static, and consigned to sexual passivity, one would expect that the heroes in the later women's novels would have to provide the active libido necessary if the love plot was to achieve consummation. Generally, however, this is not the case: women writers, no longer authorized to author female rakes, equated their heroines and heroes by feminizing the latter. Jane Spencer comments that "the unification of feeling and morality which was at the heart of [late-century] sentimental philosophy was also a characteristic of femininity as the eighteenth century defined it; and the true 'man of feeling' was therefore seen as 'feminine.'"[27] She cites Edward Rivers in Frances Brooke's *The History of Emily Montague* (1769), whose "heart has all the sensibility of woman," and the timid Henry Mandeville in Brooke's *Lady Julia Mandeville* as well as Elizabeth Griffith's subdued Charles Evelyn in *Lady Juliana Harley.*[28] To these can be added Montague De Courcy from Mary Brunton's *Self-Control* (1810/11); endowed with "feminine gentleness" and an "almost womanly modesty," De Courcy retreats from the woman he wishes to pursue, and "if she accidentally touched him, he coloured and drew back" (122, 125–26).[29]

In her introduction to *Men by Women,* Janet Todd also draws attention to the "common habit of female writers—the feminizing of men, either to master them and take [a]way their otherness or to soften their patriarchal potential by allowing them qualities usually assumed to be female: gentleness, patience, and sensitivity."[30] In the essay that opens Todd's collection, "Dreams and Nightmares: Male Characters in the Feminine Novel of the Eighteenth Century," Katharine Rogers discusses at length several exam-

26. Charlotte Smith, *The Old Manor House* (1794), introd. Janet Todd (London: Pandora Press, 1987).

27. Spencer, *Rise of The Woman Novelist,* 77.

28. Ibid., 185.

29. Mary Brunton, *Self-Control* (1810/11) (London: Pandora Press, 1986).

30. Janet Todd, ed., *Men by Women* (New York: Holmes & Meier, 1981), 3.

ples of woman-centered, woman-authored heroes, among them Charles Glanville of Charlotte Lennox's *The Female Quixote* (1752),[31] David Simple of Sarah Fielding's *The Adventures of David Simple* (1744), and the aforementioned Orlando Somerive of Charlotte Smith's *The Old Manor House,* of whom Rogers writes:

> ... when women centered their novels on men, the heroes tend to be feminized: they lack distinctively masculine characteristics, they display the virtues valued in and by women, and they often play as passive a role as women were forced into by life and literature....
>
> ... [Orlando] is tenderly considerate, not only of Monimia, but of his mother and sisters, and ever mindful of his obligations to his family. His values are the traditionally feminine ones of private virtue and domestic happiness. He explicitly rejects ambition.[32]

While these three critics establish a convincing case for the feminization of the hero in later women's fiction of the period, they do not address the fact that "feminine" is a construction that exists in opposition to another construction, "masculine." For the hero to be "feminized," he must be such in relation to some other figure that completes the binary opposition.

"Masculine" power—active libido, appropriation of the desired object,

31. Charlotte Lennox's *The Female Quixote, or The Adventures of Arabella* (1752) and Eliza Haywood's *The History of Miss Betsy Thoughtless* (1751) seem to be somewhat transitional. Arabella's reading of romances and Betsy's coquetry are temporarily empowering—both heroines retain some of the energy of the earlier "female rakes" without sharing their moral impurity. The heroes of these texts, Mr. Glanville and Mr. Trueworth, are not completely "feminized"—the latter, in fact, is forgiven for having an illicit affair in terms similar to those used in earlier Haywood fictions: "He had, indeed, done no more than any man of his age and constitution would have done, if tempted in the manner he had been ..." (*Miss Betsy Thoughtless* [London: Pandora Press, 1986], 336).

32. Katharine M. Rogers, "Dreams and Nightmares: Male Characters in the Feminine Novel of the Eighteenth Century," in *Men by Women,* 10–11. In "Inhibitions on Eighteenth-Century Women Novelists: Elizabeth Inchbald and Charlotte Smith" (*Eighteenth-Century Studies* 11 [Fall 1977]), Rogers adds, "Orlando is good in the same way the heroines are good—he is gentle, considerate, ever mindful of his obligations to his family, willing to sacrifice his own interests or put aside his own concerns to help others ..." (76).

sexual aggression and violence—is not absent from the later women's novel; it is simply displaced. The dissolving of gender difference between lovers is coupled with an increased emphasis on the savagery of rivals and, more important, on the patriarchal tyranny of fathers. Many later women's novels are concerned with prohibitions; they are texts obsessed with revealing the forces that result in thwarted, balked, and frustrated female passion. In their depictions of oppressive fathers or father surrogates, these novels dwell upon what has come to be called the *law of the father* and portray masculine sexuality as a preference for law over love, female sexuality as desire for and submission to the father.[33]

The most complex working out of such prohibitions comes in Elizabeth Inchbald's deceptively titled *A Simple Story* (1791). An analysis of the defamiliarization of familial erotics in this novel forms the subject of Chapter 4. Suffice it to say here that in this work Dorriforth/Lord Elmwood becomes the location of all that is taboo and desirable both to his ward, Miss Milner, and to his daughter, Matilda. Matilda, in her efforts to identify with and gain access to the father who is forbidden to her, engages in the rejection of the mother that forms the necessary first step of such a process. Julia Kristeva writes about this Oedipal dilemma:

> In the second case, identification with the father, the girl . . . represses the vagina and the possibility of finding someone else as her partner. (This situation can come about, for instance, by refusing the male partner, [or] by feminizing the male partner. . . .)

33. The terms are Lacan's—see, for example, "Function and Field of Speech and Language," in *Écrits: A Selection,* trans. Alan Sheridan (New York: W. W. Norton, 1977): "It is in the *name of the father* that we must recognize the support of the symbolic function which, from the dawn of history, has identified his person with the figure of the law" (67). Spacks, in *Desire and Truth,* refers to women's narratives governed by an interest in the erotics of father-daughter or surrogate father-daughter relationships as "daughters' plots" (148). Spacks specifically examines the "daughters' plots" that shape the fictions of Ann Radcliffe (147–74). While Spacks is interested in fathers and daughters, Jane Spencer examines the other half of the family dynamic, mother-daughter relationships, in " 'Of Use to Her Daughter': Maternal Authority and Early Women Novelists" (in *Living by the Pen*). She explores fictional portrayals of mother-daughter plots as a paradigm for the woman author's own literary authority (202) and notes in passing that "the ideological pattern of many women's novels in the late-eighteenth century is that of a recurrent return to the Law of the Father, whether through the mediation of the mother's authority or by avoidance of the mother's example" (206).

> ...But the daughter, on the other hand, is rewarded by the symbolic order when she identifies with the father: only here is she recognized not as herself but in opposition to her rival, the mother with a vagina who experiences *jouissance.* Thus, at the price of censuring herself as a woman, she will be able to triumph in her henceforth sublimated sadistic attacks on the mother whom she has repressed and with whom she will always fight....
>
> ...Let *jouissance* be forbidden to the mother: this is the demand of the father's daughter, fascinated by the mother's *jouissance.*[34]

In the second half of *A Simple Story,* Matilda engages in an act of amnesia, blaming and obliterating her mother's memory as an obstacle to her pursuit of the father. Rushbrook, the suitor who desires Matilda, fuels the daughter's yearning for the father; Rushbrook is easily dismissed by Matilda because he is feminized in relation to that starkly "masculine," all-powerful Lord Elmwood, whose "will was a law all around" (221).[35] When Matilda weeps, for example, she is "somewhat surprised" to find that Rushbrook "had shed tears too" (239). Rushbrook's efforts at courtship are so timid that it remains uncertain, even at the end of Inchbald's text, whether or not he ever succeeds at becoming Matilda's lover.

A Simple Story offers the fullest portrayal of the submission of female desire to patriarchal law, but other fictions of the latter half of the eighteenth century and the early nineteenth century dwell upon this theme as well. Like Matilda and Rushbrook, both hero and heroine in Jane Austen's *Northanger Abbey* (1818) adopt subservient, powerless, "feminine" positions toward a powerful, oppressive father: General Tilney is "accustomed on every ordinary occasion to give the law in his family" (201),[36] and he attempts to legislate against his son's desire. Henry Tilney, the son who admits to having read "hundreds and hundreds" of novels "with great pleasure" and who prides himself on his knowledge of fabrics (82–83, 14), is a suitable match for the heroine, Catherine Morland; like her, he

34. Julia Kristeva, *About Chinese Women,* trans. Seán Hand, excerpted in *The Kristeva Reader,* ed. Toril Moi (Oxford: Basil Blackwell, 1986), 149–50, 152.

35. Elizabeth Inchbald, *A Simple Story* (1791), ed. J.M.S. Tompkins, introd. Jane Spencer (Oxford: Oxford University Press, 1988).

36. Jane Austen, *Northanger Abbey* (1818), with *Lady Susan, The Watsons,* and *Sanditon,* ed. John Davie, introd. Terry Castle (Oxford: Oxford University Press, 1990).

remains unequal to the task of violating his father's prohibitions until the final pages of Austen's work.

In the *Memoirs of Emma Courtney* (1796), Mary Hays's hero, Augustus Harley, functions as lawgiver. Late in the text, however, this austere mentor is miraculously transformed into the feminized lover, thus combining in one person the attributes of both a Lord Elmwood and a Rushbrook. The love plot in *Emma Courtney* is symbolically Oedipal: Emma Courtney regards Harley as a surrogate father, as "my preceptor. . . . He, from whom my mind had acquired knowledge" (79).[37] When she develops "a fatal and unutterable tenderness" (5) for him, the very terms she uses to plead her forbidden passion indicate her dependent position: "Must we, then, separate for ever—will you no longer assist me in the pursuit of knowledge and truth—will you no more point out to me the books I should read, and aid me in forming a just judgment of the principles they contain" (101).[38] Harley never wholly rejects but also never fully accepts Emma's repeated importunities—he continually refuses to admit that he is attached to anyone else and "left room for the illusions of fancy, and of hope" (105). Harley retains Emma and yet refuses to acknowledge her, actions that mirror Lord Elmwood's treatment of Matilda in Inchbald's novel. For most of the text Harley avoids Emma, but when he does see her he tyrannizes over her; Emma explains,

> At length he grew captious, disputatious, gloomy, and imperious—the more I studied to please him, the less I succeeded. He disapproved my conduct, my opinions, my sentiments; my frankness offended him. . . . In company, his manners were studiously

37. Mary Hays, *Memoirs of Emma Courtney* (1796) (London: Pandora Press, 1987).

38. Note that Emma's father defined himself as such before his death by performing this task for his daughter: "[Mr. Courtney] desired I might spend one day in every week at his house in Berkley-square, when he should put such books into my hands . . . as he judged would be useful to me; and, in the intervals of his various occupations and amusements, assist me himself with occasional remarks and reflections" (19). This is analogous to the only attention Lord Elmwood pays to his banished daughter: "Lord Elmwood . . . taking up each book, examined attentively what it was.—One author he complained was too light, another too depressing, and put them on the shelves again; another was erroneous and he changed it for a better; and thus he warned . . . against some, and selected other authors; as the most cautious preceptor culls for his pupil, or a fond father for his darling child. . . . [Miss Woodley] reasonably supposed Matilda's reading, and not hers, was the object of his solicitude" (272–73). Both passages emphasize the fathers' privileged relationship to and control of language and learning.

> cold and distant; in private capricious, yet reserved and guarded. He seemed to overlook all my efforts to please, and, with a severe and penetrating eye, to search only for my errors—errors, into which I was but too easily betrayed, by the painful, and delicate, situation, in which I had placed myself. (112)

"The girl's only way to redeem her personal value, and value in general," writes Luce Irigaray of the Oedipal dilemma, "would be to seduce the father, and persuade him to express, if not admit, some interest in her."[39] Hays's work ends with a fantastic, improbable deathbed confession in which Harley takes on a feminine position in relation to his former self and acknowledges his interest in Emma: "In these last moments— . . . when human institutions fade before my sight—I may, without a crime, tell you—*that I have loved you.*—Your tenderness early penetrated my heart—aware of its weakness—I sought to shun you—I imposed on myself those severe laws of which you causelessly complained.—Had my conduct been less rigid, I had been lost" (180). Stern lawgiver throughout the text, inflexible and remote, Harley dissolves at last and utters a speech worthy of any expiring heroine.

In loving Augustus Harley, Emma Courtney feels that she has "deviate[d] from the beaten track" (90). Another heroine who "strayed from the beaten road, only to discover that all others are pathless" (873), one who also loves a forbidden father substitute named Harleigh, is Elinor Joddrel of Frances Burney's *The Wanderer; or, Female Difficulties* (1814).[40] Fathers, real and surrogate, absent and present, loom large as subjects of Burney's work; issues of patrilineal identity and patriarchal law serve as a bar to desire in every novel. The climax that *Evelina* (1778) works toward is not so much the satisfaction of the wishes of gentle, polite Lord Orville as it is the troubling reunion of Lord Belmont with his daughter. The most impassioned speeches in the text are those delivered by Belmont when he confuses the daughter with her dead mother:

39. Luce Irigaray, *Speculum of the Other Woman,* trans. Gillian C. Gill (Ithaca: Cornell University Press, 1985), 87.

40. Frances Burney, *The Wanderer; or, Female Difficulties* (1814), ed. Margaret Anne Doody, Robert L. Mack, and Peter Sabor, introd. Margaret Anne Doody (Oxford: Oxford University Press, 1991). Albert Harleigh's initials are the same as those of Hays's hero, and his last name, though spelled differently, would be pronounced identically. Burney's Harleigh plays a role similar to that of the earlier Harley, serving as the "guardian" (366) or father substitute who refuses to respond to the passion of his "ward."

> . . . in a voice scarce articulate he exclaimed, "My God! does Caroline Evelyn still live!
>
> ". . . lift up thy head, thou image of my long-lost Caroline!
>
> ". . . she lives—she breathes—she is present to my view! . . . Go, child, go," added he, wildly starting, and pushing me from him, "take her away, Madam,—I cannot bear to look at her!" And then, breaking hastily [away] . . . he rushed out of the room.
>
> . . . [He cried,] "she has set my brain on fire, and I can see her no more!" Then, with violence almost frantic, he ran up stairs. (372–73)[41]

The scene is reminiscent of Lord Elmwood's accidental first meeting with Matilda in *A Simple Story.* When Lord Elmwood surprises her on the stairs, Matilda's "voice unmanned him.—His long-restrained tears now burst forth . . . he cried out. . . . Her name did not however come to his recollection—nor any name but this—'Miss Milner—Dear Miss Milner'. . . . [With] his face . . . agitated with shame, with pity, with anger, with paternal tenderness . . . her father went away" (274). Both scenes focus upon the father's conflation of his daughter with her mother and reveal at once his desire and repression of that desire.[42]

Even more than her earliest novel, Burney's last work, *The Wanderer,* hinges upon the name and law of the father. Irigaray writes, "It is his proper name, the name of the father, that determines ownership for the family, including the wife and children."[43] If the questions of "Who or what is her 'father'? What is her 'proper name'? [and] To whom does she belong?" are not "clearly settled, the only way to maintain the economy in

41. Frances Burney, *Evelina, or The History of a Young Lady's Entrance into the World* (1778), ed. Edward A. Bloom, with Lillian D. Bloom (Oxford: Oxford University Press, 1968).

42. For a discussion of Burney's emphasis on fathers in *Evelina,* see Mary Poovey, "Fathers and Daughters: The Trauma of Growing Up Female," in *Men by Women,* 39–47. Patricia Meyer Spacks draws attention to the eroticizing of Evelina's relationship to her foster father, Mr. Villars: "The vestigially erotic father-daughter (surrogate father-daughter) relationship contrasts with the de-eroticized connection of lovers. Lord Orville values Evelina for her 'modest worth and fearful excellence' and because she is 'informed, sensible, and intelligent. . . . The aristocrat's sexuality, like Evelina's, obscures itself behind a screen of propriety" (*Desire and Truth,* 147–48).

43. Luce Irigaray, *This Sex Which Is Not One,* trans. Catherine Porter, with Carolyn Burke (Ithaca: Cornell University Press, 1985), 83.

place is by rejecting the feminine."[44] In *The Wanderer,* Juliet remains outside the patriarchal system because she has no surname. The heroine's "birth, her name, her connexions, her actual situation . . . resisted enquiry, eluded insinuation, and baffled conjecture" (41). She endeavors throughout the novel to remain free of desire until the father can reappropriate her and transfer her to a husband. When her feminized suitor, Harleigh,[45] presses her to declare whether or not she has given her heart to another, Juliet answers, "I have no heart!—I must have none!" (341). Juliet's chief desire is to be acknowledged as daughter, not as wife. An examination of the self-transformations she effects to accomplish this is undertaken in Chapter 5.

Unlike Evelina, Juliet's search for the father is symbolic rather than literal—her biological father is dead. Her efforts are rewarded symbolically as well, as the three figures who endow her with her father's name represent every branch of patriarchal power; only after these "fathers" have expressed their interest in the daughter and marked her as their property does Juliet allow herself to be handed on to her suitor. If Harleigh's desires are temporarily frustrated by Juliet's adherence to the father's law—her insistence on refusing romantic entanglements and preserving the secrecy demanded by the bishop and enforced by Lord Denmeath—other heroes in later novels are destroyed when women become the embodiment of patriarchal prohibition. In Frances Sheridan's *Memoirs of Miss Sidney Bidulph* (1761), Sidney asserts, "I think we ought always to form some laws to ourselves for the regulation of our conduct" (25).[46] Her insistence on obedience and conformity to the strictest rules of

44. Ibid., 158.

45. Although he functions as an austere, inaccessible father surrogate to Elinor, Harleigh is feminized in his relationship with Juliet. When Juliet seems to reject him, Harleigh "changed colour and looked hurt" (171). His "pride is so scrupulous, and his scruples are so squeamish" (160) that he cannot rescue Juliet from her brutal French "husband." When the Frenchman attempts to drag Juliet off, Harleigh faints (731). In *Frances Burney: The Life in the Works* (New Brunswick, N.J.: Rutgers University Press, 1988), Margaret Anne Doody writes that "Harleigh, who *should* be the hero, refrains from [the hero's traditional activities] with his own kind of impotence" (347).

46. Frances Sheridan, *Memoirs of Miss Sidney Bidulph* (1761) (London: Pandora Press, 1987). Margaret Anne Doody remarks on how "the Bidulph women in general, and Sidney most especially, . . . have a talent for transmuting experience into law" ("Frances Sheridan: Morality and Annihilated Time," in *Fetter'd or Free? British Women Novelists, 1670–1815,* ed. Mary Anne Schofield and Cecilia Macheski [Athens: Ohio University Press, 1986], 345).

male and female chastity dooms her lover, Orlando Faulkland, who "himself has a little too much of that ridiculous nicety" (272). Faulkland is condemned to feminine powerlessness—he contracts a miserable marriage with "a female libertine . . . a sly rake in petticoats" (355, 359); he weeps uncontrollably (403); he has bouts of temporary insanity; he manipulates the inflexible Sidney by threatening his own self-destruction; and he ends, presumably, by committing suicide.[47]

Another hero who suffers by a father's prohibition and the "daughter's" obedience is Delamere in Charlotte Smith's *Emmeline, The Orphan of the Castle* (1788). Threatened by her uncle, Lord Montreville, with the loss of her father's name (" . . . you must drop the name of Mowbray, to which in fact you have no right, and take that of your mother, whatever it be" [117]), Emmeline refuses to contract an engagement with his son, Delamere.[48] Delamere tries, unsuccessfully, to make Emmeline transgress the parental injunction, saying, "Your promise to my father is nugatory; for it ought never to have been given. . . . and all that you said ought not to bind *you;* since it was extorted from you by *him* who had no right to make such conditions" (180). Emmeline responds by upholding his father's right and defending "paternal authority": "What! has a father no right to decide to whom he will entrust the happiness of his son, and the honour of his posterity?" (180). Emmeline reestablishes the patriarchal order by which fathers retain ownership of the family, particularly of women, and can pass on their property, or refuse to do so, at will. Delamere at first assumes that the orphan will accompany the castle in his father's bequest: "I already begin to see great capabilities about this venerable mansion. I think I shall take to it, as my father offers it me; especially as I suppose Miss Emmeline is to be included in the inventory" (24). His father withholds

47. In "Woman's Influence" (*Studies in the Novel* 11 [Spring 1979]), Paula R. Backscheider writes about acts of female self-destructiveness in eighteenth-century novels by women: "The last step in human destructiveness is aggression turned against the self. Such an act expresses ultimate helplessness, [and] self-loathing. . . . In the final analysis, the heroine most often turns the violence against herself" (17–18). In *Sidney Bidulph,* however, roles are reversed. Sheridan's hero, Faulkland, to persuade Sidney to marry him, "drew his sword like a madman, and . . . swore that . . . he would plunge it into his breast, and die before my eyes. . . . You know, said he, the means of dying are always in my own power; take care you do not trifle with me, nor plead in excuse for falsifying your promise, that you made it to save me from immediate destruction" (390). Similar speeches would appear later in the mouth of Burney's suicidal Elinor Joddrel.

48. Charlotte Smith, *Emmeline, The Orphan of the Castle* (1788) (London: Pandora Press, 1988).

the woman, however; Delamere loses the near-Oedipal struggle, and his thwarted desires, like Faulkland's, end in his own madness and death.

Frances Sheridan dedicated *Sidney Bidulph* to Samuel Richardson, in her words "paying the tribute due to [the] exemplary Goodness and distinguished Genius" of the author of *Clarissa.* Her novel, like his, is more about separation than about union, as were the majority of late eighteenth-century novels by women. If earlier women's fictions had envisioned male sexuality as violence in the romantic sphere (seduction, rape), later works by women transferred that violence to the domestic sphere (the law of the father), rejecting explicitly, through the patriarchal figure of the tyrannical father, the aggressive sexuality of the previous generation. The displacement is logical, since the repressive moral strictures that dictated the changes in women's writing were themselves a product of male prohibitions. The later novels, however, perhaps offered more persuasive arguments against patriarchal oppression than the earlier fictions: instead of equating hero and heroine by creating improbable female rakes, later women writers feminized their heroes, putting men into the powerless position of women and showing them sharing in the misery entailed by the law of the father.

Conformity to patriarchal ideology is perhaps less obvious in the earlier women's novels, which seem to offer visions of female sexual freedom. The places where ideology has succeeded in becoming transparent are those most in need of investigation, however. As I examine masquerade in the fictions of Behn, Davys, and Haywood, I attempt to articulate how these early texts both uphold and subvert ideologies that inscribe "femininity" as the mirror double of "masculinity." Inchbald's and Burney's novels, more overtly conservative, are paradoxically clearer in their representations and exposure of patriarchal structures. As Nancy Miller writes, speaking of French literature, "sometimes even the 'old plot' rewritten by women also supplies a critique of the available cultural solutions."[49] Miller underscores the difficulty of any effort to articulate what constitutes a woman writer's feminism; every piece of women's

49. Nancy K. Miller, *Subject to Change: Reading Feminist Writing* (New York: Columbia University Press, 1988), 127. Marilyn L. Williamson, in *Raising Their Voices: British Women Writers, 1650–1750* (Detroit: Wayne State University Press, 1990), insists, "The seduction fantasies of Behn and her followers, themselves politically conservative, are revised into novels of protest at women's condition by such radicals as Elizabeth Inchbald, Mary Hays, and Mary Wollstonecraft" (210–11). Williamson, I think, overstates the case, but her refusal to define feminism as mere reversal of patriarchal ideology has merit.

fiction is a product of its age. Behn, Davys, Haywood, Inchbald, and Burney all re-create and thereby promote ideologies of female subordination within their works; they also highlight the contradictions inherent in eighteenth-century ideologies of gender, thereby subverting the dominant discourse. My purpose is not to reconcile this seeming contradiction but to analyze how, through their representations of the female body in disguise, these five writers helped both to construct and to deconstruct ideologies of female identity.

Chapter Two

Aphra Behn's *The Dumb Virgin* and Mary Davys's *The Accomplished Rake:* The Darker Side of Masquerade

Amid all of the recent interest accorded to the writings of women in the eighteenth century, two women's texts remain relatively untouched: Aphra Behn's *The Dumb Virgin; or, The Force of Imagination* (1700) and Mary Davys's *The Accomplished Rake; or, Modern Fine Gentleman* (1727). One reason these works have, as yet, managed largely to elude critical inquiry could be that their complicated, troubling plots hinge upon female victimization. *The Dumb Virgin* focuses on two sisters, one beautiful but mute, the other deformed but eloquent, who both fall in love with the same man. After he has seduced the beauty, he is found to be her brother. Davys's *The Accomplished Rake* tells the tale of a woman who is drugged by a libertine, then raped while still unconscious. Nine months later she gives birth to a son, all the while insisting "that nobody got it." Although the women are, I would argue, the chief sufferers in both texts, the two narrators focus more closely on the actions and perceptions of the main male characters. These two works, then, are unlikely candidates for the type of feminist scholarship that discusses woman-centered texts which portray empowered female characters.[1]

1. The inclination of feminist critics to work with texts that portray women subverting male domination in order to control their own lives is understandable: it stems from the desire to counterbalance the many portrayals of female victimization available in literature. Such a desire informs my own reading of Behn's *The History of the Nun; or, The Fair Vow-Breaker* in "Reworking Male Models: Aphra Behn's *Fair Vow-Breaker,* Eliza Haywood's *Fantomina,* and Charlotte Lennox's *Female Quixote*" (*Modern Language Review* 86 [October 1991]), where I argue that "early women novelists manage to embody, within conservative tales, subversive female stories, tales

The Dumb Virgin and *The Accomplished Rake* are interesting, however, to a feminism that hopes to address women's complicity in creating and maintaining the ideology that controls them. These two texts offer complex insights into the development and function of both male and female sexuality. It is difficult to tell in these narratives when women are the victims of male desire and when they are prey to their own. Patricia Meyer Spacks, in her article "Ev'ry Woman Is at Heart a Rake," discusses women writers' ambivalence toward female sexuality: "Although [female] diarists, autobiographers, letter writers, novelists all recognize that sexual impulse does exist in women, they unite in reminding themselves that it's probably evil, certainly dangerous. . . . Passion represents a shocking danger for a woman: if she admits her feelings, she may be unable to preserve her propriety, to set limits to her yielding."[2] In *The Dumb Virgin* and *The Accomplished Rake,* women who yield at all yield entirely; by losing the capacity to set limits, they end in ruin. Behn and Davys, it seems, are concerned in these texts with depicting the high cost of female sexual self-expression.

Not surprisingly, both narratives hinge upon pivotal masquerade scenes. The masquerade, as Terry Castle has pointed out in *Masquerade and Civilization,* was always associated in eighteenth-century minds with dangerous sexual license, and particularly with female sexual freedom.[3]

---

which picture heroines who are in control, both of themselves and of the men around them. Seizing men's own weapon, the pen, these female novelists push male stereotypes of women so far that they topple them" (838). Similarly, Cheri Davis Langdell asserts, ". . . Behn's heroines throughout the comedies . . . usually . . . are women capable of influencing their own destinies in sexual and political ways, patterns of the women who survived the social and political vicissitudes of late seventeenth-century England" ("Aphra Behn and Sexual Politics: A Dramatist's Discourse with Her Audience," in *Drama, Sex and Politics* [Cambridge: Cambridge University Press, 1985], 120). Writing of Mary Davys, Jean B. Kern insists, ". . . Davys's heroines are young women of good judgment and common sense," and she outlines the ways in which they use that sense to counter male oppression ("Mrs. Mary Davys as Novelist of Manners," *Essays in Literature* 10 [Spring 1983]: 37). Such readings are not incorrect, but instead are incomplete, as I hope to demonstrate in this chapter.

2. Patricia Meyer Spacks, "Ev'ry Woman Is at Heart a Rake," *Eighteenth-Century Studies* 8 (Fall 1974): 33, 36.

3. Terry Castle, in *Masquerade and Civilization: The Carnivalesque in Eighteenth-Century English Culture and Fiction* (Stanford, Calif.: Stanford University Press, 1986), notes, "Much of the fear the masquerade generated throughout the century is related to the belief that it encouraged female sexual freedom, and beyond that, female emancipation generally" (33).

"One might describe the masked assembly," Castle writes, "as a kind of machine for feminine pleasure."[4] Castle sees the masquerade as precipitating a "comic plot" within the literary work where it appears and argues,

> [The masquerade] engenders a rewarding or euphoric pattern of narrative transformation, even for characters, like the beleaguered heroines of contemporary fiction, whom one would not expect to benefit from its disarming travesties. Granted, the beneficent instrumentality of the occasion may not be immediately obvious: the narrative repercussions of the masquerade can seem painful or melodramatic on the surface. But it is important to notice how frequently the episode's ostensibly disastrous "consequences" . . . turn out to be a necessary prelude to something else: the amelioration of a central character's fortunes, the providential rewarding of the heroine.[5]

In Behn's *The Dumb Virgin* and Davys's *The Accomplished Rake,* the phantasmagoric masquerade scenes do not bring about the amelioration of the heroine's fortunes, do not result in her being rewarded. The repercussions of the masquerade in these works, instead of seeming painful "on the surface," actually are harmful for the female protagonists and appear to be so at all levels of the narratives. The sexual unions formed during the masquerade episodes prove catastrophic for Behn's and Davys's heroines.

I will examine *The Dumb Virgin* and *The Accomplished Rake,* two works that express women's fears about female sexuality, using the tools provided by theorists such as Jacques Lacan, Luce Irigaray, Mary Ann Doane, Kaja Silverman, and others. I hope to analyze the almost dreamlike logic by which these narratives proceed and to explore, in opposition to Castle, the darker side of the masquerade.

I

In his reformulation of Freudian theory, Jacques Lacan emphasizes the importance of two concepts in his account of the construction of subjectivity:

4. Ibid., 254.
5. Ibid., 122.

the mirror stage and the castration complex. For Lacan, the subject is constructed only within the terms of language and only through division. The mirror stage is the mythical moment at which the child first perceives its image in the mirror and—in conjunction with the gaze of the (m)Other whose presence, look, and naming guarantees the reality of the moment—recognizes its separateness.[6] The mirror stage offers the child an illusory sense of unity, self-mastery, and coherent identity.

Through the castration complex, the differentiation of the sexes occurs: upon recognizing that the mother does not possess the phallus, the child realizes the possibility of castration. The mediation of the third term, the father, whose law prohibits incest (castration is "the punishment for incest"),[7] then legislates against the boy's Oedipal attachment to his mother. For the girl, who identifies with the mother, her recognition of her own lack precipitates her desire for the phallus of the Other. Lacan writes, "This follows from the intervention of an 'appearing' which gets substituted for the 'having' so as to protect it on one side and to mask its lack on the other. . . ."[8] The male will "appear" to possess the phallus and the female will mask the fact that she does not—she will, in other words, masquerade to hide her lack:

> . . . I would say that it is in order to be the phallus, that is to say, the signifier of the desire of the Other, that the woman will reject an essential part of her femininity, notably all its attributes through masquerade. It is for what she is not that she expects to be desired as well as loved. . . .
>
> . . . the signifier of the phallus constitutes her precisely as giving in love what she does not have.[9]

It is because of "what she does not have" that the woman is left outside of the symbolic order, barred from access to language. Hence Lacan's notorious formulation, "There is woman only as excluded by the nature of

6. Jacques Lacan, "The Mirror Stage as Formative of the Function of the I as Revealed in Psychoanalytic Experience," in *Écrits: A Selection,* trans. Alan Sheridan (New York: W. W. Norton, 1977), 1–7.

7. Jacques Lacan, "The Meaning of the Phallus," in *Feminine Sexuality: Jacques Lacan and the "école freudienne,"* ed. Juliet Mitchell and Jacqueline Rose, trans. Jacqueline Rose (New York: W. W. Norton, Pantheon Books, 1985), 76.

8. Ibid., 84.

9. Ibid.

things which is the nature of words, and it has to be said that if there is one thing they themselves are complaining about enough at the moment, it is well and truly that—only they don't know what they are saying, which is all the difference between them and me."[10]

Lacanian theory has been criticized by feminists, particularly Irigaray, for among other things its phallocentrism;[11] a number of critics see as suspect Lacan's claim that the phallus, the signifier of desire, is not equal to the penis and is not, therefore, possessed by either sex. Mary Ann Doane, for example, writes, "But does the phallus really have nothing to do with the penis, no commerce with it at all? The ease of the description by means of which the boy situates himself in the mode of 'having' one would seem to indicate that this is not the case."[12] Phallocentrism leads to the collapse of difference. As Shoshana Felman explains,

> Theoretically subordinated to the concept of masculinity, the woman is viewed by the man as *his* opposite, that is to say, as *his* other, the negative of the positive, and not, in her own right, different, other, Otherness itself. . . .
>
> . . . Female sexuality is thus described as an absence (of the masculine presence), as lack, incompleteness, deficiency, envy with respect to the only sexuality in which value resides.[13]

The opposition thus becomes male/nonmale as opposed to male/female.

Perhaps ironically, however, their very phallocentrism makes Lacanian concepts useful in providing feminist critics with a model and a method for analyzing and critiquing the construction of the feminine within patriarchal culture. As Caroline Evans and Minna Thornton summarize,

> Current feminist theory has identified the social construction of femininity as being "other." It has used psychoanalytic theory to

10. Lacan, "God and the *Jouissance* of ~~The~~ Woman. A Love Letter," in *Feminine Sexuality,* 144.

11. See Luce Irigaray, *Speculum of the Other Woman,* trans. Gillian C. Gill (Ithaca: Cornell University Press, 1985), and *This Sex Which Is Not One,* trans. Catherine Porter, with Carolyn Burke (Ithaca: Cornell University Press, 1985).

12. Mary Ann Doane, "Woman's Stake: Filming the Female Body," in *Feminism and Film Theory,* ed. Constance Penley (New York: Routledge, 1988), 220–21.

13. Shoshana Felman, "Women and Madness: The Critical Phallacy," *Diacritics* 5 (Winter 1975): 3.

> develop a reading of how the construction of sexual difference positions the feminine as "outside" or marginal to a culture whose order and language are patriarchal. Thus masculinity is posited as the norm, femininity a *difference from* that norm. Furthermore, if psychoanalysis suggests that the construction of a gendered identity is precarious, this lends added weight to women's sense of alienation from femininity as a "fixed" identity set up as the "other" of masculinity.[14]

Feminist critics have used psychoanalytic theory to address questions about female subordination, the primacy of the male gaze, female silence, and masquerade in literary and cultural productions of the nineteenth and twentieth centuries.[15] Eighteenth-century texts dwell upon these themes as well, but few have as yet undergone similar analysis.

In its treatment of familial erotics, Aphra Behn's *The Dumb Virgin; or, The Force of Imagination* seems to demand a psychological reading. The 1916 editor of Behn's works, Montague Summers, prefaces this piece by insisting that it is based upon the "Œdipus Saga."[16] Where there is an Oedipal drama, Doane writes, there is also the "underside of the Oedipal trajectory—the maternal space it assumes as a point of departure, a scenario to be rejected."[17] This is the place where Behn's narrative begins—with a rejection of the feminine.

The Dumb Virgin opens with an account of Rinaldo, "a Senator of the great City *Venice*... [and] Master of a very plentiful Estate" (420).[18] The narrative thus starts with the father but proceeds quickly to the mother, who is immediately associated with a desire: she wishes "to view" a

14. Caroline Evans and Minna Thornton, "Fashion, Representation, Femininity," *Feminist Review* 38 (Summer 1991): 57.

15. Shoshana Felman, for example, in the article previously cited, studies Balzac's short story "Adieu." Mary Ann Doane analyzes the woman's film of the 1940s. Caroline Evans and Minna Thornton examine the fashion industry.

16. Montague Summers, Introduction to *The Dumb Virgin,* in *Oroonoko and Other Prose Narratives,* by Aphra Behn (New York: Benjamin Blom, 1967), 417.

17. Mary Ann Doane, *The Desire to Desire: The Woman's Film of the 1940s* (Bloomington: Indiana University Press, 1987), 145.

18. Aphra Behn, *The Dumb Virgin; or, The Force of Imagination* (1700), in *Oroonoko and Other Prose Narratives.* Subsequent page citations appear in parentheses.

The printing history of Behn's posthumously published *Dumb Virgin* is extremely complicated. For a detailed discussion, see Mary Ann O'Donnell, *Aphra Behn: An Annotated Bibliography of Primary and Secondary Sources* (New York: Garland, 1986), 186–204.

celebrated island twenty leagues from the Italian coast (420). The Lady (she is never given a name, only a longing) seems to assert an innocuous wish, but it is one that her husband and the narrator both perceive as dangerous: "He was unwilling to trust his treasure to the treachery of the watry element; but repeating her request, he yielded to her desires, his love not permitting him the least shew of command, and so thro' its extent, conspiring its own destruction" (421). The Lady, "with her young Son (whom she would not trust from her sight)," sets out under the charge of a male servant appointed by Rinaldo (421). Their ship is blown off course by a storm and attacked by Turkish pirates. The servant, Gasper, with "a peculiar Regard to his own Safety, and Master's Interest," straps the infant boy to two planks and leaps with them into the sea (422). Gasper is found dead and the lost infant is assumed to have drowned.

The Lady who forms the focus of the early pages of Behn's tale is depicted as having two transgressive desires, both associated with sight. She wishes to *view* the island and, simultaneously, to retain the *sight* of her son. In light of the construction of femininity described by Luce Irigaray in "The 'Mechanics' of Fluids," the "watry element" in which the Lady retains her son can be associated with her own sexual desire.[19] The Lady's look is an appropriation of the male gaze, an autonomous act of obtaining forbidden scopic pleasure. The beginning of *The Dumb Virgin* enacts what Doane refers to as "the contradictory position of the mother within a patriarchal society": the mother's is "a position formulated by the injunction that she focus desire on the child and the subsequent demand to give up the child to the social order. . . . The mother, as a mother, represents a fullness, a presence, a wholeness and harmony which must ultimately be broken."[20] In *The Dumb Virgin,* the dyadic fullness of the mother-and-son relationship is shattered first by the pirates, who transform the Lady from a spectator to a spectacle ("beauty always adds a pomp to woe, and by its splendid show, makes sorrow look greater and more moving" [421]), and next by the father's stand-in, Gasper, who tears the infant from the mother in his "Master's Interest." This forcible separation, however, proves to be

19. Irigaray, *This Sex,* 106–18. See also Doane, writing about Joan Crawford in *Humoresque:* "This emphasis on fluids seems to attach itself to . . . excessive [female] sexuality. Insofar as it signals that which exceeds set forms, boundaries, or limits, it is reminiscent of the construction of femininity described by Luce Irigaray. . . . And to have excessive female sexuality killed by its own image [through drowning] is to reveal . . . the tautological demonstration of the necessity of the failure of female desire" (*Desire to Desire,* 104).

20. Doane, *Desire to Desire,* 74, 77.

no separation at all, for the boy remains immersed in the "watry element." The narrator blames the entire situation upon the father's lack of "the least shew of command"—it was the father's responsibility to triangulate the relationship between mother and son, and he failed to do so. The son's full entry into the symbolic order is thereby not guaranteed, and the Oedipal yearnings that will bring about the catastrophe of the text are left in place.

Behn's narrative, however, proceeds by seeming to negate its opening. "Growing Hopes of another Off-spring" remove the parents' sorrow for the loss of the first, until their "Sorrows were redoubled," literally doubled, by the successive births of two daughters, one of whom is deformed and the other of whom is mute (423–24). Not only can a (castrated) daughter not compensate for the loss of a (phallic) son, but in this instance neither daughter is herself complete even as a daughter. The doubly lacking daughters are perceived as being entirely the offspring of their mother and are fully identified with her and her excesses by (presumably male) physicians: the mother "died in Child-birth, and left . . . [a] Daughter . . . naturally and unfortunately Dumb, which defect the learn'd attributed to the Silence and Melancholy of the Mother, as the Deformity of the other was [attributed] to the Extravagance of her Frights" (424). The daughters replace their mother and indeed, taken together, seem to constitute one "complete" woman, for the eldest daughter, Belvideera, although physically distorted, "understood all the *European* Languages, and cou'd speak most of 'em," while her sister, Maria, although dumb, was "the most beautiful Daughter . . . that ever adorn'd *Venice*" (424).

These two complementary halves ("Beauty" and "Wit" [431]), while raised together and kept apart from society, appear to be "whole" rather than "lacking." Belvideera's command of language seems to mark her as a "phallic" woman—a reading that her deformity allows,[21] as does the fact that, at the masquerade, she is initially taken for a man ("Sir, (said he) if you are a Man, know that I am one" [426]). Maria, though denied words, relies upon "the Language of her Eyes [which] sufficiently paid the Loss of her Tongue" (425). There was "something so Commanding in her Look" (as opposed to her father's lack of "command") that a painter who tries to finish her portrait is abashed by the "Vivacity of her Look," and "rising in great Disorder, he swore it impossible to draw that which he cou'd not look upon" (425). Maria, "sitting down to her Glass, finished it [the portrait] herself" (425). Maria thus narcissistically mirrors herself to herself,

21. Admittedly, psychoanalysis collapses the difference: the "phallic" woman is horrifying, but so is the castrated woman. The "nonmale" is monstrous in either case.

but unlike the woman who looks only-to-be-looked-at-while-looking Maria constructs her own image of herself without reference to a male spectator.[22] She seems in control of her self-image and her identity.

The masquerade scene introduces the male, Dangerfield, who triangulates the sisters' relationship and institutes rivalry between them. The masquerade functions here in a Lacanian sense—the women are precipitated into the "masquerade of femininity," a position of "otherness" and "lack." Paradoxically, the masquerade reveals what each wishes to conceal. Belvideera's "Defaults" are "not altogether hidden by her Disguise" (426), while Maria's muteness is emphasized by hers, since her masked nothing-to-see is accompanied by nothing-to-hear. Belvideera, in explaining her sister's silence, calls it a "Penance imposed by her Father-Confessor" (427). Maria deserves punishment, insists Belvideera—the fiction within the fiction will uncannily become fact when Maria violates the taboo against incest.

The masquerade scene establishes Dangerfield's desire for the sisters: "his Love was divided between the Beauty of one Lady, and Wit of another, either of which he loved passionately, yet nothing cou'd satisfy him, but the Possibility of enjoying both" (431). Dangerfield's desire, and their response to it, forces Belvideera and Maria to adopt "masks," to attempt to be what they are not in order to attract his gaze and mirror his wishes.[23] By contrast, Dangerfield himself wears "no Disguise but a *Turkish* Turbant" (427) taken from the Turkish captain he has killed. This object, which recalls the Turkish pirates, reinforces Dangerfield's connection with the mother and suggests his failure to resolve his Oedipal attachment through a recognition of the threat of castration. A second indication of this is the way in which Dangerfield fetishizes parts of the women's bodies: Belvideera's "Tongue claim'd an equal Share in his Heart with *Maria's* Eyes" (428). Dangerfield continually attempts to see each woman as whole: "Madam, (said he to her [Belvideera]) if you have the Beauty of that Lady, or if she has your Wit, I am the most happy, or the most unfortunate Man alive" (428). "The fetishist," writes Kaja Silverman,

22. See John Berger, *Ways of Seeing* (New York: Penguin Books, 1972): "Women watch themselves being looked at. . . . the subject (a woman) is aware of being seen by a spectator. . . . The real function of the mirror . . . was to make the woman connive in treating herself as, first and foremost, a sight" (47–51).

23. ". . . the masquerade permits woman to experience desire not in her own right but as the man's desire situates her"—Catherine Porter, Notes on Selected Terms, in Irigaray, *This Sex,* 220.

> is described by Freud as a man who remains incapable of accepting woman's lack, and who continues to disavow what he has seen [her absence of a penis]. He substitutes for the missing penis an adjacent object—something which was part of the original "picture" (a shoe, a garment, another part of the female anatomy). As long as this fetish is in place, woman is adequate to his pleasure. She constitutes no challenge to the sexual potency of the male subject because her "difference" has been covered over.[24]

The "woman-as-fetish may be asked to represent that phenomenal plenitude which is lost to the male subject" as he is divided from his mother.[25] Dangerfield seems trapped in a nostalgia for Oedipal or even pre-Oedipal union, while the sisters are associated with the absent maternal that forms the location of his desire. Behn's subtitle, "The Force of Imagination," might more appropriately be reconfigured with reference to Dangerfield's desire for unity as "The Force of the Imaginary."

Fetishism is a denial of the possibility of the subject's own castration and, as such, threatens patriarchal order. Without the threat of castration, the paternal prohibition against incest is ineffectual. Behn writes in *The Dumb Virgin,* "where there is no Punishment to be dreaded, the Law will prove of little Force" (430), and the ending of the narrative bears this out. Dangerfield unknowingly establishes an incestuous relationship with his sister Maria (441) and accidentally kills his father (442). The Oedipal conflict displaced from the beginning of the text is tragically resolved at the end with the destruction of the family.

What of the sisters? Their desire for Dangerfield propels them into a rivalry with each other that, by splitting them, confirms their incompleteness: "[Maria] had gather'd from her Sister's Discourse, that she was her Rival; a Rival, who had the Precedency in Age, as the Advantage in Wit, and Intreague, which want of Speech render'd her uncapable of" (434). Maria, in particular, becomes conscious of her defects. From being one who controlled her own image, she becomes one whose selfhood is constituted and constructed only by a man's view of her: Dangerfield's fetishistic scopophilia transforms Maria from the subject of the gaze into its object.

Maria's movement from being the bearer of the look to becoming the

24. Kaja Silverman, *The Acoustic Mirror: The Female Voice in Psychoanalysis and Cinema* (Bloomington: Indiana University Press, 1988), 13.
25. Ibid., 39.

object of sight begins the instant Dangerfield demands a "Sight of her Face" at the masquerade (427). Her eagerness to offer herself to his gaze makes her culpable—she desires him too, and "her own easy Inclinations" (436) bring about her ruin. When Dangerfield next sees Maria framed in the window, she is "an amazing *Sight* of Beauty, as made him doubt the Reality of the *Object*" (432; italics mine). Maria, attired only in her nightgown, "had look'd out of the Window . . . [and] cast her Eyes upon *Dangerfield*" (432). She remains in the window long enough to "captivate" the "Spectator" (433), to engage his look. Maria's offering of herself as an object of sight culminates in the meeting in the library, where Dangerfield finally recognizes her defect and stamps her as "a wond'rous Piece of Art left imperfect" (436). Maria moves from being "a Phantom only, created by the Strength of his [Dangerfield's] Fancy" to becoming "the most charming Piece of Flesh and Blood" (435). That transformation into a "real woman" renders Maria less desirable to Dangerfield—he spends the period of waiting in the closet thinking about her sister, whom he is "impatient to see" (440). Still able to fetishize Belvideera, since he has heard her without ever having seen her unmasked, Dangerfield nonetheless retains enough of his earlier passion for Maria to "assault" her, knowing that "she cou'd not tell" (440).

Just before Maria is ruined, Belvideera enters her sister's chambers and admonishes Maria, saying, "you must not appear, Sister, because 'twere a Shame to let Strangers know that you are Dumb" (437). Maria's desire to be looked at becomes, under Dangerfield's gaze, a fear of being looked at, a recognition of herself as "imperfect." Sound is conflated with sight—Maria's exclusion from language is connected to her physical appearance. She has, in other words, fully become a mute "castrated" woman, a sight of unpleasure to the male guests of her father and one who must remain hidden.

If Maria mirrored herself at the beginning of the text, after the masquerade she functions as a mirror for Dangerfield: "Poor *Maria* . . . never deplor'd the Loss of her own [speech] with more Regret, she found something so Sweet in the Mien, Person, and Discourse of this Stranger [Dangerfield], that her Eyes felt a dazling Pleasure in beholding him, and like flattering Mirrours represented every Action and Feature, with some heightning Advantage" (429). Her recognition is a misrecognition that she reflects back to Dangerfield. He, in turn, is in need of Maria's capacity to reflect himself because his own identity as a "man" is uncertain—Dangerfield has not successfully negotiated those stages necessary to the development of masculine identity. Like a woman, for example, Dangerfield has no "real" name, the descriptive appellative, "field of danger," being "a Counterfeit" (429). When Dangerfield attempts to articulate his name at the end of *The Dumb Virgin,* he does so incompletely ("my Name is not *Dangerfield;* but *Cla*— " [444]).

The ending of *The Dumb Virgin* plays out, or rather replays, the themes that came before it. When Maria kills herself with Dangerfield's sword, which is still "reeking with the Blood of her Father" (444), she realigns herself with the imaginary "phallic mother" and, for an instant, gains access to language as she utters, "Oh! Incest, Incest. . . . O my Brother, O my Love" (444). Maria's brief moment of speech is itself mirrored by her sister's loss of speech (Belvideera ends by becoming "a Recluse all the rest of her Life" [444]), a symmetry that recalls their initial complementarity.

If, as Judith Kegan Gardiner asserts, Behn's "single dominant theme in plays, novels, and poetry is human sexuality—its powers and problems,"[26] *The Dumb Virgin* is a tale that focuses on the problems. It emphasizes and exaggerates the dangerous consequences of female sexual self-expression and the transgressiveness of desire not subject to law. *The Dumb Virgin,* then, acts as a gloss to those of Behn's works which celebrate female sexual license.[27]

II

The narrator of Behn's *The Dumb Virgin* insists that she records the tragic events that form her story in order to "make him [Dangerfield] be pity'd

26. Judith Kegan Gardiner, "Aphra Behn: Sexuality and Self-Respect," *Women's Studies* 7, nos. 1–2 (1980): 68.

27. See, for example, Marilyn L. Williamson's assertion that "in poems, plays, and fiction, Behn celebrates female desire" (*Raising Their Voices: British Women Writers, 1650–1750* [Detroit: Wayne State University Press, 1990], 138). Later in her discussion of Behn's writing, Williamson modifies this claim by saying, ". . . although she frequently represents aroused female sexuality in her short fiction, she never reconciles the social structures of the stories to those representations. . . . These stories reveal that, far from challenging social convention through female sexuality, Behn simply placed female sexuality within the representation of social structures to which it is alien without an effort toward reconciliation" (216). I would argue that drawing attention to the very fact that female sexuality is alien to eighteenth-century social structures is itself an important function of Behn's writing.

for his Misfortunes, not hated for his Crimes" (444). By contrast, in Mary Davys's *The Accomplished Rake; or, Modern Fine Gentleman* (1727) the narrator expresses contempt for that creature called "a *modern fine gentleman*" who "can but whore, swear, and renounce his Maker" (244)[28] —in other words, she indicates that her unreformed protagonist *should* be hated for his crimes. Yet, in her preface to the work, Davys offers these telling sentences: "For, since passions will ever have a place in the actions of men and love a principal one, what cannot be removed or subdued ought at least to be regulated. And if the reformation would once begin from our sex, the men would follow it in spite of their hearts, for it is we have given up our empire, betrayed by rebels among ourselves" (236). "Reformation," the subduing and regulating of passion, is required of women. Women's "empire" consists in modeling the virtue of restraint, and those who fail to do so are "rebels" to their sex. While Davys's narrative ostensibly concerns itself with the *Modern Fine Gentleman,* it also seems to be a cautionary tale warning women against the dangers of female desire.

As with Behn's *The Dumb Virgin,* Davys begins *The Accomplished Rake* with an Oedipal drama. "Young Galliard, who is to be the subject of the following leaves" (241), loses his father and keeps his mother. While his father was a "wise and prudent" man, his mother possessed "an airy, roving temper, unconfined and free, [that] would know no bounds nor bear the least restraint. Pleasure was her idol" (241). Several French feminist critics—among them, Luce Irigaray, Hélène Cixous, and Catherine Clément—would reclaim for women the characteristics of excess, incoherence, and transgressive sexuality that other writers have denigrated.[29]

28. Mary Davys, *The Accomplished Rake; or, Modern Fine Gentleman* (1727), in *Four Before Richardson: Selected English Novels, 1720–1727,* ed. William H. McBurney (Lincoln: University of Nebraska Press, 1963). Subsequent page citations appear in parentheses.

29. In her famous chapter of *This Sex Which Is Not One,* "When Our Lips Speak Together," Irigaray writes, "How can I tell you that there is no possible evil in your sexual pleasure.... If we submit to their reasoning, we are guilty.... How can we speak so as to escape from their compartments, their schemas, their distinctions and oppositions ... free ourselves from their categories.... If we don't invent a language, if we don't find our body's language, it will have too few gestures to accompany our story.... They have wrapped us for so long in their desires, we have adorned ourselves so often to please them, that we have come to forget the feel of our own skin" (211–12, 214, 218). Irigaray's writing tries to imagine an impossible place in which women can be situated—outside male language and male systems of logic. Throughout, she celebrates the female body, female sexual pleasure (*jouissance*), and women's *"disruptive excess"* (78).

They celebrate women's laughter as a subversive extralingual move to counter male oppression.[30] Not so Mary Davys, whose ironic description of Lady Galliard's behavior after her husband's death condemns women's irrationality and their propensity to laughter while it reaffirms the value of male reason. Women's laughter can break through the restrictions imposed by men; instead of rupturing the limits, however, women should remain within those bounds:

> Sure unjustly are we called the weaker vessels, when we have strength to subdue that which conquers the lords of the creation, for their reason ties them down to rules, while we, like Samson, break the trifling twine and laugh at every obstacle that would oppose our pleasure. Lady Galliard had too much resolution and courage to struggle with grief but, like an expert fencer, gave it one home thrust and silenced it forever, hardly allowing so much as the common decorum of a month's confinement to a dark room, though her wild behavior told the world she was but too well qualified for such an apartment forever. (243)

In back of the reference to Samson lies the figure of Delilah, who, like Lady Galliard in her contest with grief, refuses to fight like a man. The woman's wildness—explicitly, as the text will prove, her sexual wildness—should subject her to eternal confinement. In suggesting this, the narrator records the opinion of "the world" without offering any counterpoint. The dominant ideology is left intact as Davys's narrative, like Behn's, begins with a strong rejection of the maternal.

At his death, Sir Galliard enjoins his son to "never lessen your ancestors by a misapplication of those talents Heaven has blessed you with" (242–43). If the maternal is to be rejected, the paternal is to be embraced. The Galliards' neighbor, Mr. Friendly, "long[s] to see him [Young John Galliard] in the road his worthy father travelled . . . [for] he was worthy of the name of man" (246–47). He wishes "to see him Old Sir John in behavior and principles" (297). When Mr. Friendly urges John Galliard to work to inherit his father's virtues along with his estate, Galliard responds, " . . . while

30. See Irigaray: "Isn't laughter the first form of liberation from a secular oppression?" (*This Sex,* 163). See also Catherine Clément: "Laughter breaks up, breaks out, splashes over" ("The Guilty One," in *The Newly Born Woman,* by Hélène Cixous and Catherine Clément, trans. Betsy Wing [Minneapolis: University of Minnesota Press, 1986], 33).

you make my father (whose memory I revere) a shining brilliant, you seem to call his son a worthless pebble" (248). Galliard's problem is that the *"modern fine gentleman"* (244) he becomes is only an echo of the "perfect *fine gentleman*" (243) his father was—Davys herself italicizes the words in order to highlight the ironic juxtaposition. Young Galliard's desire to take the place of his father, the boy's desire to replace the man, is the central concern of the text.

Galliard does, in a sense, replace his father: he brings home with him from Mr. Friendly's house a man who will literally "take the place of" Old Sir John in Lady Galliard's bed. This is one of the doublings or binaries that structure the narrative of *The Accomplished Rake.* Galliard's dead father, Old Sir John, is resurrected in the person of Mr. Friendly, who always treats the young man "with the tenderness of a father" (306). The two men whom Mr. Friendly sends to Young Galliard—Thomas the footman and Teachwell the tutor—serve as mediators between father and son, being identified both with Old Sir John/Mr. Friendly and with Young Sir John. The mother, Lady Galliard, is divided as well into two personas, the faulty woman and the penitent. Time is measured out in twos around the pivotal events of the narrative: two years "slipped away" after Old Sir John's death before Mr. Friendly holds the dinner party that introduces Tom (244); two more years intervene before Sir John witnesses Tom and Lady Galliard in bed together (250); two years follow that sexual transgression and bring Sir John to another—his rape of Nancy Friendly—and two more years go by before he returns to the country to marry her (366, 368).[31] Finally, two sisters (Belinda and the widow) and two sexual "fires" bring about the denouement of Davys's tale. This doubling, particularly the reduplication of father-son relationships, is significant in that it eventually allows Galliard to achieve his desired identification with the father and enter himself into the genealogy by displacing his attachment to the mother onto another woman.

Mr. Friendly, in his effort to make Young Sir John emulate Old Sir John, introduces him to Tom and immediately establishes an identity between the two young men. He explains that Tom, like Young Galliard, was left fatherless during early adolescence (a crucial time for sexual development): Tom was twelve when his father died (245), Sir John fourteen (242). Tom, born a gentleman, was ruined by the absence of his

31. Sir John remains in London for four years, and when he returns to Galliard Hall, Nancy's infant is two years old.

father and his mother's "want of care . . . towards making her son a man" (245). Mr. Friendly suggests that here, too, the boys' development is parallel.

The initial identification of the two young men is repeated and strengthened later in the text when Tom abducts Sir John's sister. Galliard is invited in by the madam of a brothel to meet "a curious fine girl in the house that was just come out of the country, brought by a fellow that would fain have ravished her" (301). Sir John is enjoined to "see her and try to gain her favor" (302). The woman in question is Galliard's sister Dolly, who further conflates her brother with her abductor: when Sir John enters, "the girl in tears thought it had been her ravisher returned" (302). As the text establishes a strong unity between Sir John and Tom, it also flirts with the subject of incest. The possibility of Sir John desiring his own sister is deflected onto the person of Tom, who indeed "would fain have ravished her."

The theme of displaced incest apparent in the later episode involving Galliard's sister can be read back into the earlier crisis that centers upon Galliard's mother.[32] When Sir John "asked Mr. Friendly if he had a mind to part with his new footman, Thomas" (249), Mr. Friendly answers that he would be willing to dismiss Thomas if he could also send Teachwell. By bringing home both of these men, Sir John unknowingly engineers his mother's fornication and his own voyeurism at the scene. As Betty Dimple will accuse her William, "[you] came in with an innocent air to find me out in the very roguery you yourself had contrived" (347), Lady Galliard could accuse her son of complicity in constructing the spectacle that he then deplores. Within this portion of the text, Tom becomes the location of those of Galliard's desires that are forbidden direct expression.

With Tom as mediator between Old Sir John and Young Sir John, a replacement for the father and stand-in for the son, Galliard is able to reconstruct the fantasy of the primal scene: Galliard at once sees his "father" copulate with his mother and also sees "himself" in the place of his father. Teachwell, Galliard's tutor and companion, who as the voice of

32. It seems not unreasonable to do so, especially since the passages are similarly worded and structured: when he finds out that Tom is the one who kidnapped his sister, Galliard instructs Dolly to pretend that no help is at hand because he "would fain see how far this dog's villainy will go" (303). He places himself in a closet so that he may witness the scene. In the episode involving Lady Galliard, Sir John asks, "is it possible for me to see that dog in my father's bed with temper?" (255). Again, Galliard places himself in a position where he can see this very thing.

reason and conscience is also associated with the father, reveals to Galliard that his mother is a "criminal" and enables Galliard to witness her crime so that he may put a stop to her "pernicious evil" (253). In a curious passage, Teachwell describes how he initially discovered Lady Galliard's faultiness:

> When I came up to bed, I cast my eye upon Molière, which lay upon my table, and got so deeply engaged in it that I read till almost two o'clock. There is a little wooden window yonder at my bed's head, which looks into the great hall and which I never opened in my life till this night, because I always took it for a cupboard which I had no use for. Before I had a mind to part with the companion in my hand . . . I thought I saw a gleam of light in the cupboard. . . . I went immediately to it, perhaps a little startled at a thing so unexpected, and, trying to open it, found it very ready to comply. Not so willing were my eyes to consent to the sight they met with, which was Lady Galliard hanging upon the arm of a man. (253)

Teachwell has never opened the cupboard because it is a thing he has no use for—he prefers the companionship of Molière. The cupboard, oddly enough, is "very ready to comply" and opens to reveal itself a window. The (sexualized?) description of inanimate objects ends in a sight of the sexual Lady Galliard with an unknown man—the anonymity allows any man to replace any other in the initial recognition. While the cupboard (something one looks into, something that contains and is sufficient in itself) is metamorphosed into a window (something that one looks through, a passageway to something else, nothing in itself), Lady Galliard undergoes a similar transformation. From one who was "resolved to be always mistress of my own actions" (248), she becomes mistress to another's actions, one across whose body men are united with each other. Lady Galliard soon laments giving "a loose to my own desires" when she recognizes that she "must now act the servile part and be subservient" (275).

As he becomes voyeur to his mother's fornication, Galliard is both fascinated and repulsed by her sexuality: he both desires and fears to see his mother's *jouissance.* By placing himself "in the dark at the little window to watch" (256), then using a key "which commands all the doors in the house," a key that had belonged to his father (again introducing the father into the scene), Sir John gains entry to his mother's "very bedchamber"

(255). The narrator, describing Galliard's anxiety to see what he expects to see, again equates him with Tom by comparing him to a lover: "no transported lover, who was to sink into the arms of his yielding mistress, ever wished for it [night] more" (256). Galliard gives the couple "time to get to bed" (257) and then enters the chamber. What he actually sees terrifies him: ". . . the blasting sight had such an effect upon him that his tongue faltered, his hand trembled, and his legs not able to support his weight, laid him speechless on the floor" (258). Since "her son had for some time been senseless," Lady Galliard attempts to explain the incident away, "to persuade him all he saw and heard was delusion or a dream" (259). Galliard, "extremely mortified with the cutting sight" (257), resolves the violent emotions that the spectacle aroused in him by expressing his "horror of the mutilated creature or triumphant contempt for her"[33] through "such reproaches as let Lady Galliard into the secret of her own character" (258). The primal scene, dream or reality, forces a separation between the son and mother and initiates his sense of loss, loss that precipitates desire—immediately after this incident, Galliard declares, "I now begin to have a taste for pleasure" (260).[34]

"If he behaves below his manhood and dignity," insists the narrator, "we must beg the mother to answer for the son, since the father left no example behind him but what was worthy of the strictest imitation" (243). The knowledge and sight of his mother's transgressive sexuality, of "women's frailty" (259) and lack, causes Galliard to ask, "are all women such?" (254).[35] Passing from one woman to another, he attempts to answer this question. His unregulated sexuality is marked by a repeated desire to "see," and what he sees convinces him that "women were made to be enjoyed" (324) and were "made for the pleasure and delight of man" (307). Every woman Galliard debauches becomes conflated with his guilty mother.

33. Sigmund Freud, "Some Psychical Consequences of the Anatomical Distinction Between the Sexes," in *The Standard Edition of the Complete Psychological Works of Sigmund Freud,* trans. and ed. James Strachey (London: Hogarth Press, 1953–74), 19:252.

34. William McBurney, in his introduction to *The Accomplished Rake,* notes this connection: "Lady Galliard's affair turns her son, after a scene of Hamletesque revulsion, into the path of debauchery" (xxxiii).

35. Kern comments, ". . . it is his mother's misalliance with her footman which shocks Sir John Galliard into distrust of female honor. . . . Lady Galliard['s] . . . promiscuity is used to motivate both her son's awareness of a double standard for sexual conduct and his own later rakish behavior" ("Mrs. Mary Davys as Novelist of Manners," 33, 36).

The identification is made explicit midway through the narrative: on one occasion when Galliard "sat considering with which of his madams he should spend the rest of the evening," he admits a woman, "not doubting but it was one of the fair ones he wanted." The "whore" turns out to be his mother ("She no sooner entered than he saw it was Lady Galliard" [304]).

Woman is equated with castration and transgression. Sir John, however, initially refuses to admit the implications of the sight of maternal lack, because it suggests the possibility of his own castration. He continually marks off the difference between himself and his mother: when his mother compares her faults to his, Galliard responds, "you will please to consider the vast disparity betwixt both our ages and sexes.... Women are naturally modest, men naturally impudent" (309). Sir John has a deep psychological stake in maintaining the sexual double standard. In his promiscuity, he defies "all laws and rules" (254), insists "rules of gravity" do not apply to "boys" (308), and despises "lawgivers who force us into fetters" and attempt to regulate erotic love (324).

The remainder of *The Accomplished Rake* traces the psychic progression by which the faithless and lawless lover becomes the faithful and lawgiving husband/father. Freud describes this trajectory:

> ... the discovery of the possibility of castration, as proved by the sight of the female genitals ... forces on him the transformation of his Oedipus complex, and ... leads to the creation of his super-ego and thus initiates all the processes that are designed to make the individual find a place in the cultural community. After the paternal agency has been internalized and become a super-ego, the next task is to detach the latter from the figures of whom it was originally the psychical representative. In this remarkable course of development it is precisely the boy's narcissistic interest in his genitals—his interest in preserving his penis—which is turned round into a curtailing of his infantile sexuality.[36]

The series of uncanny repetitions that form the bulk of the text from this point lead Galliard to occupy the place of the subject in the eighteenth-century family and force him to curtail his sexuality. The "uncanny," in Freud's formulation, is "that class of the frightening which leads back to

36. Freud, "Female Sexuality," in *Standard Edition,* 21:229.

what is known of old and long familiar."[37] Each encounter with a woman, each "fresh opportunity of acting the same villainy over again" (326), points Galliard back, either directly or indirectly, to the scene he witnessed and to the possibility of his own castration. Galliard's endeavor to answer the question, "are all women such?" becomes an effort at self-knowledge—"are all men other?" Woman's loss enables Galliard to affirm his possession and to identify symbolically with his father.

Two pivotal encounters in *The Accomplished Rake* hinge upon female masquerade: the rape of Nancy Friendly and the intrigue with the "dapper little gentleman" who is really a woman in disguise. Although the masquerade again positions the woman as one pretending to possess what she does not have, it functions differently in these episodes from the way it operated in Behn's *Dumb Virgin.* Instead of constructing an image to attract and hold the male look—to stimulate male desire, as Belvideera and Maria did—both women in Davys's text use the masquerade to confuse and redirect the male gaze. They manipulate the terms of the masquerade rather than allow themselves to be manipulated by them.

Nancy Friendly, in her choice of costume, seems to play to Galliard's desire. She says, "For my part, I intend to personate a sea nymph and dress in moss and shells. You, Sir John, may appear like Neptune, because you know he is as much obliged to take care of the ladies of his own dominions as you are to protect me" (284). Neptune was, of course, notorious for seducing the ladies of his own dominions—Miss Friendly seems to offer a tacit consent to Galliard's illicit schemes to obtain her. However, before the masquerade, she, with her friend Miss Wary, who is to accompany them to the entertainment, pursues a "frolic" designed "to cheat Sir John Galliard": "The scheme was for the two young ladies to change habits and go to the masquerade before Sir John came" (285). By means of this action, Miss Friendly discovers Sir John (despite the fact that he has changed his costume as well) and views him without his being able to view her. She masquerades in order to look, not to be looked at; in this, she reverses the power relations that had been in effect earlier at the theater, where Sir John "ogled her the whole time the play lasted" (280), and defeats completely his efforts to specularize her. By maintaining "indifference" and continuing in her "project of cheating the knight" for the duration of the masquerade (285–86), Nancy Friendly thwarts Sir John's desire and his attempt to take her to the bagnio. As she recognizes later, engineering her

37. Freud, "The 'Uncanny,'" in *Standard Edition,* 17:220.

own image provided her protection: "my own safety was owing to my change of dress" (295).

Although she appropriates the power of the gaze during the masquerade, Nancy Friendly fails to sustain her symbolic transvestism.[38] It is her desire for his desire that precipitates Miss Friendly's ruin. Even as she schemes with Miss Wary, Miss Friendly requests of her that "if the young baronet should chance to make love to her in her likeness she would use him well for her sake" (285). Miss Friendly, although she disguises her person and feigns indifference, is not actually indifferent to Sir John. In mirroring Galliard's desire, Miss Friendly relinquishes her control over herself. Just before Galliard drugs and rapes her, Miss Friendly says in his hearing, "I . . . value Sir John Galliard with all his faults" (295). This speech confirms his power over her.

The story that Sir John tells the apothecary from whom he obtains the soporific drug—that "he had a mind to a certain young lady of whom he did not despair though he should use no clandestine means" (291)—is thus not entirely false, for at some level her desire is to comply with his. Sir John, however, prefers to "have her unknown to herself than with her own consent" (291)—prefers, in other words, to reduce her completely to the state of an inanimate object rather than a self-knowing subject. "Have her he must" (283)—the words repeat those his mother used in speaking of Tom ("have him I must" [276]) and refer this encounter back to that one. In order to obtain Miss Friendly, Galliard conveys his opiate "into a few macaroons (which was what the lady greatly loved)" (291). These drugged macaroons seem to represent or signify desire itself: when she receives them Miss Friendly insists, "I know nothing I love so well as a macaroon" (294). After her son is born, Nancy Friendly calls him "her little macaroon" (356, 370), a name that both refers to his origins and reveals that her desire has been displaced.

If Nancy Friendly temporarily becomes a symbolic transvestite, the young woman who pursues Sir John in the guise of a man is the genuine article. Female cross-dressing has been variously theorized. Writing about transvestite costume at eighteenth-century masquerades, Terry Castle notes,

38. Laura Mulvey, in "Afterthoughts on 'Visual Pleasure and Narrative Cinema' Inspired by *Duel in the Sun*" (*Feminism and Film Theory,* 69–79), insists that in order to be a spectator a woman must adopt a "masculine point of view": " . . . for women (from childhood onwards) trans-sex identification is a *habit* that very easily becomes *second Nature.* However, this Nature does not sit easily and shifts restlessly in its borrowed transvestite clothes" (72).

"Historically speaking, the appropriation of the trappings of authority by those without it has usually been perceived as a threat to social structure. . . . the woman sporting male attire was a symbolic figure . . . inevitably projecting . . . radical aspirations after power, sexual prestige, and masculine authority."[39] Female cross-dressing, then, can be seen as an empowering seizure of male prerogative, as a "moving *up* the patriarchal hierarchy."[40] In its combination and confusion of the attributes of both sexes, transvestism can be regarded as undoing the hierarchy itself: Felicity Nussbaum argues that the transvestism revealed in the "scandalous memoirs" of women like Charlotte Charke and Hannah Snell "undercut[s] the ideology of the gendered subject that eighteenth-century theorists of character were attempting so desperately to preserve."[41]

In analyzing masquerade images, it is important to ask for whom the image is constructed and to whose pleasure it is addressed. Far from "undercutting the ideology of the gendered subject," the transvestism depicted in Davys's fiction reasserts the ideology of sameness. The "little dapper gentleman" (286), who in reality is a woman, comes to Sir John as a man from a man for a man. In her person, she highlights the homosocial nature of heterosexual desire: heterosexuality in *The Accomplished Rake* is a means by which Sir John can understand himself in relation to others of his own sex.[42] In his encounters with women, he derives much of his satisfaction from engaging in competition with men. Galliard insists, "I should certainly be ashamed of a fancy that nobody jumped with but

39. Castle, *Masquerade and Civilization,* 92, 256.

40. Caroline Evans and Minna Thornton, *Women and Fashion: A New Look* (London: Quartet Books, 1989), 44.

41. Felicity A. Nussbaum, *The Autobiographical Subject: Gender and Ideology in Eighteenth-Century England* (Baltimore: Johns Hopkins University Press, 1989), 198–99.

42. "The use of and traffic in women subtend and uphold the reign of masculine hom(m)o-sexuality, even while they maintain that hom(m)o-sexuality in speculations, mirror games, identifications, and more or less rivalrous appropriations, which defer its real practice. Reigning everywhere, although prohibited in practice, hom(m)o-sexuality is played out through the bodies of women, matter, or sign, and heterosexuality has been up to now just an alibi for the smooth workings of man's relations with himself, of relations among men"—Irigaray, *This Sex,* 172. Williamson writes, ". . . the libertine philosophy assumes a predatory, constantly roving male. It uses heterosexual relationships to maintain homosocial bonds, and therefore women circulate among men or are cast off when no longer desired" (*Raising Their Voices,* 208). For an extended treatment of the subject, see Eve Kosofsky Sedgwick, *Between Men: English Literature and Male Homosocial Desire* (New York: Columbia University Press, 1985).

myself" (281), and he pursues Belinda, for example, largely out of rivalry with her other suitor, Sir Combish: "Sir Combish had with his conceited speeches a little piqued him, which when joined to the liking he had for the lady, made him very industrious to get into her favor" (319).

The little gentleman, Mr. Venture-all, approaches Sir John at the masquerade to request the company of one of the latter's two female companions. Galliard responds insultingly, calling the petitioner a "Tom Thumb." This response angers Mr. Venture-all, and he challenges Sir John by telling him "he wore a sword"; Galliard replies, "for your sword, if it be no longer than yourself, it will never make work either for a surgeon or an undertaker" (286). When one later discovers that Mr. Venture-all is really a woman, the earlier remark takes on new significance: the "gentleman" possesses an inadequate sword—he, as a she, is male manqué. In her brief flirtation with lesbianism, her effort to obtain one of Galliard's ladies, the cross-dresser makes the "same gesture as the sexually aggressive man, confirming his power in her pretensions to it."[43] If transvestism is a woman's effort to "move up the patriarchal hierarchy," such a move only confirms the terms of that hierarchy and privileges "man" at the expense of "woman."

While failing to challenge the underlying terms of representation, cross-dressing allows the individual woman to obtain the privileges of a male subject: vision, movement, and speech. As Mr. Venture-all, the woman watches Sir John, follows him to the bagnio, and "bullies" him (288). Like Miss Friendly, however, the transvestite fails to sustain her appropriation of male prerogative. She acknowledges to Sir John that she is a woman and "invited [his] desires" (289) by saying, ". . . I have been eight years a wife yet have nothing to show for so much time spent in matrimony but a great estate without an heir to it. And there lies the bitter pill that takes away the sweets of life; that is the cutting blow, the smarting wound my husband always feels" (288). The woman comes to Sir John, then, to put men into relationship with each other: she comes as a man to obtain from Sir John a male heir for her husband. The entire episode of the woman's transvestism reemphasizes the themes that form the central concerns of *The Accomplished Rake:* the importance of an inheritance passing from father to son, the sameness and exchangeability of women, the "hom(m)o-sexual" (Irigaray's term) nature of heterosexual desire.

Sir John Galliard's desires throughout Davys's text are essentially solipsistic

43. Evans and Thornton, *Women and Fashion,* 86.

and self-referential. In his encounters with women, he seeks desire that will mirror his own. Irigaray writes that if the male ego

> is to be valuable, some "mirror" is needed to reassure it and re-insure it of its value. Woman will be the foundation for this specular duplication, giving man back "his" image and repeating it as the "same." . . . Woman will . . . be this sameness—or at least its mirror image. . . . through her "penis-envy," she will supply anything that might be lacking in this specula(riza)tion.[44]

Galliard's mastery over women assures him of his manhood—woman's lack forms the guarantee of his possession, of his unified, coherent identity as a man. Through the exchange of women, Galliard affirms his place among other men and, finally, situates himself in relation to his father.

The encounter with Belinda is the intrigue that makes Galliard return to the primal scene, acknowledge the possibility of his own castration, and align himself with Old Sir John Galliard. Like Miss Friendly and the female cross-dresser (who turns out to be Belinda's sister), Belinda "masquerades" as a man in the sense that she parodies male language ("Damn you, madam, you are my aversion" [323]) and embraces male reason ("I always thought man . . . had reason to regulate and govern his inordinate passions" [325]). In her refusal of Galliard's sexual advances, Belinda gives voice to the *law of the father,* saying, "But if every man were to choose as many women as he likes and take them as his proper vassals . . . I cannot but fancy it would destroy the whole system of life and the best economy must be turned upside-down" (325). Unlike the other two women, however, Belinda sustains her role and repels Sir John by pointing him back to his origins:

> "You are, 'tis true, a baronet by birth, but your mother has been some base, some faulty sinner, has violated a chaste marriage-bed, and you are the abominable product of her vice, the spawn of some of her footmen. Nothing but a channel, nay, a common-

44. Irigaray, *Speculum,* 54. See also *This Sex,* 129: " . . . the *flat mirror* . . . may be used for the self-reflection of the masculine subject in language, for its constitution as subject of discourse. Now woman, starting with this flat mirror alone, can only come into being as the inverted other of the masculine subject (his *alter ego*), or as the place of emergence and veiling of the cause of his (phallic) desire, or again as lack. . . . "

> shore, of base plebian blood, could put a man upon such low dishonorable actions. . . . "
>
> Sir John was never so stung in his life before as he was now at her bitter sharp invectives. But that which touched him the nearest was her just remarks upon his mother from whence ten thousand vexatious thoughts crowded about his heart, and (as he afterwards owned) began to ask himself whether there was not more than a bare probability of his being what she at random called him. His supposed father he knew was a man of the strictest honor and virtue. "From whence then," thought he, "does it come that I am so differently inclined? And am I then," continued he to himself, "the offspring of a nasty curry comb or horse whip, at last? . . . methinks I am not pleased to tell myself I am the son of a scoundrel." (330)[45]

Belinda reaffirms Sir John's relationship to his mother and emphasizes his affinity with Tom. By failing to align himself with his dead (symbolic) father, Galliard would remain trapped in an Oedipal circle that would deny him the power available to him if he occupied the place of the father. Galliard responds to Belinda by saying, "Though my words are invalid, I am ashamed of what I have done and which is more, you are the first woman that ever made me so" (331). Are his words invalid because he has failed to take his place in the symbolic order? Soon after this scene, Sir John is introduced to Belinda's sister and to his own daughter. He had earlier expressed the wish to see this child with the words, "methinks I long to look at something that may prove my manhood" (310). The daughter cannot fully prove his manhood in the same way that his son will, but Galliard's adoption of the position of the father in this instance prepares for the denouement of Davys's tale in which he will fully occupy his cultural place.

Forced by Belinda to (re)confront the "blasting sight" of his mother's lack, Sir John is then pushed by the two remaining episodes of the

45. An examination of issues involving class is not within the scope of this study. A materialist feminist analysis of *The Accomplished Rake* would be useful, however, in illuminating the relationship between issues of gender and issues of class. Sir John's rape of Nancy Friendly, for example, is treated very seriously in the text, while the analogous deceptive seduction of Betty Dimple by Sir Combish is portrayed as comic. The effects of Lady Galliard's fornication are dwelt upon, while the aftermath of Tom's infidelity to his wife is passed over quickly. By emphasizing the baseness of the lower classes, the upper classes can more easily victimize them.

narrative to address the possibility that he may lose his own organ. In Freud's formulation, quoted earlier, "The boy's narcissistic interest in his genitals . . . is turned round into a curtailing of his . . . sexuality." Two sexual "fires," which literalize the metaphor "burning with desire," reveal to Sir John the dangerous backlash of unregulated sexuality. The firing off of thirty "crackers" on the staircase of his mistress's house, which "set o'fire" his "wig and linen" and "scorched" his "hands, face, and bosom" (359), is juxtaposed to Sir John's amour with a "fire ship" (359), a woman with venereal disease, and his subsequent bout with illness (366). As the *"modern fine gentleman"* echoed the *"fine gentleman,"* so does Sir John's pox, his "[near-]mortal wound," balance his father's fatal smallpox. Along with Belinda's affirmation of the father's law, these two fires send Sir John back to Galliard Hall, to his point of origin, where he will claim his inheritance.[46]

Sir John aligns himself with his dead father by embracing the living "father" who is his surrogate, Mr. Friendly. Galliard, in witnessing Mr. Friendly's sorrow and receiving his blessing, "found a sudden alteration in his breast. Honor, pity, gratitude, and every noble passion of the mind had seized the whole man. . . . He could not hear such kind expressions from a man he had so greatly injured without the utmost remorse" (367–68). Galliard's Oedipal conflict is resolved. His union with Nancy Friendly that ends the work does not proceed from his desire for her but issues instead from his bond with her father and also his relationship to her son. Galliard completes his identification with the father by himself becoming a father; the child who is "a living demonstration" of his mother's guilt (371) is for Sir John a perfect mirror image. The boy has "the very face of Sir John Galliard" (368), and Galliard hails him as "my representative" and "my likeness" (370).

The ending of Davys's *Accomplished Rake* thus reaffirms patriarchal order at the expense of the woman.[47] The marriage that concludes the work is not the resolution of a "comic plot," nor a reward for its heroine, but remains ominous for Miss Friendly: the narrator closes the text with a

46. "Even the minor episodes in which Sir John is set on fire by crackers and more seriously 'burned' by Bousie's prostitute serve to turn his thoughts toward Galliard Hall and Nancy"—McBurney, introduction, xxxiii.

47. In her brief summary of this novel, Mary Anne Schofield concludes, "As is typical with these early eighteenth-century works, when confronted with the formidable male text, rhetorical strategy, and ideology, *The Accomplish'd Rake* supports the dominant power. The ambivalence that might have predominated in the novel's pages is reconciled, and male closure is assumed. The ideology of romantic love usurps its place, and the myth of female powerlessness is once more ensconced" (*Masking and*

warning that there is a possibility of "false steps or relapses" in Sir John (373).[48] The final pages of the story are unusual, however, in that they narrate the woman's recognition of and knowing consent to the terms under which her marriage is established. Miss Friendly says to Sir John, "You love my father and would take a bad bargain off his hands" (371). When Galliard presses the marriage upon her and tells her not to give herself "airs," she is angry (372). As she had previously insisted, "I do not want a husband for myself but a father for my child" (370–71), Miss Friendly closes with Sir John's proposals only to make her son heir to the Galliard estate. Her desire has been transferred from the father to the son who "is now so dear to me that the wealth of the universe should not buy him from me" (370).

The Accomplished Rake concludes, then, by setting up another Oedipal triangle and revealing that, like the first, the respective positions within that triangle are constructed and uncertain. Paternity is established amid doubt; maternity, although devalued, is more reliable. Galliard, while he claims to be the father, never completely affirms his paternity by satisfactorily explaining to Miss Friendly how he begat the child; instead he says to her, "whoever is the father, Nancy Friendly is undoubtedly the mother" (370). While Sir John's claim of paternity is couched in ambiguous language at the end of the text, no evidence is offered earlier since the narrative fails to describe what Galliard did to the unconscious Nancy Friendly. There is a gap in the text where the description of the rape would be: the narrator reports only that "Sir John had all the opportunity he expected" (296). This elision, probably introduced in the interests of delicacy, nevertheless recalls the uncertainty of Sir John's own parentage. Coming after Belinda's speech, Sir John's question—"Suppose he [the father] should prove an inferior rascal and I, in pity to your wrong and instigated by friendship, should offer to marry you, which would you take?" (371)—implies that the "inferior rascal" and Galliard are the same person.

If a feminist text is defined as one that attempts to subvert the dominant ideology and replace it with counterideology, Aphra Behn's *Dumb Virgin*

Unmasking the Female Mind: Disguising Romances in Feminine Fiction, 1713–1799 [Newark: University of Delaware Press, 1990], 89).

48. Kern writes, "Mary Davys redeems the accomplished rake, but our confidence that he will stay redeemed after his marriage to Nancy is never reinforced" ("Mrs. Mary Davys as Novelist of Manners," 33).

and Mary Davys's *Accomplished Rake* are not feminist narratives. Representing the destruction of the family brought about by the transgressive desire of the mother, *The Dumb Virgin* confirms the primacy of the father and the importance of the father's law. While Davys's *Accomplished Rake* also privileges the father, it focuses on the son's inheritance, reasserting an ideology of sameness that depicts female sexuality only as a specular duplication of male sexuality. Both texts thereby rearticulate and reaffirm patriarchal structures. At the same time, however, by emphasizing the constructedness of gender and by showing that rejection of the maternal brings about the masculine,[49] Behn's and Davys's narratives expose through reenactment, rendering invisible ideology visible and revealing the operative structures by which the feminine is suppressed: ". . . their power [is] in showing how an ideology works—not by undoing it, but by *doing* it."[50] *The Dumb Virgin* and *The Accomplished Rake* participate, in other words, in what Lennard Davis calls the "ambivalence of the novelistic experience"[51]—at once both upholding and subverting the dominant ideology, they offer complex renderings of eighteenth-century masquerade.

49. This subject is discussed at length in Nancy Chodorow's *The Reproduction of Mothering: Psychoanalysis and the Sociology of Gender* (Berkeley and Los Angeles: University of California Press, 1978).

50. Evans and Thornton, *Women and Fashion,* 100.

51. Lennard J. Davis, *Factual Fictions: The Origins of the English Novel* (New York: Columbia University Press, 1983), 222. A similar argument is proposed by Nussbaum: "I am arguing here that women's autobiographical writing, organized within prevailing discourses, helped to shape and resist the dominant cultural constructions of gender relations" (*Autobiographical Subject,* xiv).

❧ *Chapter Three*

Eliza Haywood and the Masquerade of Femininity

> Womanliness therefore could be assumed and worn as a mask, both to hide the possession of masculinity and to avert the reprisals expected if she was found to possess it—much as a thief will turn out his pockets and ask to be searched to prove that he has not the stolen goods. The reader may now ask how I define womanliness or where I draw the line between genuine womanliness and the "masquerade." My suggestion is not, however, that there is any such difference; whether radical or superficial, they are the same thing.[1]

This quotation from Joan Riviere, published in *The International Journal of Psychoanalysis* in 1929, is her summation of the case of a professional woman, a lecturer, who adopted exaggeratedly feminine gestures after her performances in an unconscious attempt to avoid the retribution she anticipated from men for her usurpation of the masculine role. Riviere's article has recently been accorded much critical attention from scholars interested in the subjects of masquerade, spectacle, spectatorship, and femininity. Her insistence that the "mask of womanliness" and "authentic womanliness" are the same thing points to the constructed nature of femininity itself—if in masquerade the woman mimics genuine womanliness, yet that "real" womanliness she dissimulates is itself also a mimicry, neither is essence and both are uncertain. This controversial aspect of Riviere's pioneering study has spawned at least "two currently circulating notions

1. Joan Riviere, "Womanliness as a Masquerade," in *Formations of Fantasy,* ed. Victor Burgin, James Donald, and Cora Kaplan (London: Methuen, 1986), 38.

of masquerade"—one that views the inevitable female disguise "as submission to dominant social codes," and another that sees masquerade as disruptive and as resistance to patriarchal norms.[2]

In her detailed study of the carnivalesque in literature and culture, *Masquerade and Civilization,* Terry Castle embraces the second theory of masquerade. For her, the masquerade is a "World Upside-Down . . . a feminocracy . . . a realm pervaded by female desire, authority, and influence."[3] Castle continues,

> With the anonymity of the mask . . . the eighteenth-century woman made an abrupt exit from the system of sexual domination. For a brief, charged moment, the masquerade suspended the archaic pattern of Western gender relations. In the exquisite round of the assembly room, a woman was free to circulate—not as a commodity placed in circulation by men, but according to her own pleasure. . . . the masquerade was indeed a microcosm in which the external forms of sexual subordination had ceased to exist. The masquerade symbolized a realm of women unmarked by patriarchy, unmarked by the signs of exchange and domination, and independent of the prevailing sexual economy of eighteenth-century culture.[4]

While she argues that the masquerade enabled women to escape or transcend patriarchal systems, Castle also admits that

> the masquerade had its undeniably provocative visual elements: one took one's pleasure, above all, in seeing and being seen. With universal privileges granted to voyeurism and self-display, the masquerade was from the start ideally suited to the satisfaction of scopophilic and exhibitionist urges. Bodies were highlighted. . . . The event put a premium on the sensuality of the visual.

2. Kathleen Woodward, "Youthfulness as a Masquerade," *Discourse* 11 (Fall–Winter 1988–89): 125. Woodward offers a useful summary of recent debate on the function of masquerade (see 125–26).

3. Terry Castle, *Masquerade and Civilization: The Carnivalesque in Eighteenth-Century English Culture and Fiction* (Stanford, Calif.: Stanford University Press, 1986), 254.

4. Ibid., 255.

> ... Not surprisingly, masked individuals were seen as fetishistically exciting.[5]

Implicit, then, in Castle's discussion are opposing views of masquerade as it relates to women. Throughout her work, Castle highlights the manner in which the obscuring of identity offered women a way of at least temporarily dismantling female roles. However, by emphasizing that the masquerade is built upon "seeing and being seen," is constructed with reference to "voyeurism and self-display," and is a practice that lends itself to fetishism, Castle raises several important questions: Who is displayed? For whom is the display/image/spectacle created? Who is the subject who obtains pleasure from looking? Who or what is the object of that gaze? While Castle does not explicitly answer these questions, she implicitly does so by means of a quotation from Wycherley that immediately follows the second passage cited above: "A Woman mask'd ... is like a cover'd Dish, giv[ing] a Man curiosity, and appetite...."[6] If it is the woman who becomes a spectacle or fetish for the man's pleasure, masquerade does not alter women's status—it leaves them inscribed in the dominant economy as objects of male vision and masculine desire.

In analyzing Aphra Behn's *Dumb Virgin* and Mary Davys's *Accomplished Rake,* I argued that Behn's Maria and Belvideera masquerade in a Lacanian sense, hiding lack and adorning the body in order to attract the male gaze. By contrast, I attempted to prove that Davys's Miss Friendly and, to a lesser extent, the cross-dresser who accosts Sir John Galliard use disguise to elude temporarily the male look and function momentarily as subjects. My discussion suggested, but did not examine, the possibility of psychological double-sidedness in the female masquerade. In what follows, I will outline more fully the opposing theories of masquerade and draw upon them in order to mark distinctions between two early masquerade fictions of Eliza Haywood—*The Masqueraders: or, Fatal Curiosity* (Parts I and II, 1724, 1725) and *Fantomina: or, Love in a Maze* (1724). I will explore the ways in which Haywood's (and, by implication, other eighteenth-century women writers') masquerade fiction helps both to construct and to deconstruct eighteenth-century cultural conceptions of femininity. Female masquerade, as it appears in Haywood's work, is more complex and ambiguous than Castle's assertions about it would suggest.

5. Ibid., 38–39.
6. Ibid., 39.

I

Following directly from Riviere's "attempt to show that women who wish for masculinity may put on a mask of womanliness to avert anxiety and the retribution feared from men"[7] comes the analysis of masquerade offered by Luce Irigaray. Countering any notion that "masquerading corresponds to woman's desire," Irigaray insists that

> masquerade has to be understood as what women do in order to recuperate some element of desire, to participate in man's desire, but at the price of renouncing their own. In the masquerade, they submit to the dominant economy of desire in an attempt to remain "on the market" in spite of everything. But they are there as objects for sexual enjoyment, not as those who enjoy.
>
> What do I mean by masquerade? In particular . . . "femininity." . . . a woman has to become a normal woman, that is, has to enter into the *masquerade of femininity* . . . [has to enter] into a system of values that is not hers, and in which she can "appear" and circulate only when enveloped in the needs/desires/fantasies of others, namely, men.[8]

Masquerade, in Irigaray's formulation, is a painful, desperate renunciation of female desire: the woman experiences desire, but it is the man's desire, not her own. She desires to be desired; by catering to male fantasies, she becomes objectified as a spectacle. Mary Ann Doane adds that "masquerade is not theorized by Riviere as a joyful or affirmative play but as an anxiety-ridden compensatory gesture, as a position which is potentially disturbing, uncomfortable, and inconsistent, as well as psychically painful for the woman."[9] She continues,

> When she masquerades, Joan Riviere's famous patient renounces her status as the subject of speech . . . and becomes the very image of femininity in order to compensate for her "lapse" into subjectivity (i.e. masculinity . . .) and to attract the male gaze. Masquerade

7. Riviere, "Womanliness as a Masquerade," 35.

8. Luce Irigaray, *This Sex Which Is Not One,* trans. Catherine Porter, with Carolyn Burke (Ithaca: Cornell University Press, 1985), 133–34.

9. Mary Ann Doane, "Masquerade Reconsidered: Further Thoughts on the Female Spectator," *Discourse* 11 (Fall–Winter 1988–89): 47.

> would hence appear to be the very antithesis of spectatorship/subjectivity. . . .
>
> . . . masquerade would seem to facilitate an understanding of the woman's status as spectacle rather than spectator.[10]

In *The Masqueraders: or, Fatal Curiosity,* Haywood exploits the sexual license allowed by eighteenth-century masquerade assemblies to analyze the dynamics of desire. Her representations of female disguise conform very closely to the negative view of masquerade as the painful submission of women to the dominant economy of male desire. Three of the four female characters in Haywood's text are rendered miserable by their efforts to transform themselves into the object of the hero's, Dorimenus's, gaze. By the end of Haywood's fiction, each is left to lament metamorphoses that result in passions "fatal to . . . Virtue . . . Reputation . . . Peace of Mind; and . . . Life" (I.45).[11] Haywood, more fully than Behn and Davys, emphasizes the constructedness of femininity through her insistent textual repetitions. At the same time, her discourse is one of the many that create eighteenth-century female consciousness and feminine roles. There is a great deal at stake in the reading of fiction: literature is both a product of ideology and a way of forming, shaping, and reshaping ideology.[12] Like Behn's and Davys's texts, Haywood's *Masqueraders* exposes female victimization and, at the same time, repeats it. Her narrative reinforces the patriarchal structures that it also subverts through enactment.

The Masqueraders opens with visual spectacle: "A fine Shepherdess, whose Bon Mien had attracted the Eyes and Addresses of a great number of the Assembly" (I.6) has fainted, revealing both by her costume and her posture the beauties of her features, mouth, eyes, complexion, neck, breasts, hands, and arms—"no part of her expos'd to view . . . did not

10. Ibid., 42, 48.

11. Eliza Haywood, *The Masqueraders: or, Fatal Curiosity,* Parts I and II (1724, 1725), in *Masquerade Novels of Eliza Haywood,* ed. Mary Anne Schofield (Delmar, N.Y.: Scholars' Facsimiles & Reprints, 1986). Subsequent page citations appear in parentheses.

12. Lennard J. Davis's *Factual Fictions: The Origins of the English Novel* (New York: Columbia University Press, 1983) concludes, "Novels cannot simply be equated with ideology, but rather must be seen as both embodying and counteracting ideology. That is, novels require the existence of the shared signifying system of ideology to 'make sense' to readers, but they oppose that system in order to reveal sense. This seemingly impossible double function has allowed the novel to have a continuing force in the history of discourse" (222). Davis stresses that ideology "constitutes a motivated, class-oriented rationalization" (221); I would add that it is also gender-oriented.

discover a Beauty peculiar to itself" (I.7). The woman is fragmented and fetishized, the threat of her image diffused into the pleasure of seeing her body in physically beautiful pieces. She is presented as a silent object of sight, a feast for the "Croud [*sic*] of Gentlemen, who had gathered round her" prone form. The foremost of these male spectators is Dorimenus, who is aroused by the "sight" and delighted to "behold Perfection, such as hers" (I.7). He narcissistically, but perhaps correctly, assumes that the fainting fit was a ploy "to make a Woman be taken Notice of" (I.6)—already eager to "attract the eye," the shepherdess has, by fainting, surrendered herself completely to become the sight/site of male visual pleasure. She is objectified again when, using the excuse of her indisposition to accompany her home, Dorimenus makes the shepherdess, Dalinda, his "Victim" and "Prize" (I.10).

This first scene is developed through language that, by focusing on the scopophilic, underscores the relative position of the lovers, his power and her submission. Dalinda has duplicated an image—that of a beautiful, helpless rustic—to engage and capture the gaze of the men around her. She particularly "wish'd to be address'd by" Dorimenus (I.8)—her desire is to be desirable to him. Haywood emphasizes that Dorimenus's appetites are the ones being satisfied. Dalinda can speak of nothing but "his Looks—his melting Pressures—his Ardours!—his Impatiences!—his Extasies!—his Languishments!" (I.12), and she unself-consciously feeds Dorimenus's narcissism: "She had not Artifice enough to disguise the Pleasure she took in his Conversation, from a Penetration so nice, and so experienc'd as his" (I.8). While Dalinda is wholly absorbed with him, Dorimenus, "the most roving and inconstant of his Sex" (I.11), is soon eagerly looking for new prey: "She may *like,* but 'tis impossible he should *love*" (I.13).

The masquerade, in this tale, rapidly becomes the arena for female loss. The women in Haywood's text, who seem differentiated and independent initially, are inevitably given tickets and called to participate in an entertainment where they are reduced to sameness and dependence. The second female character, Philecta, prides herself on her distinction from her friend Dalinda, who, she insists, has "nothing but a Face to recommend her—she has no Wit" (I.13). In her description, Philecta draws attention to the ease with which Dalinda can be objectified, reduced to a sight, a mere pretty face. Philecta marks herself off from this: while Dalinda blindly loves and trusts, Philecta remains contemptuous of Dorimenus's strategies of courtship, for she "had herself suffer'd much by Love, and the Ingratitude of a Man who had deceiv'd her with Professions of much the same nature with those her Friend seem'd now so certain were sincere . . . " (I.12).

Confident of her superior intelligence, Philecta allows the development of the "fatal curiosity" alluded to in the subtitle—she attends a masquerade impersonating Dalinda in order to examine closely her friend's lover. As she takes on the costume of subservience chosen by Dalinda,[13] that of an Indian slave, Philecta comes by degrees to resemble completely her former friend. Captivated by "the charming *Spaniard*" (I.15), the Indian slave is conquered as fully as the real peoples oppressed by Western adventurers. Initially intent on looking at Dorimenus, Philecta is soon caught up with being-looked-at-while-looking: "sometimes one sort of Glance, then its contrary seem'd the likeliest to attract" (I.22). Although she had despised Dalinda's vanity, Philecta, after her entrance into the masquerade, spends an entire day dressing and gazing at her mirror in order to reconstruct herself as an image that will please Dorimenus. Haywood underscores the specularization of the women that results from their participation at the masquerade: Dalinda wishes "to appear as amiable as she could in all Dresses in the Eyes of DORIMENUS" (I.15), while Philecta is concerned to leave "nothing undone that she thought wou'd be to the advantage of her appearing well in the Eyes of DORIMENUS" (I.22). The longing to capture the eye of the man constitutes both women's desire.

Philecta engages in a second masquerade that completes her visible entry into femininity: she imitates Dalinda's handwriting to send a letter to Dorimenus. In her forgery, Philecta "had play'd the Counterfeit so well, that 'twas scarce possible for the most discerning Eye to have discovered the difference . . . " (I.21). Difference—the "difference" that

13. Mary Anne Schofield, in *Masking and Unmasking the Female Mind: Disguising Romances in Feminine Fiction, 1713–1799* (Newark: University of Delaware Press, 1990), draws attention to the implications of the characters' choice of costume and remarks upon, but does not discuss at length, two types of female masquerade. Schofield writes, "Disguise functions in two ways in Haywood's works. First, we find . . . heroines (such as nuns, shepherdesses, and courtesans) who adopt conventional masks that further emphasize the secondary, submissive nature of the female. The disguised women do nothing to counteract this exploitation. A second and larger . . . group of masquerading women is represented by heroines whose disguises are chosen so that they can articulate the unspoken ideologies of the women themselves; their masks denote the desire for power that women have. They discard the typical, submissive shepherdess role and choose, instead, to mask themselves in disguises of aggression as the gypsy, demon, or prostitute" (44). Heroines "disguise themselves to display their hidden nature," and, in the case of Fantomina, "the disguise is a positive force working for the woman" (44).

constitutes subjectivity, that could allow a woman being in her own right rather than as man's mirror or opposite, the difference that would separate one woman from another—collapses in Haywood's text. It is as though, by "counterfeiting, as near as she cou'd, the Character of the happy DALINDA" (I.20), Philecta becomes her echo; the word "Character" in this instance means "handwriting," but the other meanings of the word resonate in the sentence. Like Dalinda, Philecta loses herself in her attempt to be what is pleasing to Dorimenus: "she remain'd unfix'd in Determination, how she shou'd Look, or Speak, or Act" (I.22). As Philecta fully participates in the masquerade of femininity, "not all her good Sense, not all her former Experience of the Passion she was now again possess'd of, had yet once reminded her, that she took all this pains for any thing more, than to triumph over the Tenaciousness of DALINDA" (I.21). Philecta reproduces the patriarchal ideology that imposes female rivalry as a cover for male control.

Dorimenus makes Philecta "his Property" (I.24)—the terms for love in this fiction nearly always allude to violent appropriation—by entering her bedroom just as she awakes from sleep.[14] Again the woman is prone, silent, vulnerable, fragmented, and fetishized—exposed as sight for "the adventurous Gazer . . . feasting his impatient Eyes with every naked Charm about her" (I.40–41). The voyeurism of the masquerade that insists on the visual objectification of the woman persists in Haywood's text even when the actual disguise is removed: "the agreeable Posture in which she lay . . . disclos'd to him Beauties, which her Dress had conceal'd" (I.40).

Part II of *The Masqueraders* offers variations on Haywood's initial themes. Two more "unhappy Victims" (II.2) of "the adventurous Gazer" (II.5), as Dorimenus will often be referred to in the remainder of the narrative, are portrayed: Dorimenus's new wife, Lysimena, and his latest mistress, Briscilla. Confusions of identity at new masquerade assemblies

14. In Behn's *Dumb Virgin* (*Oroonoko and Other Prose Narratives,* ed. Montague Summers [New York: Benjamin Blom, 1967]), Maria's objectification as spectacle is completed when "her Eyes not yet freed from the Dullness of the late Sleep, cast a languishing Pleasure in their Aspect, which heaviness of Sight added the greatest Beauties to those Suns, because under the Shade of such a Cloud, their Lustre cou'd only be view'd" (433). Sleepiness prevents the woman from looking as she is being looked at. The same situation occurs here in Haywood's narrative where sleep "left an unusual Languishment in her [Philecta's] Eyes, they had nothing of their wonted Austerity remaining, and seem'd rather to invite than forbid the adventurous Gazer" (I.40).

again emphasize that all the women in this text are interchangeable, for they function solely as repositories for Dorimenus's desire. Lysimena, for example, is unknowingly seduced by her husband when she accidentally adopts the costume of a nun, the costume Dorimenus expects to find on his mistress Briscilla. He is dressed as a friar—Haywood repeatedly uses costume to emphasize unequal power relations, since the nun is to be obedient to the priest who is her confessor. The costume of the nun serves to highlight Lysimena's absence of desire and exclusion from language:

> . . . she spoke not a Word, nor offer'd to oppose either DORIMENUS when he attempted to take her from these [two] Gentlemen [who also pursued her], nor to draw back from them; when on the other hand, they took hold of her, and prevented her from being led away by the *Fryar:* In that Confusion of her Thoughts, either Party, or if a third had interfer'd, might have done what they pleased with her, or carried her wherever they had a mind. (II.14)

Although Haywood insists that Lysimena "struggled with his Hands or Lips . . . not in a manner which a Woman who thought herself affronted would have done" (II.17), there is in this episode, as in the others, a suggestion that the scene portrays something worse than seduction, that it in fact depicts rape—the forcing of male desire upon the unresponsive or otherwise vulnerable female body. The disturbing uncanniness of Haywood's repetitions is increased as Briscilla, who had eluded Dorimenus in the guise of a gypsy, succumbs to him at the next masquerade in the costume of a shepherdess, "BRISCILLA herself having made choice of that innocent Resemblance, which she told him she hoped might be an Omen of his Constancy and Faith" (II.33–34). The unrelenting circularity of Haywood's text, its metamorphosis of Briscilla into a replica of Dalinda, is broken by only one positive note—the work ends with Briscilla finding unusual "Methods to retain the Heart of this gay Inconstant, which none of her Sex before were ever Mistress of" (II.45). Haywood hints, through Briscilla's early efforts to frustrate Dorimenus's desires and satisfy her own, and through Briscilla's successful evasion and refocusing of Dorimenus's gaze when she is cloaked as a gypsy, that the masquerade can function differently from the way it does for the first three women in this text.

II

The second theory of masquerade is most clearly articulated by Mary Ann Doane in her important article "Film and the Masquerade: Theorising the Female Spectator." In this early work, Doane argues that

> The masquerade, in flaunting femininity, holds it at a distance. Womanliness is a mask which can be worn or removed. The masquerade's resistance to patriarchal positioning would therefore lie in its denial of the production of femininity as closeness, as presence-to-itself, as, precisely, imagistic.... To masquerade is to manufacture a lack in the form of a certain distance between oneself and one's image.... masquerade is anti-hysterical for it works to effect a separation between the cause of desire and oneself....
>
> ... By destabilising the image, the masquerade confounds this masculine structure of the look.... masquerade [is]... a type of representation which carries a threat, disarticulating male systems of viewing.[15]

Doane posits that masquerade, when adopted intentionally, can be a form of resistance to male voyeurism. By providing distance between the self and the consciously constructed image, masquerade can destabilize the male gaze, refocusing it upon the manufactured identity. This notion seems similar, though not identical, to Irigaray's concept of mimicry:

> There is, in an initial phase, perhaps only one "path," the one historically assigned to the feminine: that of *mimicry.* One must assume the feminine role deliberately. Which means already to convert a form of subordination into an affirmation, and thus to begin to thwart it....
>
> To play with mimesis is thus, for a woman, to try to recover the place of her exploitation by discourse, without allowing herself to be simply reduced to it. It means to resubmit herself—inasmuch as she is on the side of the "perceptible," of "matter"—to "ideas," in particular to ideas about herself, that are elaborated

15. Mary Ann Doane, "Film and the Masquerade: Theorising the Female Spectator," *Screen* 23 (September–October 1982): 81–82.

> in/by a masculine logic, but so as to make "visible," by an effect of playful repetition, what was supposed to remain invisible: the cover-up of a possible operation of the feminine in language.[16]

Masquerade encompasses this effort to play the game knowingly, to "assume the feminine role" deliberately in order to point to its exploitativeness while setting it apart from oneself.

In *Fantomina: or, Love in a Maze* (1724), Haywood's protagonist employs masquerade in this empowering way: she ensures the constant ardent embraces of a man of her own choosing, Beauplaisir (his name itself bespeaks pleasure), by assuming a new disguise whenever he tires of the old one. By this method, Fantomina satisfies her own wishes at the same time as she destabilizes the gaze of her lover, refocusing his look upon her four intentionally manufactured selves. The first three of these disguised selves produce the gap or distance between Fantomina's real self and her constructed image necessary for the emergence of her subjectivity:[17]

> She was told by 'em all [all the men], that she was the most lovely Woman in the World; and some cry'd, *Gad, she is mighty like my fine Lady Such-a-one,* —naming her own Name. She . . . receiv'd no small Pleasure in hearing herself prais'd, tho' in the Person of another, and a suppos'd Prostitute. . . . [Beauplaisir] look'd in her Face, and fancy'd, as many others had done, that she very much resembled that Lady whom she really was. . . . (258–59)[18]

16. Irigaray, *This Sex,* 76. Doane herself notes the similarity of her concept of specular distance to Irigarayan mimicry in *The Desire to Desire: The Woman's Film of the 1940s* (Bloomington: Indiana University Press, 1987), 182. Here, she writes, ". . . the process of remirroring reduces the mirror effect . . . [and] it demonstrates that these are poses, postures, tropes—in short, that we are being subjected to a discourse on femininity" (181).

17. "Masquerade seems to provide that contradiction insofar as it attributes to the woman the distance, alienation, and divisiveness of self (which is constitutive of subjectivity in psychoanalysis) rather than the closeness and excessive presence which are the logical outcome of the psychoanalytic drama of sexualized linguistic difference. The theorization of femininity as masquerade is a way of appropriating this necessary distance or gap, in the operation of semiotic systems, of deploying it for women, of reading femininity differently"—Doane, "Masquerade Reconsidered," 47.

18. Eliza Haywood, *Fantomina: or, Love in a Maze,* 2d ed. (1725), in *Masquerade Novels of Eliza Haywood.*

The separation that Fantomina consciously creates between her image and herself protects her from all reprisals for her actions: "It will not be even in the Power of my Undoer himself," she exults, "to triumph over me" (266). As men gaze at the beautiful prostitute, Fantomina laughs at her intentional production of a spectacle for their sight: "She listen'd to 'em all, and was not a little diverted in her Mind at the Disappointment she shou'd give to so many . . . " (258).

Fantomina does "in every Thing as her Inclinations or Humours render'd most agreeable to her" (258) and remains "INDEFATIGABLE in the Pursuit of whatsoever her Humour was bent upon" (280). Instead of constructing images solely to gratify Beauplaisir, she acts upon her own desires, the "Strange and unaccountable . . . Whimsies she was possess'd of,—wild and incoherent . . . Desires" (261). Fantomina is more concerned with procuring her own sexual enjoyment than with being attractive to her lover for his sake; she is intent upon "gratifying the Inclination she had for his agreeable Person" (277) and "assumed this Manner of Behaviour only to engage him" (262) for her own satisfaction. Her disguises do, however, cater to Beauplaisir's fancies and fantasies.[19] Three of Fantomina's constructed selves—the prostitute, the country maid, and the widow—are lower in status and power than her hidden identity and serve to mask Fantomina's ultimate control in order to make her an acceptable object for Beauplaisir's desire.[20] Furthermore, as Fantomina's characters rise in rank, they also become easier of access. This feature, which directly opposes the conditions of the eighteenth-century world, serves to increase and enhance Beauplaisir's pleasure.[21]

19. Stephen Heath, in his study "Joan Riviere and the Masquerade" (in *Formations of Fantasy*), writes, "the masquerade is the woman's thing, hers, but is also exactly *for* the man, a male presentation, as he would have her" (50).

20. Note Riviere's comment about her patient's " . . . 'disguising herself' as merely a castrated woman. In that guise the man found no stolen property on her [the penis] which he need attack her to recover and, further, found her attractive as an object of love" ("Womanliness as a Masquerade," 38).

21. I am indebted to one of my seminar students, Jennifer Luke, for this observation. Lawrence Stone, in *The Family, Sex, and Marriage in England, 1500–1800* (New York: Harper & Row, 1977), notes that, "because of their concern to defend and pass on their property," members of the aristocracy were troubled by "the ease with which penniless adventurers could entice or seduce their daughters and heiresses and irrevocably marry them without parental knowledge or consent" (35); hence, laws were passed to limit access to heiresses, and it became a criminal offense to abduct an heiress. The fiction of the period reflects the sexual class distinctions: in Frances Burney's *Wanderer* (1814), for

Fantomina, in her effort to attract Beauplaisir and keep him "always raving, wild, impatient, longing, dying" (283), repeats many of the behaviors of the women in Haywood's *Masqueraders* and reconstructs traditional images of subordinate, helpless femininity. As a prostitute, although Fantomina reverses their roles by choosing the place of the rendezvous and paying for the supper (261), she maintains sexual conventions: "*He* was bold;—he was resolute: *She* fearful,—confus'd, altogether unprepar'd to resist in such Encounters . . . " (262). When impersonating Celia, the country maid, Fantomina feigns extreme youth, innocence, and naïveté:

> [Beauplaisir] ask'd her, how long she had been at Service?—How many Sweethearts she had? If she had ever been in Love? and many other such Questions, befitting one of the Degree she appear'd to be: All which she answer'd with such seeming Innocence, as more enflam'd the amorous Heart of him who talk'd to her. . . . He laughed at her Simplicity. . . . (269–70)

Fantomina appears helpless and poor when she takes on the guise of Widow Bloomer. Her first action is to appeal to Beauplaisir for aid: "You have the Appearance of a Gentleman, and cannot, when you hear my Story, refuse that Assistance which is in your Power to give to an unhappy Woman, who without it, may be render'd the most miserable of all created Beings" (271). To entice him further, Fantomina finally has recourse to Dalinda's ploy: " . . . she counterfeited a fainting, and fell motionless upon his Breast" (274).

How, then, is Fantomina's masquerade different from that of Dalinda and Philecta? In her defloration, Fantomina seems to enact sincerely a submissive female role, but in other meetings with her lover she mimics it. It is this mimicry—this choreographed deception or conscious self-display—that separates Fantomina from the women of Haywood's *Masqueraders.* Unlike the latter, Fantomina does not wear her femininity with conviction, does not take on the roles "for real."[22] She inhabits the costumes

example, when the heroine, Juliet, disguises herself as the lower-class Debby Dyson, she is accosted by men on the street. On the other hand, when Juliet is acknowledged to be the heiress, Miss Granville, she is only accessible to men through the permission of her guardians.

22. " . . . femininity is a masquerade, a matter of dressing up, but it is also a costume that must be worn with conviction—for real"—Caroline Evans and Minna Thornton, *Women and Fashion: A New Look* (London: Quartet Books, 1989), 99.

knowingly—while reproducing the very same behaviors as the other women, Fantomina maintains an ironic distance, a detachment from her representations. Fantomina

> was so admirably skill'd in the Art of feigning, that she had the Power of putting on almost what Face she pleas'd, and knew so exactly how to form her Behaviour to the Character she represented, that all the Comedians at both Playhouses are infinitely short of her Performances: She could vary her very Glances, tune her Voice to Accents the most different imaginable from those in which she spoke when she appear'd herself. (274)

Completely adept at playing the game to her own advantage, Fantomina chooses for herself what guise of femininity she will display. By manipulating the terms of her own representation instead of being manipulated by them, Fantomina avoids being "deceiv'd and cheated" (277), escapes the role of "all neglected Wives, and fond abandon'd Nymphs" (283), and has a remedy when she begins "to grow . . . weary of receiving his . . . insipid Caresses" (286) when Beauplaisir tires of one of her personas. She "could not forbear laughing heartily to think of the Tricks she had play'd him" (283) and exults in having "outwitted even the most Subtle of the deceiving Kind, and while he [Beauplaisir] thinks to fool me, is himself the only beguiled Person" (277).

When she poses as a prostitute, Fantomina not only maintains an ironic distance between herself and her created image but also, by the very nature of her disguise, undoes and undermines those invisible "commonsense" hierarchical oppositions that constitute the ideology of the feminine.[23] After watching the conduct of a prostitute in the theater, Fantomina adopts the role herself, "practising as much as she had observ'd, at that Distance, the Behaviour of that Woman" (258). Beauplaisir and the other men recognize the prostitute's resemblance to "the vi[r]tuous, the reserv'd . . . the Haughty Awe-inspiring Lady" (266–67) Fantomina is during the day, "but the vast Disparity there appear'd between their Characters, prevented him from entertaining even the most distant Thought that they cou'd be the same" (259). The "two" vastly disparate women of course are the same woman—the ambiguity of Fantomina's temporary transforma-

23. ". . . ideology works to appear as a natural, unprejudiced truth—a commonsense notion"—Davis, *Factual Fictions,* 220.

tion unites the two parts of binary oppositions such as "mistress" and "heiress," "prostitute" and "virgin." "When an equivalence . . . is proposed between two halves of an antithesis, when one pole can no longer be fully distinguished from the other, an ideological ranking of terms within the pair can no longer be performed."[24] By conflating the lady with the tramp, Fantomina challenges the underlying terms of representation itself.

Fantomina's masquerade is more complicated and powerful than any of the female masquerades spoken of earlier. Unlike Haywood's Dalinda, whose mask is removed when she faints, or Behn's Maria, who takes off her mask to give Dangerfield a sight of her face, or Haywood's Philecta, who "pluck'd off her Mask" (I.16) to let Dorimenus see his mistake, Fantomina keeps her "mask" on and does not allow her lover to penetrate her disguises. In the way that she eludes the male gaze while retaining her own "Power of seeing" (260), Fantomina is similar to Davys's Nancy Friendly and to Haywood's Briscilla, the latter of whom "resolved to disappoint him [Dorimenus]; and instead of appearing in the Habit she had made him believe, put on the Resemblance of a *Gypsy*" (II.9). By not letting the man into the secret of what her costume will be, the woman acquires the ability to see rather than be seen. If, however, the masquerade scene is pushed no farther than simple reversal, as I would argue it is not in Davys's *Accomplished Rake,* the woman merely becomes a transvestite, "reversing the relation and appropriating the gaze for her own pleasure."[25] Mary Ann Doane emphasizes that such a move "remains locked within the same logic . . . whose acknowledgment simply reinforces the dominant system of aligning sexual difference with a subject/object dichotomy. And an essential attribute of that dominant system is the matching of male subjectivity with the agency of the look."[26] Role-reversal does not deconstruct the dominant ideology; by leaving in place the same logic, the logic of sameness, role-reversal risks reverse role-reversal. Haywood's *Fantomina,* by destabilizing dichotomies instead of overturning them, poses a greater threat to patriarchal order than perhaps any other masquerade text of the early eighteenth century.

Like *The Masqueraders,* though, *Fantomina* is still to a certain extent doomed to reproduce the dominant discourse even as it challenges it. Any

24. Castle, *Masquerade and Civilization,* 78.
25. Doane, "Film and the Masquerade," 77.
26. Ibid.

attempt to represent the feminine within patriarchy is problematical,[27] as Fantomina's last disguise illustrates. Her frolic as the mysterious aristocratic Incognita is Fantomina's only literal masquerade—the only transformation in which she is actually masked. This nameless guise, however, in which Fantomina endeavors to say almost nothing about herself, is paradoxically the least successful because in it there is some slippage: Fantomina here comes closest to revealing to Beauplaisir that her semblance of womanly weakness is just that, a semblance—her femininity is a masquerade. Fantomina sends Beauplaisir a letter that states her desire for him directly but denies him "the Knowledge of my Name . . . [and] Sight of my Face" (281). When he comes to her, "she yeilded [*sic*] without even a Shew of Reluctance" (284) yet refuses to allow him the privilege he demanded of "gazing" upon her (282). Fantomina insists upon "concealing from *Beauplaisir*... the Knowledge [of] who she was" (266). Although she allows her body to be fetishized ("Her fine Shape, and Air, and Neck, appear'd to great Advantage" [284]), she maintains the psychic distance necessary to avoid objectification by repeatedly denying Beauplaisir "the Sight of her Face"—the phrase is repeated over and over, for Beauplaisir is "wild with Impatience for the Sight of a Face which belong'd to so exquisite a Body" (284).

While Fantomina's earlier efforts at concealment had left Beauplaisir "surpris'd and troubled" (263), her last intrigue makes the masquerade overt and, although arousing desire, also produces fear: Beauplaisir, for the first time in their amours, "resolv'd never to make a second Visit. . . . he went out of the House determin'd never to re-enter it, till she should pay the Price of his Company with the Discovery of her Face and Circumstances" (286). Riviere insists that "womanliness [is] . . . a mask, behind which man suspects some hidden danger."[28] Stephen Heath adds, "As indeed he would: if there is a mask, then there is a behind-the-mask and we need to know what is behind, to be *sure*."[29] Beauplaisir's scopic obsession

27. Doane acknowledges this in "Masquerade Reconsidered": "But it [masquerade] is a curious norm, which indicates through its very contradictions the difficulty of *any* concept of femininity in a patriarchal society" (43).

28. Riviere, "Womanliness as a Masquerade," 43.

29. Heath, "Joan Riviere and the Masquerade," 50. See also Michèle Montrelay: "But what we must see is that the objective of such a masquerade is to say nothing. Absolutely *nothing*. And in order to produce this nothing the woman uses her own body as disguise. . . . man has always called the feminine defences and masquerade *evil*. . . . It is this evil which scandalizes whenever woman 'plays out' her sex in order to

is analogous to Dorimenus's in *The Masqueraders:* when Dorimenus "endeavour'd with a complaisant Force to pull off" the mask of the "nun" he had just violated, she was "infinitely less assiduous to preserve her Virtue, than her Face from Discovery" (II.18, 20). This inability to see behind the mask "fill'd him with an equal share of Surprize and Curiosity" (II.20). Both texts emphasize the voyeurism inherent in the masquerade and move relentlessly toward exhibiting what lies behind the mask.

The ending of *Fantomina: or, Love in a Maze* appears to expose the "real" woman: Beauplaisir seems to be allowed to penetrate Fantomina's disguises when she gives birth to their child and is forced by her mother to summon the father of it. Yet at the end Beauplaisir is left "full of Cogitations, more confus'd than ever he had known in his whole Life" (290). In describing the partial failure of Fantomina's role as the masked Incognita, the narrator insists, "she comforted herself with the Design of forming some other Stratagem, with which to impose on him a fourth Time" (286). *Fourth* time? The aristocratic disguise *was* the fourth disguise—presumably Haywood erred in her count. Or did she? Is one of Fantomina's performances "real"? It is impossible to know—the reader never finds out Fantomina's true name nor learns anything substantial about her identity. From the ambiguous motto, "In Love the Victors from the Vanquish'd fly. / They fly that wound, and they pursue that dye,"[30] to the troublesome final sentences—what does become of Fantomina after she is sent to a French monastery?[31]—Haywood's text remains a puzzle. It is impossible, in this fiction, to say exactly what lies behind the mask. By embodying inconsis-

evade the word and the law. Each time she subverts a law or a word which relies on the predominantly masculine structure of the look" ("Inquiry into Femininity," trans. Parveen Adams, in *French Feminist Thought: A Reader,* ed. Toril Moi [Oxford: Basil Blackwell, 1987], 239).

30. The epigraph is from Waller and is also found in George Etherege's *The Man of Mode* (1676). Mary Anne Schofield draws attention to the fact that victor and vanquished in Haywood's *Fantomina* are difficult to determine: "Beauplaisir is the victor; she [Fantomina], the vanquished, but not for long. . . . Haywood subtly inverts the persecuted innocence theme, and victim and victimizer exchange roles in her effort to show how to control the male" (" 'Descending Angels': Salubrious Sluts and Pretty Prostitutes in Haywood's Fiction," in *Fetter'd or Free? British Women Novelists, 1670–1815,* ed. Mary Anne Schofield and Cecilia Macheski [Athens: Ohio University Press, 1986], 191).

31. Schofield insists that Fantomina "does not seem to be at all subdued" ("Descending Angels," 192), and her "imprisonment in the convent is only a temporary setback in her continued high-spirited life" (*Quiet Rebellion: The Fictional Heroines of Eliza Fowler Haywood* [Washington, D.C.: University Press of America, 1982], 62).

tency and refusing to resolve it, by preserving ambiguity and challenging the idea of a unified central subject, by refusing to make meanings explicit or coherent, Haywood's *Fantomina* works against an ideology whose smooth functioning calls for the elimination of contradictions.

III

If *The Masqueraders* posits masquerade as woman's submission to patriarchal constructions of the feminine, *Fantomina* counters by destabilizing the terms of that construction. Another of Haywood's fictions, *The City Jilt; or, The Alderman Turn'd Beau* (1726), while not overtly a masquerade text, nevertheless embodies many of the ideas Haywood developed in the two earlier narratives. A work not frequently discussed, *The City Jilt* merits careful scrutiny; this brief narrative provides a useful coda to the study of female identity articulated in Haywood's masquerade writings.

The City Jilt falls roughly into two parts, the first portion outlining Glicera's victimization at the hands of her lover Melladore and the second relating her method of revenge. The two halves of the narrative together trace one woman's submission to patriarchal inscriptions of the feminine and her eventual efforts to play her way out of the predicament that is femininity. The first section of *The City Jilt* is thus in some ways analogous to *The Masqueraders,* while the latter portion can fruitfully be compared to *Fantomina.*

The City Jilt begins by offering Glicera as an unwitting object of exchange between two men, her father and her lover. Melladore had been "well received by the Father of *Glicera*" (2) because he had a substantial fortune; Melladore, in turn, is pleased to contract nuptials with Glicera, not out of tenderness for her, but because of "the real Love he had . . . to the Wealth of which he expected she would be possess'd" (6).[32] The woman, mistakenly thinking that she has value in herself, is nonplussed when, after her father dies and leaves her portionless, her lover abandons her. The narrator remarks, "Ah! how little is Youth sensible of what it owes to Age, and how far are we unable to conceive what is due to the Care of a tender Parent, or how greatly we suffer in the loss of such a one! But soon was this fond Maid made sensible of her Error" (4). Glicera's

32. Eliza Haywood, *The City Jilt; or, The Alderman Turn'd Beau,* 2d ed. (London: J. Roberts, 1726). Subsequent page citations appear in parentheses.

error is in not understanding that her position in the patriarchal economy is one of an object of barter, a commodity equivalent to the money that was supposed to change hands, something to put men into relationship with each other.[33] As in Davys's *Accomplished Rake,* heterosexual love in Haywood's *City Jilt* is really homosocial: when Glicera's father dies, she ceases to have value to Melladore because the exchange of property between the men becomes impossible. As Irigaray writes, "there is no such thing as a commodity . . . so long as there are not *at least two men* to make an exchange. In order for a product—a woman?—to have value, two men, at least, have to invest (in) her."[34]

Failing to grasp the dynamics of male desire, Glicera tries to enforce the "deal" herself. Crediting Melladore's professions of constancy "because she wish'd it so, and had before set down in her own Heart for Truth, all that he now professed" (6), Glicera allows herself to be seduced by him under the assumption that he will marry her afterward. Like Dalinda and Philecta, she is objectified and falls "Victim" to her lover's "brutal Appetite." Her desire is to be desired, her concern is "that of giving Pleasure to the dear Undoer" (7). The narrator describes her action as "the Crime she had been guilty of to Heaven and to herself" (8)—the addition of "to herself" is an innovation. Haywood's narrative stresses the complicity of the woman in allowing her own self-destruction.

Melladore refuses to keep his vows. Desire, he insists, is constituted by lack, not possession, "for who can wish for what he has already?" Melladore explains, "The very word *Desire* implies an Impossibility of continuing after the Enjoyment of that which first caused its being" (16). Melladore's behavior and letters convey to Glicera knowledge of the terms underlying heterosexual relationships. Her newly acquired understanding of the "Perfidy" and "undoing Artifices of deluding Men" (10) transforms Glicera into an eighteenth-century "she-devil":

> The Memory of her Wrongs, however, left her not a Moment, and by degrees settled so implacable a hatred in her Nature, not

33. This analogy was originally formulated by Irigaray: "For woman is traditionally a use-value for man, an exchange value among men. . . . Woman has functioned most often by far as what is at stake in a transaction, usually rivalrous, between two men, her passage from father to husband included. She has functioned as merchandise, a commodity passing from one owner to another, from one consumer to another, a possible currency of exchange between one and the other" (*This Sex,* 31, 157–58).

34. Irigaray, *This Sex,* 181.

> only to *Melladore,* but to that whole undoing Sex, that she never rejoic'd so much as when she heard of the Misfortunes of any of them.
>
> . . . the Hatred which his Ingratitude had created in her Mind was so fix'd and rooted there, that it became part of her Nature, and she seem'd born only to give Torment to the whole Race of Man. . . . (20, 29)

What is especially interesting about Haywood's narrative is that Glicera does not simply wait for misfortunes to fall upon men but actively pursues means of bringing those misfortunes about: ". . . she had already experienced Mankind, and was not to be deceived again by the most specious Pretences: despising therefore the whole Sex, she resolved to behave to them in a manner which might advance both her Interest and Revenge" (21). For the remainder of the text, Glicera masquerades. Where earlier she had enacted femininity "for real," Glicera now begins to mimic her former behavior, creating images of femininity believable to the men around her. Glicera becomes a self-exhibiting subject rather than an exhibited object—she manipulates others rather than becoming manipulated herself: ". . . as nothing is capable of giving more Vexation to a Lover, than a Disappointment when he thinks himself secure from the Fears of it, she gave Encouragement to the Hopes of as many as sollicited her,—She received their Treats and Presents, [and] smil'd on all . . . " (21).

Mary Anne Schofield, in her article " 'Descending Angels': Salubrious Sluts and Pretty Prostitutes in Haywood's Fiction," insists that Glicera "prostitutes her body in order to gain wealth, power, and most especially, control which she exercises over the duped male. . . . Glicera vows to get even. She does so by selling her body to all men."[35] This seems to me a serious misreading: it is precisely because she does *not* prostitute her body that Glicera is capable of exercising power.[36] Glicera flaunts femininity and holds it at a distance; she attracts the male gaze to a misleading constructed display, not to the hidden self: ". . . never did a Woman passionately in love take greater Pains to captivate the ador'd Object of her

35. Schofield, "Descending Angels," 193–94.

36. Note Glicera's final admonishment to Grubguard: "It is not in the power of the loveliest, wittiest, and most engaging of all your Sex, to tempt me to an Act of Shame . . . " (53).

Affections than did this fair *Jilt,* to appear amiable in the Eyes of Mankind" (29). Having come to understand fully the mechanisms of male desire through her experience, Glicera consciously engages in "the forbidden activity of confusing sexual messages"[37]—like Fantomina, she seems to be a mistress but is not. Glicera's masquerade is, if anything, more complex than Fantomina's, for she manages to attract and retain male desire not by repeatedly satisfying it, but by never satisfying it. Glicera, "having as large a Share of Sense as Beauty, knew . . . well how to manage the Conquests she gain'd" (28)—she keeps old men and young men alike in competition with each other. Glicera knowingly offers herself as a bridge to put men into relationship with each other—she assumes the feminine role deliberately in order to reconfigure it.

It is thus that Glicera turns male desire against itself for her own advantage. She feeds the narcissism of her elderly suitor, Alderman Grubguard, by allowing him to believe that her desires mirror his own; Glicera treats him "with a double Portion of seeming Kindness" (22). "But vastly different," says the narrator, "were the Designs which made her treat him in the sort she did, from those which he imagined them to be" (22). Glicera, through her friend Laphelia, drops hints that stir Grubguard's jealousies toward her other, younger suitors. His efforts to compete lead him to adopt elaborate, ridiculous fashions in order to attract Glicera's gaze to himself (24). By skillfully manipulating his narcissism, and by encouraging competition with other men, Glicera finally intimates that she can be had "by way of Bargain" (48). Her representation of herself as the object of exchange between men is a representation Grubguard believes

37. Caroline Evans and Minna Thornton, "Fashion, Representation, Femininity," *Feminist Review* 38 (Summer 1991): 58. I am indebted to their discussion of British punk fashion here, and in their book *Women and Fashion,* for many of my own ideas about the function of disguise in Haywood's fiction. The ahistorical parallel may seem initially unlikely; however, in their account of punk as "the fashion parody of pornography," which allowed a woman "autonomous control over her self-presentation," Evans and Thornton describe a collapse of categories very similar to those that occur in *Fantomina* and *The City Jilt:* "Bondage dress allowed women to express the crudest will to sexual power, or, indeed, to sexual victimization, while preserving a central ambiguity. Punk girls—and they were girls—engaged *en masse* in the forbidden activity of confusing sexual messages: they looked like prostitutes but were not. They were women but were not 'feminine,' 'tarty' but not tarts. This was an exercise of power, not in the literal sense of what could be done, but on the level of representation, of what could be signified" ("Fashion, Representation, Femininity," 58).

because it is the one he expects[38]—he is duped into giving up the mortgage he holds to Melladore's estate in the belief that, once he parts with this, he will receive his mistress. When she has obtained the power over Melladore that she wants, Glicera sends Grubguard away by enacting another female role, that of the prude, and delivering a lecture on morality (53–54). Grubguard dies soon after (55), as does Melladore, who is forced to join the army to raise money to pay his debt to Glicera (59).

The narrator insists, "how severely did the unerring Hand of Providence revenge the Injuries he [Melladore] had done *Glicera!*" (38). What is remarkable in Haywood's *City Jilt* is that Providence, in fact, has very little to do with Glicera's vengeance. Glicera's own ability to distance herself from her feminine gestures is combined, in this text, with a strong female solidarity that assists her in overcoming her initial disadvantages. *Fantomina* had offered hints of female unity: few patriarchal figures inhabit the world of this masquerade text. For example, when Fantomina's mother travels to a foreign country she leaves her daughter to the care of an aunt, not a father or uncle (265). The landlady of the first lodging Fantomina rents helps the young woman maintain her reputation and does not need a bribe to do so: "The Landlady assur'd her she would do every Thing as she desired, and gave her to understand she wanted not the Gift of Secrecy" (265). *Fantomina* ends with the birth of a daughter whose mother and grandmother refuse Beauplaisir's offer to take care of "the new-born Lady" (290), and Fantomina is finally sent to "a Monastery in *France,* the Abbess of which had been her [mother's] particular Friend" (291). If bonds between women are subtly established in *Fantomina,* in *The City Jilt* the female unity is overt; while female relationships form interesting tangents in *Fantomina,* they are instrumental to the plot of *The City Jilt.* If Melladore's wife unwittingly aids Glicera by pursuing those extravagances and excesses that plunge Melladore into debt, Glicera's friend Laphelia is "let into the Secret of her Thoughts" (22) and knowingly assists her companion with all of her schemes: it is Laphelia "to whose Friendship and ready Wit she [Glicera] was chiefly indebted for her good Fortune" (60). When Glicera obtains "a sufficient Competency to maintain her for her Life" she does not turn back to Melladore as "some of her weak Sex would" (59)—the narrator's tone is contemptuous here—but maintains "a State of happy Indifference" (59) and lives with Laphelia "in a fine House, which formerly

38. Notice how analogous this is to Glicera's own experience: she believed Melladore's protestations because they matched her own expectations.

belong'd to *Melladore*" (60). Haywood gestures, perhaps, toward lesbianism but moves away from this suggestion to report Laphelia's marriage, her "exchanging the Pleasures of a single Life, for the more careful ones of a married State" (60). The conclusion of the text does not, however, privilege heterosexual union. The pleasures available from marriage are qualified, rendered uncertain, and the single felicity of Glicera is cautiously celebrated. *The City Jilt* closes by saying, "Few Persons continue to live in greater Reputation, or more endeavour by good Actions to obliterate the memory of their past Mismanagement, than does this Fair Jilt; whose Artifices cannot but admit of some Excuse, when one considers the Necessities she was under, and the Provocations she received from that ungrateful Sex" (60). Glicera's "crime" is renamed "mismanagement," a failure to understand the unspoken terms upon which heterosexual relations are established. Haywood's *City Jilt,* together with *The Masqueraders* and *Fantomina,* articulates and exposes those terms while undermining them. There are real gains for women in Haywood's reformulation of female disguise: Fantomina and Glicera, unlike other seduced women in fiction of the period, are not defined and do not define themselves as "guilty." They remain economically and verbally empowered. They do not end in ruin or in death. Through her fictions, as Haywood both reconstructs and deconstructs the masquerade that is femininity, she prepares the way for later women writers to explore further the establishment of female identity in the eighteenth century.

❧ Chapter Four

Elizabeth Inchbald's Not So Simple Story

> There are, however, women who write. Is their writing different from men's? *In what ways does their writing call attention to the fact that they are women?...*
>
> If, however, "replete" words (*mots pleins*) belong to men, how can women speak "otherwise," unless, perhaps, we can *make audible* that which agitates within us, suffers silently in the *holes of discourse,* in the unsaid, or in the non-sense....
>
> And then, blank pages, gaps, borders, spaces and silence, holes in discourse: these women emphasize the aspect of feminine writing which is the most difficult to verbalize because it becomes compromised, rationalized, masculinized as it explains itself.... If the reader feels a bit disoriented in this new space, one which is obscure and silent, it proves perhaps, that it is women's space.
>
> —Xavière Gauthier, in *New French Feminisms,* ed. Elaine Marks and Isabelle de Courtivron

In *Masquerade and Civilization,* Terry Castle argues that Elizabeth Inchbald's *A Simple Story*

> offers an unfamiliar image of female plot. Here the heroine's desires repeatedly triumph over masculine prerogative; familial,

> religious, and psychic patterns of male domination collapse in the face of her persistent will to liberty. . . .
>
> The irony . . . is that threatened punishments are never executed —or at least never completely executed—in Inchbald's imaginative world.[1]

Focusing upon Miss Milner's entry into the forbidden zone of the masquerade, and dwelling upon the fact that this act of defiance does not result in "the catastrophic undoing of the plot of heterosexual romance," Castle sees the second half of Inchbald's work as a "displaced recapitulation" of the first: "The burgeoning November of the last pages is indeed the green world of romance, the beautiful image of Inchbald's permanent World Upside-Down. For the second time in *A Simple Story,* patriarchal violence is quelled, and feminine delight made paramount."[2] Such a reading, while it correctly emphasizes the subversive nature of Inchbald's text, fails to take into account such troubling aspects of the work as the emotional anguish of both heroines, Miss Milner's final capitulation to patriarchal authority, and Matilda's continual submission to the tyranny of the father.[3]

A Simple Story is not simple at all. Inchbald's work cannot be defined as an unambiguously feminist masquerade text in the way that Castle wishes to define it. Inchbald's presentation is complicated and ambivalent; it is often vehement in its denial of the possibility of female power and equally vehement in its portrayal of male violence directed at women. Miss Milner *is* punished for defying the commands of her mentor/lover Dorriforth. She does not marry him until he has obtained complete mastery over her through a psychological manipulation that results in physical illness: Miss Milner's ailing body functions as a visible sign that the coquette has been "reformed" into a sober woman. When that sober woman errs again, she

1. Terry Castle, *Masquerade and Civilization: The Carnivalesque in Eighteenth-Century English Culture and Fiction* (Stanford, Calif.: Stanford University Press, 1986), 292, 295.

2. Ibid., 308, 323, 325.

3. In her recent book, *Desire and Truth: Functions of Plot in Eighteenth-Century English Novels* (Chicago: University of Chicago Press, 1990), Patricia Meyer Spacks also departs from Castle: "The female 'freedom' Castle celebrates has found little scope. . . . Taking a rather less rosy view than Castle's, I find in Matilda's career not a narrative of female freedom and power but one of necessary acceptance and limited reconciliation" (199).

has internalized her oppression sufficiently to have learned to punish herself. Lady Elmwood's sufferings and death are not sufficient to satisfy Lord Elmwood's resentment: the sins of the mother must be visited upon the daughter, whom he virtually imprisons. Unlike other eighteenth-century texts, where fathers confine daughters so that they do not have access to forbidden lovers, in *A Simple Story* Lord Elmwood confines Matilda so that she does not have access to him. The eventual reunion between father and daughter, which Castle applauds as "a celebration of feminine delight," appears instead to be merely another instance of male violence: when Matilda is forcibly abducted, Lord Elmwood just as forcibly reclaims her—as his property. Matilda, whose will is entirely subsumed within her father's, restores the status quo initially disrupted by her mother, so that *A Simple Story* ends as it began, with patriarchal control firmly in place.

If Inchbald's book is feminist, it is not so in its triumph of female desire over masculine prerogative, as Castle believes. Like other women's texts of the 1790s, notably Mary Hays's *Memoirs of Emma Courtney* (1796) and Mary Wollstonecraft's *Maria, or The Wrongs of Woman* (1798), Inchbald's work is disturbing in its portrayal of balked female desire and in its rendering of intense female suffering. Unlike Ann Radcliffe, whose *Mysteries of Udolpho* (1794) and *The Italian* (1797) appeared soon after *A Simple Story* (1791), Elizabeth Inchbald found no need to transport her heroines to exotic climes and haunted castles in order to have them experience violence—the struggles and anguish in *A Simple Story* occur completely within the domestic sphere, defamiliarizing the familial and poignantly emphasizing the problems inherent in the existing structures of late eighteenth-century society.

A Simple Story is subversive, then, not because it succeeds in undermining patriarchal authority but because it questions and probes the psychological underpinnings of that authority in subtle and sophisticated ways. Inchbald's subject is not unique—several of the masquerade texts I have analyzed expose oppression through reenactment—but her treatment of that subject is: her text speaks through silences and gaps, from between the lines, in what Luce Irigaray refers to (in her *Speculum of the Other Woman*) as the "*blanks* in discourse."[4] In what follows I shall draw on the work of

4. Luce Irigaray, *Speculum of the Other Woman,* trans. Gillian C. Gill (Ithaca: Cornell University Press, 1985), 142. See also her *This Sex Which Is Not One,* trans. Catherine Porter, with Carolyn Burke (Ithaca: Cornell University Press, 1985): "This

Continental feminists to examine the critique of patriarchal systems offered by *A Simple Story* through its enactments of destructive male authority and pathological female submission.

I. The Guilty One

In "Sorties: Out and Out: Attacks/Ways Out/Forays," Hélène Cixous insists, "Thought has always worked through opposition. . . . Through dual, hierarchical oppositions. . . . Everywhere (where) ordering intervenes, where a law organizes what is thinkable by oppositions (dual, irreconcilable; or sublatable, dialectical). . . . Logocentrism subjects thought—all concepts, codes and values—to a binary system."[5] All thought about women during the eighteenth century was certainly organized by binary opposition, as Patricia Meyer Spacks states in "Ev'ry Woman Is at Heart a Rake": ". . . at the century's end as at its beginning, society drew an absolute line between virtuous and nonvirtuous sexual conduct in

process of interpretive rereading has always been a *psychoanalytic undertaking* as well. . . . What is called for . . . is an examination of the *operation of the 'grammar'* of each figure of discourse, its syntactic laws or requirements, its imaginary configurations, its metaphoric networks, and also, of course, what it does not articulate at the level of utterance: *its silences*" (75).

A number of perceptive critics have noted Inchbald's successful manipulation of textual silences. In a letter to Inchbald (14 January 1810), Maria Edgeworth wrote: ". . . I am of [the] opinion that it is by leaving more than most other writers to the imagination, that you succeed so eminently in affecting it. By the force that is necessary to repress feeling, we judge of the intensity of the feeling; and you always contrive to give us by intelligible but simple signs the measure of this force" (quoted in Gary Kelly's *English Jacobin Novel, 1780–1805* [Oxford: Clarendon Press, 1976], 78). More than a century later, Jane Spencer writes, "Drawing on her long experience as a dramatist, Inchbald uses lively dialogue and telling gesture to convey her meaning with a lightness of touch rare in the fiction of her time. . . . Only Inchbald's extreme delicacy of handling could have made her theme [the disruptive potential of female desire] acceptable to her readership. . . . Inchbald renders desire sparingly and obliquely. . . . hers is an art of excision and compression" (Introduction to *A Simple Story,* by Elizabeth Inchbald [Oxford: Oxford University Press, 1988], vii, xv).

5. Hélène Cixous, "Sorties: Out and Out: Attacks/Ways Out/Forays," in *The Newly Born Woman,* by Hélène Cixous and Catherine Clément, trans. Betsy Wing (Minneapolis: University of Minnesota Press, 1986), 63–64.

women."[6] Alice Browne, in *The Eighteenth-Century Feminist Mind,* concurs: "One consequence of the double standard is that women are divided into 'good' and 'bad' on the basis of their sexual history, regardless of their other moral qualities."[7] The position of the "good" woman was quite precarious: sex outside of wedlock was far from being the only thing that condemned a woman to the category of "bad." Any self-centeredness, a desire to be amused rather than to amuse, was condemned in women, as the portraits offered by influential Joseph Addison in *The Spectator,* no. 15 (17 March 1711), illustrate:

> *Aurelia,* tho' a Woman of Great Quality, delights in the Privacy of a Country Life, and passes away a great part of her Time in her own Walks and Gardens. Her Husband . . . is her Bosom Friend, and Companion in her Solitudes. . . . They both abound with good Sense, consummate Virtue, and a mutual Esteem. . . .
>
> How different to this is the Life of *Fulvia!* she considers her Husband as her Steward. . . . She thinks Life lost in her own Family, and fancies her self out of the World when she is not in the Ring, the Play-House, or the Drawing-Room: She lives in a perpetual Motion of Body, and Restlessness of Thought . . . [and] grows Contemptible by being Conspicuous.[8]

The "good" woman possesses a taste for solitude and domestic felicity that will protect her from the snares laid for her reputation in the frivolous pleasures of the town; the "bad" woman eschews solitude and domesticity and appreciates only herself and those pursuits that can add to her own enjoyment, in spite of their dangers.

This binary opposition of the characters of women was a bane for writers attempting to create interesting female characters in novels. In the preface to *Maria,* Mary Wollstonecraft complained that "In many works of this species, the hero is allowed to be mortal, and to become wise and virtuous as well as happy, by a train of events and circumstances. The heroines, on the contrary, are to be born immaculate, and to act like

6. Patricia Meyer Spacks, "Ev'ry Woman Is at Heart a Rake," *Eighteenth-Century Studies* 8 (Fall 1974): 27.

7. Alice Browne, *The Eighteenth-Century Feminist Mind* (Detroit: Wayne State University Press, 1987), 140.

8. Joseph Addison and Richard Steele, *The Spectator,* ed. Donald F. Bond (Oxford: Clarendon Press, 1965), 1:68–69.

goddesses of wisdom, just come forth highly finished Minervas from the head of Jove."[9] While male and female authors struggled to create heroines for their works who reflected as many of the attributes of the good woman as possible, Inchbald refused to conform to such a simple categorization. While the attempt to judge Miss Milner forms a large and important part of the first two volumes of her text—Dorriforth, his tutor Mr. Sandford, Miss Milner's companion Miss Woodley, and all of the other characters who surround the heroine attempt to form a solid judgment about Miss Milner's essential character—the successful placement of the heroine into the binary of either good or bad is impossible.[10] A woman of "lively elegance and dignified simplicity," Miss Milner combines extraordinary beauty "with sense and with virtue" (14).[11] While she partakes

9. Mary Wollstonecraft, *Maria, or The Wrongs of Woman* (1798) (New York: W. W. Norton, 1975), 21. See also Paula R. Backscheider's "Women Writers and the Chains of Identification," *Studies in the Novel* 19 (Fall 1987): "The heroes had correctable faults, but the heroines were paragons. . . . Women writers observe this convention throughout the period. Delarivière Manley's 'To the Reader' in *The Secret History of Queen Zarah* complains that heroes may have faults but heroines are 'exempted from all the Weakness of Humane Nature, and much above the Infirmities of their Sex.' Nearly a hundred years later, Mary Wollstonecraft resented the fact that 'the hero is allowed to be mortal' while the heroines 'are to be born immaculate' . . . " (246, 259n.). Katharine M. Rogers adds, "For the chastity, propriety, sense of duty, delicacy enjoined on women in real life were doubly enjoined on the fictitious woman who was not worthy to be a heroine if she could not serve as a model. Moreover, since the main concern was to keep the heroine beyond criticism by the most rigorous standard of female virtue, the emphasis tends to fall on the errors she avoids rather than the good qualities she has. Her chastity must not only keep her chaste but keep her from strong feelings for any man to whom she is not married, her prudence must keep her from entering any situation wherein she might conceivably be compromised, her modesty must keep her from showing even the least sign of egotism" ("Inhibitions on Eighteenth-Century Women Novelists: Elizabeth Inchbald and Charlotte Smith," *Eighteenth-Century Studies* 11 [Fall 1977]: 65).

10. It must be noted, however, that Inchbald encourages the *attempt* to judge even as she refuses its success: Miss Milner is not introduced to the principal characters or to the reader until the third chapter of the text. This delayed revelation allows both characters and reader to speculate about the heroine. Miss Milner, when she does appear, dares others to evaluate her: "The whole world is welcome to hear what I say, and every different judge welcome, if they please, to judge me differently" (56). Inchbald's narrative appeals to the reader—"Yet let not our over-scrupulous readers be misled, and extend their idea of her virtue so as to magnify it beyond that which frail mortals commonly possess; nor must they cavil, if, on a nearer view, they find it less . . . " (14)—and challenges the reader to form a judgment.

11. Elizabeth Inchbald, *A Simple Story* (1791), ed. J.M.S. Tompkins (Oxford: Oxford University Press, 1988). Subsequent page citations appear in parentheses.

"with delight" of all the London pleasures of "balls, plays, incessant company," visiting, and operas, and "thought those moments passed in wasteful idleness during which she was not gaining some new conquest" (15), she also shows great "satisfaction" in the "tranquillity" of life at her country house (47). Miss Milner's resemblance to Addison's Fulvia is as marked as her similarity to his Aurelia, and for a great part of the text she defies all attempts at categorization and remains interesting, vital, and elusive.

Of all those who attempt to judge her, the most relentless is Miss Milner's guardian and self-styled mentor, Dorriforth, who cannot see her in any other terms except those of binary opposition. Before he is introduced to his ward, Dorriforth tries to decide which sort of woman she shall be, a "good" or a "bad" one. When Lady Evans tells him that Miss Milner is a "young, idle, indiscreet, giddy girl, with half a dozen lovers in her suite," Dorriforth wishes never to meet her (9). Just a few moments later, when he is told by Mrs. Hillgrave that Miss Milner was the benefactress of the financially distressed Hillgraves, interceding with her father on their behalf and, when that failed, selling "some of her most valuable ornaments to satisfy his [Mr. Milner's] demand," Dorriforth is pleased and seems to agree with his visitor's opinion that Miss Milner is an "angel" (12). Every judgment Dorriforth makes concerning his ward's character is based on a conventional sense of duality: Miss Milner is good when she obeys him and refrains from going out (33); she is good or evil depending on whether or not she is willing to leave London for the country (42–44); she is evil whenever she shows signs of levity, disobedience, or self-contradiction, especially when she disobeys Dorriforth to attend a masquerade (156–65) and disobliges him by refusing to specify her attitude toward Lord Frederick (56–58, 69–70). Dorriforth thinks in categories and vacillates between extremes. He does not understand his ward, yet he insists upon maintaining control over her.

Miss Milner, however, mocks male binaries and control. She refuses to accept male authority simply because it asserts itself as such. When Sandford offers a discourse on angels and devils, asserting that beauty combined with evil is a mark of the most extreme wickedness, just as "Lucifer was the most beautiful of all the angels in paradise," Miss Milner responds by tauntingly asking, "How do you know?" (117). If Sandford had responded by citing male authorities—Milton or Genesis, for example—Miss Milner probably would have asked, "How do they know?" She may also have offered her characteristic response to phallocratic discourse—laughter, the sort of laughter that Catherine Clément speaks of when she says, "She laughs, and it's frightening—like Medusa's laugh—petrifying and shattering constraint. . . . Laughter breaks up, breaks out, splashes over. . . . It is the moment at which the woman crosses a dangerous line, the cultural demarcation beyond which she will find herself excluded."[12] This is also the laughter Hélène Cixous writes about: "They riveted us between two horrifying myths: between the Medusa and the abyss. That would be enough to set half the world laughing. . . . You only have to look at the Medusa straight on to see her. And she's not deadly. She's beautiful and she's laughing."[13]

Miss Milner's laughter defies the binary system of those around her. It is laughter that enables her to break convention apart instead of simply asserting another version of convention. As Irigaray puts it, "To escape from a pure and simple reversal of the masculine position means in any case not to forget to laugh."[14] The clearest example of Miss Milner's escape from patriarchy through laughter appears when Dorriforth asserts that the dogma of Roman Catholicism is true and that Miss Milner should "trust to persons who know better than yourself." Miss Milner responds to his authority and the pious subservience of the others by "freely . . . indulg[ing] that risibility which she had been struggling to smother; and without longer suffering under the agony of restraint, she gave way to her humour, and laughed with a liberty so uncontrolled, that in a short time left her in the room with none but the tender-hearted Miss Woodley" (17). Miss Milner laughs when Dorriforth attempts to press the case of a suitor she dislikes (24); she laughs again at the advice of Miss Woodley that she "not fall in love without the approbation of" her guardian (26); she cannot "restrain her laughter" when Sandford stresses the importance of his "counsel" and his "interest at Rome" (87); and she laughs at Dorriforth, now Lord Elmwood, when he tells her sternly "Not to think of being there" at the masquerade (151–52). Any form of masculine constraint or animosity is subject to Miss Milner's mirth, as laughter becomes her woman's weapon against oppression. She sustains and returns Sandford's

12. Catherine Clément, "The Guilty One," in *The Newly Born Woman,* 32–33.

13. Hélène Cixous, "The Laugh of the Medusa," trans. Keith Cohen and Paula Cohen, in *New French Feminisms: An Anthology,* ed. Elaine Marks and Isabelle de Courtivron (New York: Schocken Books, 1981), 255. See also: "If she's a her-she, it's in order to smash everything, to shatter the framework of institutions, to blow up the law, to break up the 'truth' with laughter" (258).

14. Irigaray, *This Sex,* 163.

attacks by mocking him: "She now commenced hostilities on all his arguments, his learning, and his favourite axioms; and by a happy turn for ridicule, in want of other weapons, threw in the way of the holy Father as great trials for his patience, as any his order could have substituted in penance" (40–41). Only when she is disarmed of her weapon of laughter, when she falls in love with the enemy, can Miss Milner be subdued. Her love for Dorriforth deprives her of her "laugh of ridicule" (24), as she tells her companion: "It is that tenderness which frightens me, Miss Woodley; that intimidates, and strikes me dumb—is it possible I can return impertinence to the language and manners Mr. Dorriforth uses? and as I am debarred from that, what can I do but stand before him like a guilty creature, acknowledging my faults" (49). Disarmed, Miss Milner is reduced to the role imposed on women by men, the role of "the guilty one," to use Catherine Clément's phrase. The reduction is so complete as to seem physical: "In the last mentioned situation [awaiting Dorriforth's censure], she was shorter in stature than in the former [surrounded by admirers in the drawing room]—she was paler—she was thinner—and a very different contour presided over her whole air, and all her features" (50).

The love plot, often treated unambiguously as the desirable goal in eighteenth-century novels, receives bizarre twists in *A Simple Story.* Love is not to be sought but is to be avoided in the first part of Inchbald's work, for Miss Milner has fallen in love with the forbidden; she has developed a passion for her guardian, a Roman Catholic priest. The problem is complex: as long as Miss Milner is not in love, the notion of "forbidden" does not apply, for she is removed from patriarchal codes and rules. However, as soon as she falls in love with Dorriforth, Miss Milner enters the patriarchal system and is forced to accept the masculine binary code and to see herself as the bad woman.

In *A Simple Story,* priesthood forms the location of all that is prohibited and taboo. The very first words of Inchbald's text offer an account of Dorriforth's extremely atypical vocation:

> DORRIFORTH, bred at St. Omer's in all the scholastic rigour of that college, was by education, and the solemn vows of his order, a Roman Catholic priest.... He refused to shelter himself from the temptations of the layman by the walls of a cloister, but sought for, and found that shelter in the centre of London, where he dwelt, in his own prudence, justice, fortitude, and temperance. (3)

Elizabeth Inchbald was a Catholic herself,[15] and as such she was probably familiar with the position of the Catholic clergy in England. The First Catholic Relief Act of 1778 made Catholic priests "no longer subject to prosecution through common informers," while the Second Catholic Relief Act of 1791 "legalized the public celebration of Mass."[16] With the easing of persecution, Roman Catholic clergy in England could behave more in accord with their vows and less in disguise as private gentlemen. Yet Dorriforth, a Jesuit priest in name, is not one in practice. As Roger Manvell notes, "Dorriforth, the gentleman priest, never officiates at a service (however clandestine) in *A Simple Story,* or seems to observe the rites of his faith."[17] The Society of Jesus was founded as an order that "would not retire into monasteries to spend their days in chanting and prayer. They would remain in the world." Still, the rites of Dorriforth's faith and the demands of his vocation would involve, among other things, the vows of "poverty, chastity, and obedience."[18] Dorriforth, living alone under his own management, seems absolved from the vow of obedience,

15. Castle, *Masquerade and Civilization,* 291. See also Roger Manvell, *Elizabeth Inchbald: A Biographical Study* (Lanham, Md.: University Press of America, 1987), 72–73.

16. Manvell, *Elizabeth Inchbald,* 72. See David Mathew, *Catholicism in England: The Portrait of a Minority: Its Culture and Tradition,* 2d ed. (London: Eyre & Spottiswoode, 1948): "In June 1778 the first Catholic Relief Act received the royal assent. In consequence of this measure . . . the prosecution of the clergy by common informers and the penalty of imprisonment for life were abolished. . . . [In 1791] Catholic chapels became legal on registration and Mass could be celebrated by all priests who had taken a form of oath (the Irish Oath of 1774) acceptable both to the vicars apostolic and the government. The celebration of Mass was forbidden in any building possessing a bell or steeple. It was, however, permitted in a private house if not more than five outsiders were present. No Roman Catholic ecclesiastic was allowed to exercise any of the rites or ceremonies of his religion except in such a private house or in a registered chapel. The habits of religious orders might not be worn in the streets. . . . With the passing of the Relief Act of 1791 the acute difficulties within the Catholic body diminished" (146, 160).

17. Manvell, *Elizabeth Inchbald,* 73.

18. Manfred Barthel, *The Jesuits: History and Legend of the Society of Jesus* (New York: William Morrow, 1984), 28, 53. Along with the initial vows of poverty, chastity, and obedience, Jesuits also take a special fourth vow "to obey every instruction of the Pope of Rome, to go in whatsoever direction he might choose to send us" (48). Dorriforth does make a trip to the West Indies, but he does not go as a missionary; instead, after he becomes Lord Elmwood, Dorriforth travels in order "to save from the depredation of his steward, a very large estate" (196). Inchbald is subtly ironic in her use of Catholicism in this fiction: the heroine's father, a man who chooses Dorriforth as his

while he dispenses with that of poverty: "Mr. Dorriforth was nearly related to one of our first catholic peers; his income was by no means confined, but approaching to affluence" (6). Dorriforth allows a "liberal stipend" for his apartments and board (7), keeps a carriage (12), summers at Miss Milner's country seat (42), and fights a duel (63ff.). While it can beargued that Inchbald was offering social commentary on the vices and hypocrisy of Jesuits, such an attack would be inconsistent with her continual narrative attempts to emphasize Dorriforth's rectitude and virtue, such as the following: "he possessed qualities not unworthy the first professors of Christianity—every virtue which it was his vocation to preach, it was his care to practise" (3). Even as Inchbald describes his violation of the vow of poverty, she emphasizes that Dorriforth's "attention to those in poverty, and the moderation of his own desires were such, that he lived in all the careful plainness of œconomy" (6). There are no elements of clerical satire in Inchbald's treatment of Dorriforth.

If Dorriforth is not made a priest for the purposes of social commentary, why then is he a Jesuit? Dorriforth's vocation seems to serve a sexual purpose in Inchbald's text: the only priestly vow that remains inviolable is the "religious vow of celibacy" (7). Chastity is the only religious constraint explicitly mentioned in the text and the only one stressed during the opening pages of the work. In *A Simple Story,* then, priesthood seems to be offered as an enticement to desire: Dorriforth, as a priest, is learned, masculine, virtuous, and ostensibly virginal. As *Father* Dorriforth, he is forbidden; as Miss Milner's guardian or surrogate father, he is doubly prohibited. To seduce a priest was represented, in pornographic works of the century, as a Catholic woman's desire, and the seduction of the priest in this case would defy and overthrow all patriarchal boundaries. Miss Milner's declaration that she loves Dorriforth "with all the passion of a mistress, and with all the tenderness of a wife" (72) is,

---

sole friend, shares the name of Bishop John Milner (correspondent to the Press, 1779–1826), a clergyman "particularly attached to the Jesuits" (Mathew, *Catholicism in England,* 154). (On Inchbald's knowledge of Bishop Milner, see J.M.S. Tompkins's notes on *A Simple Story:* "The name Milner may conceivably have been suggested by J. P. Kemble. John Milner . . . had been at school with him" [340n.].) Dorriforth is a Jesuit bred at St. Omer's in France—Mathew states that the Jesuits were expelled from St. Omer's in 1763 (138) (Tompkins puts the date at 1762 [340n.]). Dorriforth's vocation is made to appear chimerical in its very formulation.

like her laughter, a shocking disruption of male hierarchy and order.[19] The very coupling of the two words "mistress" and "wife" undoes their hierarchical opposition.

Inchbald makes the seduction possible by transforming the Father/father into Lord Elmwood. Having established the taboo in her first volume, she can then remove the overt bonds of priesthood while retaining the resonance of the proscription in Dorriforth's character. For, although "there are no religious vows, from which the great Pontiff of Rome cannot grant a dispensation . . . [so] that this earldom should continue in a catholic family" (101), nothing can remove the attributes of a priest from Dorriforth. Since he retains a position of patriarchal dominance, Dorriforth/Lord Elmwood's submission to Miss Milner's charms would be an astonishing female triumph. Such is the passion Miss Milner wishes to create in him, an unconditional love:

> "Are not my charms even more invincible than I ever believed them to be? Dorriforth, the grave, the sanctified, the anchorite Dorriforth, by their force is animated to all the ardour of the most impassioned lover—while the proud priest, the austere guardian, is humbled, if I but frown, into the veriest slave of love." . . . These thoughts . . . of being beloved in spite of her faults, (a glory proud women ever aspire to) was, at present, the ambition of Miss Milner. (138)

19. "Miss Milner feels love for Dorriforth when it is doubly forbidden, by the code of feminine delicacy and by his priesthood, and her frank declaration, 'I love him with all the passion of a mistress, and with all the tenderness of a wife' . . . heralds the return of women's sexuality to the women's novel"—Jane Spencer, *The Rise of the Woman Novelist: From Aphra Behn to Jane Austen* (Oxford: Basil Blackwell, 1986), 160. In her introduction to the novel, Spencer adds, "Her [Miss Milner's] emotions are doubly forbidden, by the code of feminine delicacy and by Dorriforth's religious vows. The Catholic interest in the novel is important mainly because it adds the shocking hint of sacrilege to the heroine's desire: that desire and its prohibition are Inchbald's main concerns" (vii). See also Castle: "But by far and away the most important aspect of Miss Milner's character is her yearning, intractable and unerring, for that which is taboo. She longs, as though by reflex, for that which is denied her, banned by convention, edict, or scruple. She is undoubtedly capricious and often desires what is forbidden precisely because it is forbidden. She exemplifies what Georges Bataille calls the 'absurd proposition' at the heart of desire—that 'the forbidden is there to be violated.' 'Monastic vows, like those of marriage,' Miss Milner overhears someone remark early in the novel, 'were made to be broken' " (*Masquerade and Civilization,* 299).

At first, Miss Milner retains a seductive indifference similar to that of Eliza Haywood's Briscilla, Fantomina, or Glicera: "As my guardian, I certainly did obey him; and I could obey him as a husband; but as a lover, I will not. . . . for if he will not submit to be my lover, I will not submit to be his wife—nor has he the affection I require in a husband" (154). The similarities of Miss Milner to Haywood's masquerade heroines, however, are merely superficial, for, unlike the truly indifferent coquetry of Haywood's trio, Miss Milner's unconcern is feigned. The problem is not that Miss Milner falls in love with what is forbidden—it is that she falls in love at all.

Inchbald's pivotal masquerade scene has, as Terry Castle points out, "only one real purpose: to disclose relations of power, of dominance and submission."[20] Unable to be indifferent to the outcome of her defiance, Miss Milner is reabsorbed into the patriarchal structure and, as Irigaray puts it, "has to become a normal woman, that is, has to enter into the *masquerade of femininity*" where she will "participate in man's desire, but at the price of renouncing . . . [her] own."[21] Miss Milner's contradiction of Lord Elmwood's will brings her no pleasure. Instead, it results in her envisioning herself as Lord Elmwood sees her and entering into the binary system he controls:

> She . . . was at the scene of pleasure she had pictured to herself, and all the pleasure it gave her was, that she was sure she should never desire to go to a masquerade again.—The crowd and bustle fatigued her—the freedom offended her delicacy—and though she perceived she was the first object of admiration in the place, yet there was one person still wanting to admire; and the remorse at having transgressed his injunctions for so trivial an entertainment, weighed upon her spirits, and added to its weariness. (161)

From this point onward with few interruptions, Miss Milner sees herself as a "bad" woman, guilty within the patriarchal system. Her diminishment through masquerade is analogous to the objectification that transforms the female protagonists in Behn's *Dumb Virgin* and Haywood's *Masqueraders.* When Lord Elmwood's formal letter of parting comes, Miss Milner begins a period of suffering that fulfills the desires of men but robs her of any

20. Castle, *Masquerade and Civilization,* 309.
21. Irigaray, *This Sex,* 133–34.

desires and pleasures of her own. Gone is her "immoderate enjoyment of the art of pleasing, for her own individual happiness, and not for the happiness of others" (19)—her sole concern is to please one who will only be satisfied with the complete submission of all her inclinations to his direction.[22] Inchbald's innovative, complex female protagonist is reabsorbed into the system that she had, during the greater part of two volumes, defied. While *Fantomina*'s fantastic plot allowed for the heroine's extended freedom, the realism of *A Simple Story* offers no possibilities beyond the restoration of the oppressive status quo.

II. Mirror and Commodity

In *The Rise of the Woman Novelist,* Jane Spencer discusses many women's novels that focus upon the reform of the heroine through the intervention of a lover-mentor, among them Mary Davys's *Reform'd Coquet* and Frances Burney's *Evelina* and *Camilla.* Of Inchbald's *Simple Story,* Spencer writes,

> . . . the novel casts doubt on the whole notion of reform by the lover-mentor. Miss Milner's reform, based not on reflection and self-knowledge but on passion, is incomplete, and her austere guardian, also under the influence of passion for the first time in his life, is the worst person to make allowances for her imprudences. . . .
>
> Lord Elmwood's inability to be both lover and mentor is symptomatic of *A Simple Story*'s challenge to the fundamental assumptions behind the didactic tradition. A novel like *Evelina* suggested that the tutor and lover could properly be found in the

22. If his own desire for dominance is to be fulfilled, if his "horror of . . . a family without subordination" (142) is to be avoided, Dorriforth must force Miss Milner to renounce her own desires, desires which she often cannot defend because she finds it impossible to put them into words. Irigaray and other Continental feminists stress the impossibility of expressing female desire in the language that men speak and understand; yet, at the same time, they realize that such an inability to express "what it is that women want" makes it possible for men always to win the struggle for "mastery of power": "A whole strategy has to be worked out so that her, their, instincts remain inhibited . . . in their aims, so that women work at reproduction without pleasure or property rights over the product" (*Speculum,* 95). Inchbald shows such inhibition taking over in Miss Milner and reveals the gradual stages by which desire and pleasure are lost.

> same person, and that the right husband was one who would take over the functions of father and guardian. Only by giving her heroine such an excess of delicacy that she seems quite impervious to sexual desire did Burney avoid the incestuous implications of this relationship.[23]

Inchbald, while stressing how the "incestuous implications" of the lover-mentor relationship could precipitate desire,[24] criticizes the idea that a husband should function as the guardian or mentor of his wife. While Burney's heroines, for example, are tutored in prudence and polite manners, Inchbald's heroine is systematically broken and transformed from a vital woman into a soulless object. Inchbald's work emphasizes the ruinous results—for both men and women—of allowing one person so much power over another and establishing such a dangerous inequality within marriage.

In *A Simple Story,* Dorriforth never questions his right to "reform" Miss Milner. Twelve years her senior and male, he immediately exercises the prerogative to impress his value for the quiet, reflective life upon her, "notwithstanding that dissimilarity of opinion . . . in almost every respect, subsisted between Miss Milner and her guardian" (23). Although Mr. Milner had asked Dorriforth simply to "protect without controlling, [and] instruct without tyrannizing" (5), since Miss Milner is old enough to choose for herself, Dorriforth issues peremptory commands and dares her to defy them, as when he, knowing she has a previous engagement, says, "I command you to stay at home this evening" (29). The order is purely arbitrary, a test of his power. Once assured of Miss Milner's obedience, he tells her to "keep your appointment, and be assured I shall issue my commands with greater circumspection for the future, as I find how strictly they are complied with." When Miss Milner responds by weeping, "it gave satisfaction to Dorriforth.—He was charmed to find her disposition so little untractable—forboded the future prosperity of his guardianship, and her eternal, as well as temporal happiness from this specimen" (33).

It is well to ask in what the prosperity of Dorriforth's guardianship consists and why he is a better judge of what will constitute Miss Milner's

23. Spencer, *Woman Novelist,* 159–60.

24. Inchbald alludes to incest twice: "to see her guardian at her feet, struck her [Miss Milner] with the same impropriety as if she had beheld a parent there" (62), and "[his priesthood was] a prohibition to her love . . . as . . . that barrier which divides a sister from a brother" (74).

"eternal, as well as temporal happiness" than she is herself. His changes seem calculated to reduce Miss Milner from subject to object: she is to adopt his wishes and deny her own, thereby becoming his mirror. Lacan insists that the formation of the "I" can only be accomplished with reference to the mirror offered by the desire of the "other"; Irigaray takes this one step farther to insist that "*Commodities, women, are a mirror of value of and for man....* They yield to him their natural and social value as a locus of imprints, marks, and mirage of his activity."[25] Inchbald portrays this complex psychological development as she shows Dorriforth using Miss Milner's desire to discover himself: "Again he searched his own thoughts, nor ineffectually as before.—At the first glance the object was presented, and he beheld *himself*" (130).

Dorriforth is Machiavellian in his efforts to transform Miss Milner: he delegates the unpleasant task of breaking her spirit to his second, Sandford, while he stands on the sidelines, pretending to deplore the very things he sets in motion. The reader is at first encouraged to see Sandford as the leader when the elder Jesuit is introduced as Dorriforth's feared tutor (38–39). The fact that Sandford is subordinate to Dorriforth becomes apparent only in the second half of Inchbald's text, as Sandford admits, " 'In a word, I am more at my ease when I am away from him [Lord Elmwood]—and I really believe,' added he with a smile, but with a tear at the same time, 'I really believe I am more afraid of him in my age, than he was of me when he was a boy' " (223). It can be argued that their relationship has changed over time, and that the ruled has usurped the position of ruler. A careful examination of the text, however, offers evidence against such an argument. When Dorriforth decides to fight a duel, he is "unshaken by the arguments, persuasions, and menaces of Sandford" (66). As Lord Elmwood, wishing to marry Miss Milner, he "with the utmost degree of inflexibility, resisted all his [Sandford's] good counsel" and refused to "flatter the *supposed* authority he [Sandford] possessed over him" (136–37; italics mine). Finally, in the second half of *A Simple Story,* Lord Elmwood insists that his implacability represents not so much a change of temper as a return "to what it was originally" (214). Sandford's activities must meet with Dorriforth's approbation, or else he would not tolerate them.

Sandford's sole occupation seems to be that of oppressing Miss Milner.

25. Jacques Lacan, "The Mirror Stage," in *Écrits: A Selection,* trans. Alan Sheridan (New York: W. W. Norton, 1977), 1–7; Irigaray, *This Sex,* 177.

He is "eager to draw upon him her detestation, in the hope he could also make her abominate herself" (39). Miss Milner feels the effects of his repeated attacks on her independence of mind: "This behavior of Mr. Sandford's had its desired effect; it humbled Miss Milner in her own opinion. . . . She felt an inward nothingness she never knew before, and had been cured of all her pride, had she not possessed a degree of spirit beyond the generality of her sex, and such as even Mr. Sandford with all his penetration did not expect" (40). Miss Milner realizes that the struggle is for control. When Sandford says he will never enter any house where she is the mistress, she responds, "Nor any house I am certain, Mr. Sandford, but where you yourself are the master" (44). Miss Milner dislikes the repeated confrontations but understands that she can end them only by offering complete subservience: "But though she had generosity to forgive an affront, she had not the humility to make a concession; and she foresaw that nothing less than some very humble atonement on her part, would prevail upon the haughty priest to be reconciled" (47).

Miss Milner is also aware, at some level, that what Sandford finally wants is to reduce her to being a mirror for the men around her, to deprive her of her own identity in order to serve their desire to dominate. When questioned by Sandford about her knowledge of Lord Frederick's arrival in the country, Miss Milner responds,

> "But I hope, Mr. Sandford, you will permit me to know?" cried Miss Milner.—For as she now meant to torment him by what she said, she no longer constrained herself to silence —and as he harboured the same kind intent towards her, he had no longer any objection to make a reply, and therefore answered,
>
> "No, madam, if it depended upon my permission, you should *not* know."
>
> "Not *any thing,* sir, I dare say;—you would keep me in utter ignorance."
>
> "I would."
>
> "From a self-interested motive, Mr. Sandford—that I might have a greater respect for you." (48–49)

In *Speculum of the Other Woman* Irigaray insists, "Now, if this [male] ego is to be valuable, some 'mirror' is needed to reassure it and re-insure it of its value. Woman will be the foundation of this specular duplication, giving man back 'his' image and repeating it as the 'same.'"[26] Clearly, Sandford wishes to have Miss Milner serve this replicating function.

Dorriforth claims to be impartial during all of these very serious struggles, as he comments to Miss Milner:

> "For in respect to all those little disputes between Mr. Sandford and you," said he, "I should be partial if I blamed you more than him—indeed, when you take the liberty to censure him, his character makes the freedom appear in a more serious light than when he complains of you—yet, if he provokes your retorts, he alone must answer for them; nor will I undertake to decide betwixt you." (51)

In one clever move, Dorriforth belittles the attacks of Sandford upon Miss Milner, ignoring the fact that the stakes are very high—Miss Milner is fighting for her very identity; he claims to blame them equally but immediately asserts that her responses are more blameworthy than Sandford's complaints, once again casting Miss Milner as "the guilty one"; Dorriforth insists upon his own impartiality, which leaves Miss Milner in a hopeless position. For if she is to be a properly submissive woman, she needs a man who will undertake to defend her against the insults of others. Dorriforth is the only man in a position to provide that defense. By remaining impartial he is really taking Sandford's side, since he leaves Miss Milner to defend herself, which automatically makes her blameworthy.

The irony is, of course, that Dorriforth is not impartial at all. He always offers aid to his fellow Jesuit. Yet the aid is given in such a way as to leave Sandford with the taint of malignancy and absolve Dorriforth from the charge of unkindness. In some cases, Dorriforth changes the subject when Miss Milner's responses are getting the better of Sandford (44), while at other points he uses the power of silent frowns (49). At those times when Sandford has reduced Miss Milner to tears Dorriforth says nothing, seeing her weeping as "a new reproach to his friend Mr. Sandford, and to suffer himself to be moved by it, he considered would be a tacit condemnation of his friend's conduct," which Dorriforth rarely offers (45). Instead, he unnecessarily subjects Miss Milner to Sandford's judgment (55) and allows Sandford to enter the house that belongs to his ward (66), thereby silently encouraging confrontations between them under conditions favorable to his friend.

26. Irigaray, *Speculum,* 54.

Dorriforth is the hidden controlling patriarchal force behind all of Sandford's and Miss Milner's skirmishes. His insistence on bringing the two together and his quiet interference fuel their animosity. In every case, however, Dorriforth is careful to protect his own good relation with each combatant. The claim of impartiality that he offers to Miss Milner is an instance of his attempt to palliate her, as is his rare but gallant defense of her. At one point, although he has invited Sandford into her house, Dorriforth censures the very attack he has brought about, saying, "Hold, Mr. Sandford . . . the lady is under my protection, and I know not whether it is not necessary you should apologize to her, and to me, for what you have already said." Sandford very rightly responds, "You asked my opinion, or I had not given it you." Dorriforth counters by leading Miss Milner "kindly to the door, as if to defend her from his [Sandford's] malice" (87–88). In this defense, Dorriforth removes Miss Milner from Sandford instead of banishing the latter from the house of the former, an act calculated to placate the Jesuit. At another time, Dorriforth earns Sandford's goodwill at Miss Milner's expense: " . . . perceiving Sandford was offended at what had passed [a request that he not censure Miss Milner], as the only means of retribution, his lordship began himself to lament her volatile and captious propensities; in which lamentation Sandford, now forgetting his affront, joined with the heartiest concurrence . . . " (106). Playing one side against the other, Dorriforth "reforms," or rather crushes, Miss Milner with a minimum of his own effort.

Absolute control of Miss Milner is the objective. When she says to her guardian, "I am not mistress of my inclinations, sir, or they should conform to yours," he avidly replies, "Place them under my direction, madam, and I'll answer they will" (53). Dorriforth desires her compliance, not her happiness—during those times when "her melancholy humour was . . . predominant; and for several days she staid entirely at home, and yet was denied to all her visitants. . . . Lord Elmwood could not but observe this change . . . and applaud it" (109). Pleased to find her sad and bored, Dorriforth employs a rigid behaviorist system of rewards and punishments calculated to transform Miss Milner from subject to "worthy object" (113): "he watched her as he would a child . . . [or] his darling bird" (134).

Luce Irigaray, in her essay "Women on the Market," employs the image of the market to explain how women function as a type of commodity for men:

> The society we know, our own culture, is based upon the exchange of women. . . . men, or groups of men, circulate women among themselves. . . .
>
> . . . The law that orders our society is the exclusive valorization of men's needs/desires, of exchanges among men. . . .
>
> . . . Men make commerce *of* them [women], but they do not enter into any exchanges *with* them. . . . The economy—in both the narrow and the broad sense—that is in place in our societies thus requires that women lend themselves to alienation in consumption, and to exchanges in which they do not participate, and that men be exempt from being used and circulated like commodities.[27]

Miss Milner, during the first part of *A Simple Story,* is revealed as having such an exchange and use function. Eager at first to pursue her own desires, by the end of the second volume she has no will but that which conforms to Lord Elmwood's wishes and whims. Miss Milner is potentially dangerous: strong-willed and an heiress, were she outside the control of men she could disrupt the hierarchical patriarchal system.[28] Handed from father to guardian, Miss Milner is never actually free of male domination, even when she attempts to defy Dorriforth's control. However, until she is entirely subdued, until even her attempts at defiance are at an end, Miss Milner produces fear: "Though Mr. Sandford was not a man easily intimidated, he was on this occasion [of Miss Milner's rising to challenge him] evidently alarmed; and stared about him with so strong an expression of surprise, that it partook in some degree of fear" (125). Until she is seen to be a commodity, firmly established as the property of Lord Elmwood, Miss Milner poses a threat to the entire society. When she is reduced to "dead silence" and "a flood of tears," Sandford "then heaved a sigh of content that it had so ended" (125).

Once Miss Milner is broken, silent, tearful, and submissive, Sandford's mission is over. He can then offer her a plate of biscuits (182), hold her hand (184), comfort her (185), and finally unite her to Lord Elmwood (191–92). Mrs. Horton's speech emphasizes the fact that this behavior is

27. Irigaray, *This Sex,* 170–72.

28. Irigaray tries to imagine such a state: "For, without the exploitation of women, what would become of the social order? What modifications would it undergo if women left behind their condition as commodities—subject to being produced, consumed, valorized, circulated, and so on, by men alone—and took part in elaborating and carrying out exchanges?" (*This Sex,* 191).

possible only when Miss Milner is no longer a threat: "Ay . . . good Mr. Sandford may show his kindness now, without any danger from its consequences" (186).

Miss Milner's capitulation and visible entry into the patriarchal system of exchange are indicated by her movement from vivacious speech to tearful silence and by her passage from self-willed to other-dominated. She also reveals her function as commodity by being the object of male competition and by herself entering into female rivalry. Irigaray again offers an appropriate analogy:

> The price of the articles, in fact, no longer comes from *their* natural form, from *their* bodies, *their* language, but from the fact that they mirror the need/desire for exchanges among men. To do this, the commodity obviously cannot exist alone, but there is no such thing as a commodity, either, so long as there are not *at least two men* to make an exchange. In order for a product—a woman?—to have value, two men, at least, have to invest (in) her.[29]

Competition with other men allows Dorriforth to estimate Miss Milner's price. Dorriforth credits Sandford's investment in Miss Milner as giving the first impetus to his interest:

> Mr. Sandford . . . I [will not] suffer myself to be again prepossessed in her favour by your prejudice against her—for I believe it was compassion at your unkind treatment of her, that first gained her my heart. . . .
>
> . . . Now, I will no longer . . . have an enemy such as you have been, to heighten her charms. . . . (141)

Rivalry with Miss Milner's suitor Lord Frederick provides a second incentive. The blow that Dorriforth bestows upon the face of Lord Frederick, and the subsequent threat of a duel, precipitates Miss Milner into the marriage market, as she is blamed for the event and forced then to choose (59–71). Miss Milner's initial unconcern—"Miss Milner observed, but observed with indifference, the sensations of both [Dorriforth and Lord Frederick]" (19)—is forfeited as Dorriforth's rash behavior makes her regard him as a lover.

29. Ibid., 181.

From this point in the text onward, Miss Milner becomes a commodity within a violently competitive male system. Her submission to that system is complete when, fearful of losing Dorriforth, she invites Lord Frederick to the house in hopes of making her guardian jealous (172). Far from being a break in the continuity and unity of the text,[30] then, Miss Milner's (now Lady Elmwood's) infidelity—which opens the second part of Inchbald's work—is a very appropriate confirmation of her status as an object given value only by exchange. Since commodities are encouraged to "be preoccupied with their respective values,"[31] it is a sign of Lady Elmwood's coming to see herself as object that in the absence of one consumer she turns to the other, being unable in solitude to draw upon any inherent value in herself.

Miss Milner's commodity status also appears in her relations with other women. Having at first "a heart affectionate to her sex, even where she saw them in the possession of charms superior to her own" (38), she comes to enter into a rivalry with Miss Fenton. "Men," says Irigaray, "have organized a *de facto* rivalry among women. . . . the interests of businessmen require that commodities relate to each other as rivals."[32] Such is the case with Miss Milner—Dorriforth, as he masterminds the other projects intended to reduce her to an object, sets in motion this female rivalry,

> and frequently, *sometimes inadvertently,* held up . . . [Miss Fenton] as a pattern for her to follow—for, when he did not say this in direct terms, it was insinuated by the warmth of his panegyrics on those virtues in which Miss Fenton excelled, and his ward was obviously deficient. Conscious of her inferiority in these subjects of her guardian's praise, Miss Milner, instead of being inspired to emulation, was provoked to envy. (37; italics mine)

30. Many critics see the second part of *A Simple Story* as a separate work clumsily tacked on to the first part. See James Boaden, *Memoirs of Mrs. Inchbald* (London: Richard Bentley, 1833), 1:286; J.M.S. Tompkins, Introduction to *A Simple Story,* by Elizabeth Inchbald (Oxford: Oxford University Press, 1967), x, xiii; Manvell, *Elizabeth Inchbald,* 70–71; Rogers, "Inhibitions," 68, 71; Spacks, *Desire and Truth,* 196–97. Even Castle flirts with the possibility of textual discontinuity (*Masquerade and Civilization,* 321–22). Mary Anne Schofield, in *Masking and Unmasking the Female Mind: Disguising Romances in Feminine Fiction, 1713–1799* (Newark: University of Delaware Press, 1990), insists that "Part One tries to present the feminine text, while Part Two is the man's story" (180).

31. Irigaray, *This Sex,* 179.

32. Irigaray, *This Sex,* 164, 196.

And what are those virtues that Dorriforth "sometimes inadvertently" (and therefore sometimes deliberately) holds up for Miss Milner to imitate?

> That serenity of mind which kept her [Miss Fenton's] features in a continual placid form, though enchanting at the first glance, upon a second, or third, fatigued the sight for want of variety; and to have seen her distorted with rage, convulsed with mirth, or in deep dejection had been to her advantage. . . . there was more inducement to worship her as a saint, than to love her as a woman. (37)

Placid and cowlike, given to loading any "poor frail being . . . with . . . calumny" as long as that being is female (75), seeing it as her "duty" to become a wife yet incapable of really caring for anyone, she is "as much in sorrow as her nature would suffer her to be" when her fiancé is dangerously ill (91). Miss Milner's supposition that "a trial of her [Miss Fenton's] fortitude, might be more flattering to her vanity than to be Countess of Elmwood" (95) might be unkind, but every character in the book finds Miss Fenton unnatural. Lord Frederick calls her "the most insufferable of Heaven's creatures" (38); Miss Milner finds her "gloomy" (123); the narrator uses the words "insipid" and "cold indifference" when describing her (137); and, ironically, even Dorriforth *secretly* disparages her as "dreary winter" when set against Miss Milner's "perpetual spring" (137). Miss Fenton is, however, the perfect commodity, subservient to men and competitive with women. She can easily be used to "mortify" the "proud spirit" of Miss Milner and to force her to "suffer by immediate comparison—men, can scarcely bear this humiliation, but to women the punishment is intolerable" (37). Miss Fenton, who ends up immured in a convent while her brother enjoys her fortune (138), is the goal to which Miss Milner is encouraged to aspire. When, as Lady Elmwood, Miss Milner voluntarily retires to a "single house by the side of a dreary heath" in "a lonely country on the borders of Scotland" (199), she proves that she has successfully internalized the attributes of the model Dorriforth set before her.

Elizabeth Inchbald recognized, as few authors before her had, that the result of adding the manipulative ability of a lover to the power of a husband and the force of a guardian would be the destruction of a woman's independence.[33] The story of Miss Milner is the story of a woman's subjugation to the system of patriarchal dominance, to the practices of the marketplace. It is the story that comes to pass when the mentor/ward relationship is seen as a paradigm for marriage, as it often was in eighteenth-century society.

The irony of *A Simple Story*—an irony that strongly reinforces Inchbald's critique of complete patriarchal dominance in marriage—is that, had Dorriforth and Miss Milner *not* married, they stood a chance of being contented and virtuous people. Taken singly, Dorriforth's austere rectitude and Miss Milner's spritely sensibility are each attractive. Put together, Dorriforth becomes a priggish despot and Miss Milner a languishing neurotic. Inchbald begins the second part of her novel with this description:

> ...The beautiful, the beloved Miss Milner—she is no longer beautiful—no longer beloved—no longer ... virtuous.
>
> Dorriforth, the pious, the good, the tender Dorriforth, is become a hard-hearted tyrant. The compassionate, the feeling, the just Lord Elmwood, an example of implacable rigour and injustice. (194–95)

This passage clearly emphasizes that *both* protagonists are destroyed by the unequal union.

Dorriforth clearly becomes more imperious with every increase in love and attention that Miss Milner bestows upon him. From the start, there are hints of a dark side to his composition: "Although Dorriforth was that good man that has been described, there was in his nature shades of evil—there was an obstinacy; such as he himself, and his friends termed firmness of mind; but had not religion and some opposite virtues weighed heavy in the balance, it would frequently have degenerated into implacable stubbornness" (33–34). As Miss Milner comes to make her happiness depend on his kindness, Dorriforth's "firmness of mind" transforms itself into inflexible, implacable tyranny. As he comes to consider her spontaneity as "pernicious caprice" (90), her vivacity as coquetry, and her gaiety as dangerous levity, he begins the systematic imposition of his will upon her,

33. Inchbald is explicit on this—Miss Woodley warns Miss Milner of the risk she runs by attempting to gain power over Dorriforth: "consider, he is your guardian as well as your lover, he means also to become your husband; and he is a man of such nice honour, he will not give you a specimen of that power before marriage, which he does not intend to submit to hereafter" (166).

using behaviorist rewards and punishments, encouraging Sandford's attacks, and instituting rivalry with Miss Fenton in order to fit Miss Milner to his own desires.

Miss Milner, in turn, becomes unable to express her desires. She is cut off from access to language, being encouraged by both her guardian and his minion Sandford to "never speak" (123). Miss Milner begins to express with her body those things she can no longer put into words. From being a spirited woman "privileged to say any thing she pleased" (39), Miss Milner becomes one who "for the world . . . could not have spoken with a sprightly accent . . . not three words could she utter, before her tones sunk into the flattest dejection" (179). Miss Milner fades and sickens because she loves: "her health became impaired from the indisposition of her mind; she languished, and was once in imminent danger" (96). As the time of Dorriforth's departure nears, "Not only her colour, but her features became changed; her eyes lost their brilliancy, her lips seemed to hang without the power of motion, her head drooped, and her dress was wholly neglected. . . . never had she [Miss Woodley] yet seen her look so ill. . . . his [Sandford's] attention was caught by her deathly countenance" (179, 181–82).

As her own relationship to language becomes attenuated, Miss Milner becomes obsessed with the words of others. Like Brontë's Lucy Snowe, Miss Milner, during her stay at Bath—an enforced separation from Dorriforth that exiles Miss Milner from her own home—takes an abnormal interest in letters (I quote the passage at length to reveal its close similarity to the later treatment of the same subject in Charlotte Brontë's *Villette*):

> In the wide prospect of melancholy before her, Miss Milner's fancy caught hold of the only comfort which presented itself; and this, slender as it was, in the total absence of every other, her imagination pictured as excessive. The comfort was a letter from Miss Woodley—a letter wherein the subject of her love would most assuredly be mentioned, and in whatever terms, must still be the means of delight.
>
> A letter arrived—she devoured it with her eyes.—The post mark on the outside denoting from whence it came, the name of "Milner Lodge" written on the top, were all sources of pleasure—and she read slowly every line it contained to procrastinate the pleasing expectation she enjoyed, till she should arrive at the

> name of Dorriforth. At last her impatient eye, caught the word three lines beyond the place she was reading—irresistibly, she skipped over those lines, and fixed on the point to which she was attracted.
>
> Miss Woodley was cautious in her indulgence; she made the slightest mention of Dorriforth, saying only, "He was extremely concerned, and even dejected, at the little hope there was of his cousin, Lord Elmwood's, recovery."—Short and trivial as this passage was, it was still more important to Miss Milner than any other in the letter—she read it again and again, considered, and reflected upon it.—Dejected, thought she, what does that word exactly mean?—did I ever see Mr. Dorriforth dejected? —how I wonder does he look in that state?—Thus did she muse. . . .
>
> But her guardian wrote to her, and though the subject was sorrowful, the letter gave her joy—the sentiments it expressed were but trite and common-place, yet she valued them as the dearest effusions of friendship and affection; and her hand trembled, and her heart beat with rapture while she wrote the answer, though she knew it would not be received with one emotion, such as those which she experienced. (94–96)

As Lucy Snowe will later do, Miss Milner pores over every aspect of her friend's letter, from the postmark to the vocabulary. If she does this with a letter from Miss Woodley, how much more must she read and reread, muse over, and anatomize a letter from Dorriforth. Inchbald is effectively mute on that point, dwelling on Miss Milner's response to the letter from her female companion and allowing the reader to imagine the excesses implied by the phrase, "the letter [from her guardian] gave her joy." Yet Dorriforth's letters, like those of John Graham Bretton, are clearly not worth the expenditure of that much emotion and energy, being merely the expression of "trite and common-place" sentiments. Miss Milner, again like Brontë's heroine, writes rapturous responses that will be wasted on their receiver.

Miss Milner exaggerates the qualities of Dorriforth's letters in the same way that she magnifies the number of his virtues—she says at one point, "I believe, his being faultless, was the first cause of my passion" (149). Kaja Silverman points out that woman's "obligatory receptivity to the male gaze is what establishes its superiority, just as her obedience to the male voice is what 'proves' its power."[34] Miss Milner's objectification is completed when she becomes an "acoustic mirror" as well as a visual one, offering Dorriforth a heightened view and echo of himself.

Miss Milner's objectification clearly foreshadows the crisis that will form the second part of Inchbald's work. Having submitted herself so completely to Dorriforth "like a person insane . . . like a lunatic" (96), Miss Milner, as Lady Elmwood, does extravagant penance for her infidelity to him. The catastrophe that begins the second half of *A Simple Story* is not that Lady Elmwood has been unfaithful—it is that, because of her excessive guilt over her adultery, she willingly submits her daughter to Lord Elmwood's control and allows Matilda to continue to expiate her mother's sin. Unlike Haywood's Fantomina, who rejects Beauplaisir's offer to take his daughter and who establishes a community of women to raise her child, Lady Elmwood leaves Matilda behind when she flees her husband's house (197). When he sends the infant after her, Lady Elmwood, instead of rearing the child, "fell sick and lingered . . . till ten years decline, brought her to" death (199), again leaving Matilda prey to her father's despotism: "She [Lady Elmwood] had no will, she said, but what she would wholly submit to Lord Elmwood's; and, if it were even his will, her child should live in poverty, as well as banishment, it should be so" (203).[35]

On a second reading, knowing the outcome of the marriage, the reader realizes that the continually threatened dissolution of the engagement is a desirable event. Inchbald, playing upon the expectations of readers, makes that separation seem disastrous at first. Showing how both characters confront and test one another, Inchbald calculates that the reader will want the marriage to come about regardless of the outcome of the trials.

Dorriforth is determined to examine Miss Milner, noting to Sandford, "I will watch her closely myself—and if I find her mind and heart (such as my suspicions have of late whispered) too frivolous for that substantial happiness I look for with an object so beloved; depend upon my word—the marriage shall yet be broken off" (141–42). Since Dorriforth can only value what is like himself, and since Miss Milner's tastes and disposition are

34. Kaja Silverman, *The Acoustic Mirror: The Female Voice in Psychoanalysis and Cinema* (Bloomington: Indiana University Press, 1988), 32.

35. Compare this to the fragment that ends Wollstonecraft's *Maria:* in the midst of her attempt to commit suicide, Maria is told that her daughter is still alive. Wanting, in her own misery, to flee the world, she nevertheless concludes, "The conflict is over!—I will live for my child!" (153).

wholly dissimilar to his own, she has no chance of satisfying his scrupulous surveillance.

Miss Milner, on the other side, wishes to put Dorriforth "to the proof" (148). Desiring that love be unconditional, she wishes him to surrender his reason to his feelings, as she explains to Miss Woodley: "I mean, I will do something that any prudent man ought *not* to forgive; and yet, with that vast share of prudence he possesses, I will force him still to yield to his love" (148).[36] Considering that Dorriforth is a man who prides himself on the fact that "I have never yet . . . been vanquished by them [my passions] . . . my reason shall combat to the last" (131), he is certain to fail her test.

Miss Milner's defiant attendance at the masquerade decides the issue, or so it should. Both hero and heroine prove to each other and to themselves that they are entirely unsuited for one another as partners for life. In spite of all clear evidence of incompatibility, however, every character in the book still assumes that the two will marry, including Miss Milner herself: "In the various, though delicate, struggles for power between Miss Milner and her guardian, there was not one person witness to these incidents, who did not suppose, all would at last end in wedlock" (151). Even after the masquerade incident, Miss Milner insists, "I have been counterfeiting indifference to *him;* I now find all *his* indifference has been counterfeit too, and we not only love, but we love equally" (172). Only after receiving Lord Elmwood's final, abrupt letter does Miss Milner despond—again emphasizing the power Dorriforth's letters have over her (176).

Still, Inchbald is confident that the reader will wish for the marriage to take place and to succeed, in spite of the fact that she shows it to be constructed upon a foundation of repeated trials and countertrials. Courtship and marriage in *A Simple Story* do not involve tenderness—instead, they are revealed as erotically charged power struggles that contain implications of dissolution in their very origin. Many of the primary gaps in *A Simple Story* involve passages that would describe Miss Milner's and Dorriforth's happy and tender moments of courtship and marriage. The description of the joyous portion of the engagement is over in two sentences: "Within a few days, in the house of Lord Elmwood, every thing, and every person wore a new face.—His lordship was the profest lover of Miss Milner" (136). Four years of happy wedded life take up only

36. Notice that the pattern of transgression—doing something that any prudent man ought *not* to forgive—is repeated in Lady Elmwood's adultery, but at that point, bereft of will and desire, she makes no attempt to force Lord Elmwood to yield to his love and flees the estate at his approach (197).

one sentence (196).[37] The bulk of the text is about necessary separation, and the movement of the novel is toward breaking apart. Volume I begins with the meeting of Dorriforth and Miss Milner and ends with the enforced separation of guardian and ward. The second volume begins with their meeting again and moves inexorably toward their second parting. Stylistically, Volume II *should* end with Lord Elmwood's departure for the Continent.[38] The coda that joins the two protagonists is, on all counts, undesirable. Inchbald makes this clear through the only instance of transparent symbolism offered in her novel—Lady Elmwood's wedding ring is "a—MOURNING RING" (193).

III. The *No(m)* of the Father

Inchbald's examination of patriarchal authority and its implications continues through a second generation; the last two volumes of *A Simple Story* trace Dorriforth's, or Lord Elmwood's, transformation from an austere, dominating guardian into a rigid, uncommunicative husband, and finally into a tyrannical, despotic father. If the first part of Inchbald's text showed Miss Milner's desires becoming absorbed into those of her

37. There is a question, however, as to whether or not Miss Milner is at all happy in the marriage. The "delight" of the impetuous marriage is said to subsist in the fact that "every joy was doubled by the expected sorrow" (193). Irigaray defines the obsession with "pain as a necessary component of pleasure" as being particularly male (*This Sex,* 199–201). Inchbald is mute on the subject of Miss Milner's pleasure, although she does imply, through presumably ironic overstatement, that there was a falling off: "We left Lady Elmwood in the last volume at the summit of human happiness; a loving and beloved bride" (195). The main focus in Inchbald's description of the marriage is Dorriforth: "Lord Elmwood, after four years passed in the most perfect enjoyment of happiness, the marriage state could give; after seeing himself the father of a beautiful daughter . . . was then under the indispensable necessity of leaving them both for a time . . . " (196). Spacks points out that marriage "implies immense social power for its male participants. It provides the definitive means to quell female insubordination" (*Desire and Truth,* 198).

38. *A Simple Story* is structurally symmetrical: Part I, Volume I, begins with the death of Mr. Milner, who leaves his offspring under the protection of Dorriforth. The first two volumes explore the relationship of Miss Milner and her surrogate father. Part II, Volume III, begins with the death of Lady Elmwood, who leaves her offspring under the protection of Lord Elmwood. The last two volumes explore the relationship of Matilda and her biological father.

guardian/husband, the second portion of *A Simple Story* specifies what his desires are: Lord Elmwood *"seems to get more sexual satisfaction from making laws than love."*[39]

After four years of marriage Lord Elmwood leaves, as the newspapers phrase it, "a most captivating young woman . . . without a protector" (204). Early acquainted with her propensity to feel "immediate resentment of . . . neglect" (15), he nonetheless remains abroad for three years (196) and is furious to discover upon his return that Lady Elmwood has committed adultery. Without making any effort to forgive his wife (the Catholic element of the novel being abandoned) and repair the marriage, he seeks a vengeance that, for the greater part of two volumes, seems as though it will be endless. The narrator insists that Lord Elmwood's "love to his lady had been extravagant" (197), yet that "love" finds its expression only in revenge:

> . . . [Lord Elmwood] determined upon his own death, or the death of the man who had wounded his honour and his happiness. A duel with his old antagonist was the result of this determination; nor was the Duke of Avon . . . Lord Frederick Lawnly . . . backward to render all the satisfaction that was required. . . . [Lord Frederick's] triumph however was but short . . . his Grace was called upon to answer for his conduct, and was left upon the spot where they met, so maimed, and defaced with scars, as never again to endanger the honour of a husband. (198)

The outcome of the duel fought in the first half of *A Simple Story* is more than reversed in the second half. The sexual competition fittingly ends with what seems a sexual mutilation: Lord Frederick, who had quoted Pope's *Eloisa to Abelard* (22), is himself the lover who is castrated, symbolically and perhaps literally as well. Such a finale reestablishes the patriarchal supremacy of Lord Elmwood: "from the ample and distinguished vengeance he had obtained upon the irresistible person of the duke, in a short time [Lord Elmwood] seemed to regain his usual tranquillity" (199). Enforcing law, for him, is better than making love.

Once Lord Frederick is emasculated, Lady Elmwood is no longer

39. "And if for him [the father] the law guarantees an increment of pleasure, and power, it would be good to uncover what this implies about his desire—*he seems to get more sexual satisfaction from making laws than love*"—Irigaray, *Speculum,* 38–39.

desired by two men; as a commodity, her stock has fallen. The notice of Lady Elmwood's death causes Lord Elmwood to pause in his reading of the paper, nothing more. The narrator's comment seems ironic:

> Nor let the vociferous mourner, or the perpetual weeper, here complain of his want of sensibility—but let them remember Lord Elmwood was a man . . . and who shall say, but that at the time he leaned his head upon his hand, and rose to walk away the sense of what he felt, he might not feel as much as Lady Elmwood did in her last moments.
>
> Be this as it may, his lordship's susceptibility on the occasion was not suspected by any one—he passed that day the same as usual; the next day too, and the day after. (204–5)

His lordship's susceptibility is not suspected, the narrator implies, because it does not exist. Lord Elmwood has no more trouble enforcing Lady Elmwood's exile and hearing of her death than he had in cutting off a "once beloved sister" who married against his consent (34). The death of the latter had no force with him either: "He loved his sister too, tenderly loved her, and yet when he had taken the resolution; passed his word he would never see her again; even upon her death-bed he would not retract it—no entreaties could prevail upon him" (144). Law, again, has greater attraction for Lord Elmwood than love.

With his sister and with his wife, Lord Elmwood is implacable. With his daughter he is, if possible, more tyrannical. Matilda, the infant sent after Lady Elmwood, is "the perpetual outcast of its father" (197). The all-powerful father decrees that his child is to be banished and only mitigates the punishment when appealed to in the name of another father—Mr. Milner.

Relations among men are what matter in the patriarchal system,[40] especially when the relations are between men who are as nearly allied as Mr. Milner and Dorriforth. The elder man, like the younger, is a tyrant—his despotism is revealed by his determination to seize all the effects of the destitute Hillgraves (11–12). It is fitting that Mr. Milner chooses Dorriforth as his heir and transfers his daughter to him. For all of her seeming independence, it must be remembered that Miss Milner has no other name

40. On this head, note that Sandford "loved her [Matilda] more that she was Lord Elmwood's child, than for any other cause" (322).

but that of her father and then, as Lady Elmwood, that of her husband: she is passed from one to the other. Miss Milner's role is to "resemble, to copy" her father: "It is from that resemblance, from that imitation of what represents paternal authority, that commodities [women] draw their value—for men."[41] Miss Milner earns Dorriforth's initial approval because she looks like her father: "You have a greater resemblance of your father, Miss Milner, than I imagined you had from report: I did not expect to find you so like him" (15). When she defies her guardian and attends the masquerade, wearing a costume of ambiguous gender,[42] Miss Milner paradoxically fails to be a mirror of her father, and her appeal to Lord Elmwood in her father's name, while affecting him, cannot influence him: " 'Appeal to your father in some other form, in that [pointing to her dress] he will not know you.—Reflect upon him too in your moments of dissipation, and let his idea control your indiscretions—not merely in an hour of contradiction call peevishly upon his name, only to wound the dearest friend you have' " (164–65). When Lady Elmwood dies with the word "Father" on her lips (201) and begs Lord Elmwood to read her letter *"for her father's sake"* (208), she conforms to the strictures of the father's law, and Lord Elmwood grants the petition "in the name of her father, (a name I reverence)" (213): "For Mr. Milner's sake I would do much—nay, any thing, but that to which, I have just now sworn never to consent.—For his sake I have borne a great deal—for his sake alone, his daughter died my wife.—You know, no other motive than respect for him, prevented my divorcing her" (209). Only exchanges among men give value to women—Lady Elmwood recoups a vestige of value when she puts Lord Elmwood into relation with her father. Her pleas for Matilda—"as the grand-daughter of Mr. Milner . . . [f]or her grandfather's sake do not refuse this—to the child of his child whom he trusted to your care, do not refuse it" (210–11)—have just enough force to revoke partially the child's banishment. Lord Elmwood agrees to "give his [Mr. Milner's] grandchild the sanction of my protection" but refuses "ever [to] see or hear from her" (213). Retained at the estate as one of Lord Elmwood's household goods, Matilda is to serve as the "angel in the house," an unseen female presence that makes Lord Elmwood "feel myself more attached to this house at present, than ever I did in my life" (243). By placing Matilda in this position, Lord Elmwood can enjoy both

41. Irigaray, *This Sex,* 178.

42. For a detailed and profitable discussion of Miss Milner's costume, see Castle, *Masquerade and Civilization,* 310–13.

her presence and his law—Matilda is at once rendered desirable and prohibited, invisible to Lord Elmwood's sight but present to his mind's eye.[43]

Rendered both unseen and mute, the daughter is given to unaccountable silent excesses, such as reverencing Lord Elmwood's hat: "But a hat, lying on one of the tables, gave her a sensation beyond any other she experienced on this occasion—in that trifling article of his dress, she thought she saw himself, and held it in her hand with pious reverence" (246). Matilda also worships her father's portrait:

> There was one object, however, among all she saw, which attracted her attention above the rest, and she would stand for hours to look at it—This was a full length portrait of Lord Elmwood, esteemed a very capital picture, and a great likeness—to this picture she would sigh and weep; though when it was first pointed out to her, she shrunk back with fear, and it was some time before she dared venture to cast her eyes completely upon it. (220)

Matilda's fetishizing of these objects is the sign of her own desire, which is forbidden expression in patriarchal discourse—an erotic attachment to her father.

Matilda's obsessive devotion indicates the development of what Freud calls the "typical Oedipus complex in women," a violent rejection of her mother and wish to "take her [mother's] place with her father."[44] Freud

43. Lord Elmwood's treatment of his daughter seems to bear an affinity to "the first game played by a little boy of one and a half and invented by himself" ("Beyond the Pleasure Principle," in *The Standard Edition of the Complete Psychological Works of Sigmund Freud,* trans. and ed. James Strachey [London: Hogarth Press, 1955], 18:14). When his mother is absent, the boy throws his toys away "into a corner, under the bed" and then, in some cases, retrieves them. Freud calls his play *"fort-da"* ("gone there") and links the behavior to the boy's "instinct for mastery" as well as to his desire "to revenge himself on his mother for going away from him. In that case it would have a defiant meaning: 'All right, then, go away! I don't need you. I'm sending you away myself' " (16). Lord Elmwood's law banishes his daughter just as the boy's game removes his toy: in both cases, the desirable object is out of sight but within reach. Like the child's game, Lord Elmwood's prohibition procures him both the pleasure of exerting mastery and the satisfaction of obtaining revenge upon the wife/mother (Lady Elmwood) who fled from him.

44. Sigmund Freud, "Femininity," in *Standard Edition,* 22:120, 134.

specifies, "Her [the daughter's] love was directed to her *phallic* mother; with the discovery that her mother is castrated it becomes possible to drop her as an object" and transfer her attachment to the one who possesses the phallus, the father.[45] If "possessing the phallus" is seen as a representation of entry into the symbolic order, Lady Elmwood's transformation from the vibrant Miss Milner to the "fallen" Lady Elmwood would represent a type of castration, a loss of speech, will, power, and control. Since Matilda is "perfectly acquainted with the whole fatal history of her mother" (216), it is particularly easy in this case for the daughter to reject her mother in favor of the father.[46] The lingering death of Lady Elmwood is calculated to remove the mother, both physically and psychologically, from the daughter, while it also serves to privilege the father: Lady Elmwood, who saw herself as worthless, imparted that vision to Matilda while encouraging "that respect and admiration of her father's virtues which they justly merited" (216). In her obsession with gaining access to her father, Matilda does sacrifice her relationship to her mother: "In the bitterness of her grief, she once called upon her mother, and reproached her memory . . . " (244).[47]

If erotic power underlies the attachment of Matilda to Lord Elmwood—the daughter's "phantasy of being seduced by the father"[48]—the reversal that Irigaray posits should also be taken into account:

> And it is odd that, in the whole adventure of female sexuality as described by Freud, the father makes his appearance only at the

45. Freud, "Femininity," 126.

46. In *About Chinese Women,* Julia Kristeva writes, " . . . this pursuit of the father's cause has a darker side to it: hatred of the mother, or, more precisely, hatred of her *jouissance*" (trans. Seán Hand, in *The Kristeva Reader,* ed. Toril Moi [Oxford: Basil Blackwell, 1986], 152).

47. "Woman's rebellions are never aimed at the paternal function—which is sacred and divine—but at that powerful and then castrated mother, because she had brought a castrated child into the world"—Irigaray, *Speculum,* 106.

48. Freud, "Femininity," 120. Many critics have noted the Oedipal tensions in Inchbald's second volume. For example, Castle writes, " . . . the sustained erotic tension, the frisson at the heart of Inchbald's psychological drama . . . is present in the second half of the novel, though in perhaps even more elemental form, deriving as it does from the charged Oedipal attachment between Dorriforth/Elmwood and his daughter. . . . in Matilda's Oedipal absorption with this invisible tyrant-father, we see the outlines of classic Romantic psychodrama . . . " (*Masquerade and Civilization,* 297, 321). Spencer notes, "The novel's denouement suggests the infantile fantasy of union with a powerful father . . . " (Introduction to *A Simple Story,* xviii).

> end and in such a dim . . . role. With no desires, no instincts, no dealings, of any kind, in regard to his daughter.
>
> . . . it is neither simply true, nor indeed false, to claim that the little girl fantasizes being seduced by her father, since it is equally valid to assume that the father *seduces his daughter* but that, because (in most cases, though not in all) he refuses to recognize and live out his desire, *he lays down a law that prohibits him from doing so.* That said, it is his desire which, come what may, prescribes the force, the shape, the modes, etc., of the law he lays down or passes on, a law that reduces to the state of "fantasy" the little girl's seduced and rejected desire—a desire still faltering, barely articulate, silent perhaps, or expressed in signs or body language, a desire that must be seduced to the discourse and law of the father. . . .
>
> . . . Her duty would be to sustain with her desire the enticing delusion of a legislative discourse, of a legal text that would state, among other things, that the father has no desire for her.[49]

Such desire and law of prohibition are at the core of Inchbald's last two volumes. Lord Elmwood fears "to form another attachment near to his heart; more especially so near as a parent's, which might a second time expose him to all the torments of ingratitude, from one whom he affectionately loved" (202), and he insists, "Never, for her mother's sake, [will I see her and] suffer my heart to be again softened by an object I might doat on" (208). Lord Elmwood establishes a law that forbids Matilda to look upon him and threatens her with abandonment "should she dare to break through the limits he prescribed" (218). His prohibition serves to make Matilda believe "that the father has no desire for her"—she is actually told, "It is always proper . . . for *you* to think of him, though he should never think on you" (217)—when in fact his law exists clearly to prevent Lord Elmwood from desiring her too much.[50] Matilda's own desires, hidden and silent, must then take the form of adoration for his

49. Irigaray, *Speculum,* 62, 38–39. See also: "while he alone can satisfy her and give her access to pleasure, he prefers the added sexual enjoyment to be derived from laying down the law, and therefore penalizes her for her (or his own?) 'seduction fantasies' " (60).

50. "With this highly neurotic psychic blackmail, the stricken Elmwood legislates against love itself, armoring himself against human contact even as he claims to protect his unfortunate daughter"—Castle, *Masquerade and Civilization,* 323.

belongings: "In the breakfast and dining rooms she leaned over those seats with a kind of filial piety, on which she was told he had been accustomed to sit. And in the library she took up with filial delight, the pen with which he had been writing; and looked with the most curious attention into those books that were laid upon his reading desk" (245–46). If the pen can substitute for the phallus by signaling the father's privileged relationship to language, Matilda's obsession can be read as a desire to enter the symbolic order. While she is silent and powerless, her father speaks and commands: "Lord Elmwood's will was a law all around" (221).[51]

Despite her efforts to align herself with her father, for Lord Elmwood Matilda is a surrogate for her mother:

> [Although] in the features of her father she was proud to discern the exact moulds in which her own appeared to have been modelled; yet Matilda's person, shape, and complection were so extremely like what her mother's once were, that at the first glance she appeared to have a still greater resemblance of her, than of her father.... and [she] looked just as her mother at her age often times had done.... (220, 222)

As the replacement for Lady Elmwood, Matilda is both desired and hated by Lord Elmwood. His punishment, which keeps her within his household while denying her his presence, perfectly reflects his ambivalence. This pattern of retention combined with rejection appears again in the scene that recounts their eventual meeting:

> When she [Matilda] had descended a few stairs, she heard a footstep walking slowly up; and, (from what emotion she could not tell,) she stopt short, half resolved to return back.—She hesitated a single instance which to do—then went a few steps farther till she came to the second landing place; when, by the sudden winding of the staircase,—Lord Elmwood was immediately before her!
>
> ... her *fears* confirmed her it was him.—She gave a scream of terror ... and fell motionless into her father's arms.

51. "It is in the *name of the father* that we must recognize the support of the symbolic function which, from the dawn of history, has identified his person with the figure of the law"—Lacan, "Function and Field of Speech and Language," in *Écrits: A Selection,* 67.

> He caught her. . . . when he found her in his arms, he still held her there—gazed on her attentively—and once pressed her to his bosom.
>
> At length, trying to escape the snare into which he had been led, he was going to leave her . . . when . . . [h]er voice unmanned him.—His long-restrained tears now burst forth . . . he cried out. . . . Her name did not however come to his recollection—nor any name but this—"Miss Milner—Dear Miss Milner."
>
> That sound did not awake her; and now again he wished to leave her. . . .
>
> . . . [with] his face . . . agitated with shame, with pity, with anger, with paternal tenderness . . . her father went away. (273–74)

The meeting seems accidental, and yet Matilda says, "I know I have done wrong—I know I had but one command from my father, and that I have disobeyed" (275). She believes herself culpable, at some level, for bringing the meeting about—and she is partly responsible. The event itself offers a picture of Matilda's hesitation and then movement, a movement toward what she has desired.[52] Lord Elmwood, conflating mother and daughter, holds her then tries to release her, retains her then eventually abandons her—a recapitulation of his behavior throughout the text, particularly his approach-avoidance behavior during his courtship of Miss Milner. Lord Elmwood's fear is here exposed—his daughter's voice "unmans" him, robs him of his iron control, of his ability to repress desire. Like her mother before her, Matilda is seen as a threat to Lord Elmwood's patriarchal

52. Remarking upon this "accidental meeting of Lord Elmwood and his daughter," Gary Kelly says, "The fainting scene, stock in trade of every romance-writer and discreet substitute for the swoon of sexual ecstasy, is here given new and complex meaning" (*English Jacobin Novel,* 77). His statement has interesting implications if one argues that Matilda's swoon is *not* given a new meaning.

Spacks writes that "Matilda's longing for a father by and large conceals its erotic components. When she faints in her father's arms . . . she hints at an emotional identity between filial and romantic relationship. But Lord Elmwood's rescue of his daughter from a would-be ravisher reestablishes the appropriate sublimations" (*Desire and Truth,* 200). I would only argue that the erotic component is thinly concealed at best—when father and daughter are reunited, the language Inchbald uses to describe their journey home is that which typically brings to a close the conventional eighteenth-century love plot: ". . . she experienced the extreme joy of . . . receiving during his conversation, a thousand proofs of his love, and tokens of her lasting happiness" (331).

dominance, a female force at once wished for and terrifying that must be controlled and contained. To love "one so nearly allied to her [Lady Elmwood] as her child. To bestow upon that his affections, would be, he imagined, still in some sort, to divide them with the mother" (197).

The problem is largely one of gender, for while Lord Elmwood cannot bring himself to look upon his daughter Matilda, he receives his nephew Rushbrook: "The child Rushbrook is become a man, and the apparent heir of Lord Elmwood's fortune; while his own daughter, his only child by his once adored Miss Milner, he refuses ever to see again, in vengeance to her mother's crimes" (195). Never, "for her mother's sake" (208), will Lord Elmwood accept Matilda as his offspring; yet he can be as a father to Rushbrook, who ought also to remind him of Miss Milner/Lady Elmwood since she was the one to bring that nephew home (34–36) and "by her kindness preserved [him] there . . . [and] intreated [Lord Elmwood] . . . to take him, and through her caresses and officious praises of him to his uncle, first gave him that power he now possesses over him" (230, 232). Lord Elmwood himself had confirmed the bond by saying, "you [Miss Milner] shall be a mother, and I will, henceforward, be a father to him" (151).

Rushbrook, as a male, cannot stand in for the absent mother in the same way that Matilda, as a woman, can. And as long as that mother is effectually removed, dead and never to be named, no Oedipal struggle can exist to make Rushbrook in any way dangerous to Lord Elmwood. So long as Lady Elmwood remains unmentioned, nothing can threaten Lord Elmwood's authority: "Love, that produces wonders, that seduces and subdues the most determined and rigid spirits, had in two instances overcome the inflexibility of Lord Elmwood . . . but the magic which once enchanted away this spirit of immutability was no more—Lady Elmwood was no more, and the charm was broken" (251). Part of the law that Lord Elmwood creates, then, is a prohibition against speaking Lady Elmwood's name. He banishes a poor elderly dependent and his family when the man inadvertently does so (270–72) and almost exiles Rushbrook when the youth acknowledges gratitude for "her, who first introduced me to your protection" (290), even though Rushbrook does not actually utter the fatal name. No one must speak the words that remind Lord Elmwood that there were moments when he had lost control.

Not only is Rushbrook less dangerous than Matilda, he is also preferred as the naturally superior male offspring. Lord Elmwood married to obtain an heir (99), and a female child is useless for that purpose. As Irigaray writes,

> For the patriarchal order is indeed the one that functions as the *organization and monopolization of private property to the benefit of the head of the family.* It is his proper name, the name of the father, that determines ownership for the family, including the wife and children. And what is required of them—for the wife, monogamy; for the children, the precedence of the male line, and specifically of the eldest son who bears the name—is also required so as to ensure "the concentration of considerable wealth in the hands of a single individual—a man." . . . [53]

Ownership, which had been Lord Elmwood's primary concern in his treatment of Lady Elmwood on her violation of monogamy, is once again of primary interest in his choice of offspring. Rushbrook, although not his biological child, is Lord Elmwood's chosen child because he is male. Although he agrees to provide for his daughter, Lord Elmwood insists that Rushbrook will remain his heir, while he laments that the youth is only his adopted son: "Could any thing but a son have preserved my title? . . . Henry Rushbrook I leave my heir" (214). Even after being reconciled to his daughter, "never for a moment did he [Lord Elmwood] indulge . . . the idea of replacing her exactly in that situation to which she was born, to the disappointment of all his nephew's expectations" (334).

In her appeal to Lord Elmwood, Lady Elmwood cited "the unfortunate child in the scripture" and quoted the biblical passage, *"I will go to my father; how many servants live in my father's house, and are fed with plenty, while I starve in a foreign land?"* (211). She forgets that the story is about the prodigal *son*—no one wastes the fatted calf on the daughter, certainly not Lord Elmwood:

> The twenty ninth of October arrived; on which a dinner, a ball, and supper, was given by Lord Elmwood to all the neighbouring gentry—the peasants also dined in the park off a roasted bullock;

53. Irigaray, *This Sex,* 83. See also *Speculum:* "This boy child is the sign of the seed's immortality, of the fact that the properties of the sperm have won out over those of the ovum. Thus he guarantees the father's power to reproduce and represent himself, and to perpetuate his gender and his species. What is more, the son, as heir to the name, ensures that the patrimony will not be squandered. . . . The son is remade by the father in his own likeness and woman is thereby inscribed in an economic calculus she has no control over" (74, 79).

> several casks of ale were distributed, and the bells of the village rung.—Matilda, who heard and saw some part of this festivity from her windows, inquired the cause. . . . Miss Woodley . . . soon learnt the reason, and groaning with the painful secret, informed her, "Mr Rushbrook on that day was come of age."
>
> "My birth day was last week," replied Matilda; but not a word beside. (235)

Rushbrook has inherent value as a male heir, while "the girl's only way to redeem her personal value, and value in general, would be to seduce the father, and persuade him to express, if not admit, some interest in her."[54] At the end of *A Simple Story* such a resolution comes about—not because Matilda succeeds in proving her worth to Lord Elmwood, but because she becomes the prey of Lord Margrave. Her abduction by that evil peer gives her commodity value, for it shows to Lord Elmwood that his property is once again in danger of being appropriated by a rival. The end of the second half of Inchbald's text is an uncanny recapitulation of its beginning. Once again, Lord Elmwood's neglect of his goods results in market competition:

> . . . the behavior of Lord Elmwood to his child . . . [indicated to Lord Margrave that] it was more than probable he would be utterly indifferent to any violence that might be offered her. . . .
>
> . . . [Seeing her discarded state,] Lord Margrave . . . was no longer fearful of resentment from the Earl, whatever treatment his daughter might receive. . . . (249, 299)

Lord Margrave, the uncivilized, country-booby version of Lord Elmwood, lacks the latter's refinement and must resort to physical rather than mental force to subdue women, "for he had much rather have encountered the piercing cries of a female in the last agonies of distress, than the fatigue of her sentimental harangues" (299). Both men operate in the same system, however; thus, as Lord Elmwood proved himself a husband by maiming

54. Irigaray, *Speculum,* 87. See also *This Sex:* "Indeed, in this view, woman never truly escapes from the Oedipus complex. She remains forever fixated on the desire for the father, remains subject to the father and to his law, for fear of losing his love, which is the only thing capable of giving her any value at all" (87).

Lord Frederick, he "proves himself a father" by taking up his pistols and seeking out Lord Margrave (324). The outcome of the transaction between the two men is that Lord Elmwood repossesses his daughter:

> That moment her father entered—and with the unrestrained fondness of a parent, folded her in his arms.
>
> Her extreme, her excess of joy on such a meeting; and from such anguish rescued, was still, in part, repressed by his awful presence.—The apprehensions to which she had been accustomed, kept her timid and doubtful—she feared to speak, or clasp him in return for his embrace, but falling on her knees clung round his legs, and bathed his feet with her tears.—These were the happiest moments she had ever known—perhaps the happiest *he* had ever known....
>
> She could only turn to him with a look of love and duty; her tongue could not utter a sentence. (328–29)

Completely abject, Matilda has (like her mother) lost access to language. She speaks with looks and gestures, with tears and illness. As was the case with Lady Elmwood, Matilda's mental anguish results in physical impairment: "Lady Matilda . . . [was] considerably altered in her looks and in her health;—she was become very thin, and instead of the most beautiful bloom that used to spread her cheeks, her whole complexion was of a deadly pale—her countenance no longer expressed hope or fear, but a fixed melancholy—she shed no tears, but was all sadness" (304). Matilda's silent mouth and "speaking" body conform to Irigaray's description of the speech of the hysteric:

> I should like to ask what it means "to speak (as) hysteric." Does the hysteric speak? Isn't hysteria a privileged place for preserving—but "in latency," "in sufferance"—that which does not speak? And, in particular (even according to Freud . . .), that which is not expressed in woman's relation to her mother, to herself, to other women? Those aspects of women's earliest desires that find themselves reduced to silence in terms of a culture that does not allow them to be expressed. A powerlessness to "say," upon which the Oedipus complex then superimposes the requirement of silence.
>
> Hysteria: *it speaks* in the mode of a paralyzed gestural faculty,

> of an impossible and also a forbidden speech. . . . It speaks as *symptoms* of an "it can't speak to or about itself." . . . [55]

Matilda's excessive sufferings and excessive joys, forbidden verbal expression in masculine language, find their outlet in the language of gesture, of the body—the only language such desires are allowed.

Matilda can finally be admitted into the presence of the father because her mutism proves that she has received, as Inchbald emphasizes in capital letters set off from the paragraph as the very last words of her text, "A PROPER EDUCATION":

> He [the reader] has beheld the pernicious effects of an improper education in the destiny which attended the unthinking Miss Milner—On the opposite side, then, what may not be hoped from that school of prudence—though of adversity—in which Matilda was bred?
>
> And Mr. Milner, Matilda's grandfather, had better have given his fortune to a distant branch of his family—as Matilda's father once meant to do—so he had bestowed upon his daughter
>
> A PROPER EDUCATION. (337–38)

The final paragraphs of Inchbald's novel implicate the "PROPER EDUCATION" of woman, the type of education promoted by writers such as Sarah Scott, Jane West, and Hannah More, as one intended to suppress female desire—like the "cure" of the hysteric that is "intended to adapt them . . . to masculine society."[56] Matilda, bred in adversity, receives her education in

55. Irigaray, *This Sex,* 136. Note that Miss Milner/Lady Elmwood takes hysteria to its utmost extreme—she uses her dead body as a final appeal, writing to her husband, "nor should I dare to offer you even this humble petition, but that at the time you receive it, there will be no such person as I am in existence. . . . Farewell Lord Elmwood—and before you throw this letter from you with contempt or anger, cast your imagination into the grave where I am lying. . . . Behold *me,* also—in my altered face there is no anxiety—no joy or sorrow—all is over.—My whole frame is motionless—my heart beats no more. . . . ask yourself—whether I am an object of resentment?" (210–12).

56. Irigaray, *This Sex,* 137. Lessons in self-restraint were, for example, the type of instruction advocated by Hannah More: "That bold, independent, enterprising spirit, which is so much admired in boys, should not, when it happens to discover itself in the other sex, be encouraged, but suppressed. . . . [Girls] should acquire a submissive temper, and a forbearing spirit: for it is a lesson which the world will not fail to make them

subjugation through suffering and accepts her mute role. Miss Milner, reared at first in the illusion of freedom, experiences the "pernicious effects" of not being overtly oppressed from the start when, forced—as she must be—to enter the patriarchal system, she cannot adapt and is destroyed. The reference to Mr. Milner reminds the reader that the first father was as powerful as the second, while the remarks about Lord Elmwood recall the fact that in each successive role he increases at once in power and in tyranny: as guardian, Dorriforth is harsh; as husband, he is unfeeling and unyielding; as father, Lord Elmwood is relentless and cruel, "haughty, impatient, imperious, and more than ever, implacable" (230). The references to grandfather and father end the book, privileging the male as Inchbald saw the male indulged in her society. The ending of *A Simple Story,* read in the light of what precedes it, seems Inchbald's way of calling that male primacy into question.

The conclusion of Inchbald's novel shows male desires privileged in another way. If Lord Elmwood's desires for power and dominance are satisfied, Rushbrook's desires seem also to be on the point of fruition. The

---

frequently practise, when they come abroad into it, and they will not practise it the worse for having learnt it the sooner" (*Essays on Various Subjects, Principally Designed for Young Ladies* [1777], quoted in Patricia Meyer Spacks, *The Adolescent Idea: Myths of Youth and the Adult Imagination* [New York: Basic Books, 1981], 120).

Spencer offers an insightful analysis of the theme of woman's education in *A Simple Story.* She writes, "The novel has a feminist interest, not because it shares the contemporary advocacy of a rational education for women, but because it reveals what was repressed in order to make that case. Miss Milner embodies the female sexuality that women writers of Inchbald's time were busy denying in the interests of their own respectability, and women's claims for better treatment. . . . The significant difference between Miss Milner's education and her daughter's is that Miss Milner's failed to subdue the sexual desire and the will to power which make her such a disruptive figure. . . . because she has not been seriously educated at all she cannot suppress her desire. . . . it is clear that education in this novel functions negatively, not adding wisdom but imposing taboos. The female desire which it is meant to stifle is the novel's more fundamental concern" (Introduction to *A Simple Story,* xiv–xv). Katharine M. Rogers echoes Spencer in "Elizabeth Inchbald: Not Such a Simple Story" (*Living by the Pen: Early British Women Writers,* ed. Dale Spender [New York: Teachers College Press, 1992]): "In contrast to her faulty and ruined mother, Matilda is supposed to illustrate the results of 'A Proper Education.' . . . What this actually means is that her cheerless childhood has inhibited her from developing her mother's will and passion; Matilda's rational self-control is indistinguishable from the dutiful self-suppression that eighteenth-century convention prescribed for women" (86).

second romance plot of the text is as problematic as the first, but in this case the forbidden desires are the man's: Rushbrook's longing for Matilda acts out his own Oedipal fantasies. His plot, then, is a shadowy reproduction of the two other plots of the text.

Matilda is continually conflated with her mother. If Lord Elmwood "can[not] divide those two objects in his mind" (229), nobody else can either. Miss Woodley's "imagination pictured Matilda as her [mother] risen from the grave in her former youth, health, and exquisite beauty" (221). Lord Margrave sexually equates Matilda with Lady Elmwood and offers the daughter "Such [proposals] . . . as the Duke of Avon made to her mother" (301). It is not surprising then that when Rushbrook first meets Matilda, he "cast his eyes upon her, and stood motionless" (238), seeing in her the reincarnation of her dead mother. Before the end of the page he is on his knees to her, and few chapters go by before Rushbrook's heart whispers to him "that pity, gratitude, and friendship, strong and affectionate as these passions are, are weak and cold to that, which had gained the possession of him—he doubted, but he did not long doubt, that which he felt was love" (250). Rushbrook himself is dimly aware of the source of his passion: " . . . it is love of that kind . . . arising from causes independant of the object itself. . . . Did I not love Lady Matilda before I beheld her?—for her mother's sake I loved her. . . . [But] the tenderness he felt towards her . . . were yet cool and dispassionate sensations, compared to that which her person and demeanour had incited . . . " (250). "In order to correspond to man's desire, woman must play the part of or identify with his mother";[57] Matilda's resemblance to her mother suits her to Rushbrook's wishes.

If the first forbidden match was made possible by Dorriforth's dispensation from his priestly vows, the second is acceptable because, although Matilda is essentially Rushbrook's sister since both have been raised by the same parents, she is not his biological sister. The second marriage, however, seems to hold more promise than the first because, in his relationship to the all-powerful father, Rushbrook is feminized. He, like Matilda, cannot give voice to his desires: Rushbrook lies with ease, employing an "art of dissimulation, cunning, and duplicity" (234) that is most often credited to women. Economically dependent and in danger of being disinherited, he is required to please Lord Elmwood at all times. Like Miss Milner, Rushbrook

57. Irigaray, *Speculum,* 31. See also: "the little boy's first love object was his mother and 'she remains so until she is replaced by someone who resembles her or is derived from her' [Freud, 'Female Sexuality,' 228]. . . . throughout his life man remains fixated to his 'primary object,' his mother, or wife-mother . . . " (63).

"magnifies trifles" in composing a letter (251). Like Matilda, he is completely "subservient to his [Lord Elmwood's] will" (254) and, in his subservience, is deprived of language: he, too, is reduced to speaking with gestures. When Lord Elmwood demands to know if his heir is in love and will not allow him to dissimulate, "Rushbrook stood silent, confused, alarmed, and bewildered in his thoughts" (252). Subsequently, fear of his "father" throws the youth into a severe high fever: "Divided between the claims of obligation to the father, and tender attachment to the daughter, his sickness was increased by the tortures of his mind, and he once sincerely wished for that death, of which he was in danger, to free him from the dilemma into which his affections had involved him" (254–55). Upon meeting Rushbrook, Matilda "burst into a flood of tears"; she was "somewhat surprised to see, he had shed tears too" (239).

Rushbrook's similarity to Matilda in his relationship to the father—he says to her at one point, "with all my seeming good fortune, I am not happier than yourself" (239)—serves as the only way out of the dilemma of patriarchal tyranny. If society remains in its present form, if existing institutions are left intact, then this union, it seems, is the best compromise Inchbald can envision. As Matilda's lover, Rushbrook is considerate and self-sacrificing. Eager to please and fearful to offend, Rushbrook respects Matilda's right to a room of her own and, unlike Dorriforth in his courtship of Miss Milner, fears to intrude into the house that should belong to her: "how could he support the idea that his visit had placed the daughter of his benefactor as a dependant stranger in that house, where in reality he was the dependant, and she the lawful heir.—For two or three days he suffered the torments of these reflections, hoping to come to an explanation of all he felt" (258). The mutuality and equality of the second relationship in some ways remedy the oppression and inequality of the first. Rushbrook risks being abandoned when he defends Matilda to her father: " 'Lady Matilda,' resumed Rushbrook, 'is an object that wrests from me the enjoyment of every blessing your kindness bestows.—I cannot but feel myself as her adversary—as one who has supplanted her in your affections—who supplies her place, while she is exiled, a wanderer, and an orphan' " (289–90). Matilda, in turn, is only willing to brook the displeasure of Lord Elmwood in order to supplicate for Rushbrook: " 'Mr. Rushbrook is my relation,' she cried in a pathetic voice, 'my companion, my friend—before you loved me he was anxious for my happiness, and often visited me to propose some kindness.—I cannot see him turned out of your house without feeling for him, what he once felt for me' " (335–36).

The relationship between Rushbrook and Matilda is reciprocal. In a world of patriarchal domination, the best that women can achieve is to marry a man who is as powerless as a woman. Yet even here Inchbald is ambivalent. Matilda considers Rushbrook her relation, companion, and friend—she has no desire to marry him. When he, with the father's somewhat unwilling sanction—Lord Elmwood feigns (displays?) anger at Rushbrook's presumptuous request (335)—asks her not to doom him to misery by refusing herself to him, Matilda is shocked and does not answer. The outcome is left uncertain, as Inchbald writes, "Whether the heart of Matilda, such as it has been described, *could* sentence him [Rushbrook] to misery, the reader is left to surmise—and if he supposes that it did not, he has every reason to suppose their wedded life was a life of happiness" (337). Inchbald gives the reader the desired closure, but it is worded ambiguously. Furthermore, Rushbrook's longing, "Then let us be joined . . . till death alone can part us" (337), ominously echoes Sandford's earlier command, which coupled Lord and Lady Elmwood in their disastrous union: "Separate this moment . . . Or resolve never to be separated but by death" (190). There are many reasons given in *A Simple Story* to suppose that no wedded life is a life of happiness for the woman and that the institution itself only offers the satisfaction of male desire through denial of female desire. If the "happy" ending of *A Simple Story* consists of the successful resolution of the masculine subject's Oedipus complex, Inchbald's work is comparable to Davys's.

Unlike her contemporary, Mary Wollstonecraft, Elizabeth Inchbald did not make a direct statement for the rights of women and against patriarchal oppression. Instead, in *A Simple Story* Inchbald constructs a complicated and disturbing narrative that exposes defects in the patriarchal system not through explication, but through enactment—showing troubling relationships between men and women and thereby forcing readers to examine the foundations, assumptions, and implications of masculine domination. Her novel achieves its strongest effect in what it does not say—in its silences and repetitions: the relationship between father and daughter, for example, reworks many elements of the relationship between guardian and ward and makes explicit the problematic nature of that first union. Miss Milner, seemingly free and independent, is actually as little in control as is Matilda—the former's apparent autonomy is just a more sophisticated form of oppression, for her forbidden desire for the Father/guardian is actually analogous to her daughter's Oedipal obsession; both passions are consigned to silence as both women are devoted to suffering. Inchbald's *Simple Story,* offering itself as a familiar, straightforward domestic novel, is deceptively titled and compellingly complex.

Chapter Five

Feminine Excess: Frances Burney's *The Wanderer*

> They should not put it, then, in the form "What is woman?" but rather, repeating/interpreting the way in which, within discourse, the feminine finds itself defined as lack, deficiency, or as imitation and negative image of the subject, they should signify that with respect to this logic a *disruptive excess* is possible on the feminine side.
>
> —Luce Irigaray, in *This Sex Which Is Not One*

In 1814, a novel entitled *The Wanderer; or, Female Difficulties* appeared. It was to be the last work of the celebrated author of *Evelina,* Frances Burney, Madame d'Arblay. Unlike her earliest novel, the later work was not a critical success. The *British Critic* (April 1814) commented that the book was "tedious and tiresome" and filled with "dull and uninteresting adventures."[1] John Wilson Croker, for the *Quarterly Review* (April 1814), insisted that Burney "has been gradually descending from the elevation which the vigour of her youth had attained."[2] He went on to compare Burney's last work to her first and thereby glance insultingly at her aging, sixty-two-year-old body:

1. Quoted in Joseph A. Grau, *Fanny Burney: An Annotated Bibliography* (New York: Garland, 1981), 29.

2. John Wilson Croker, review of *The Wanderer; or, Female Difficulties,* by Madame D'Arblay, *Quarterly Review* 11 (April 1814): 124.

> The Wanderer has the identical features of Evelina—but of Evelina grown old; the vivacity, the bloom, the elegance, "the purple light of love" are vanished; the eyes are there, but they are dim; the cheek, but it is furrowed; the lips, but they are withered. And when to this description we add that Madame D'Arblay endeavours to make up for the want of originality in her characters by the most absurd mysteries, the most extravagant incidents, and the most violent events, we have completed the portrait of an old coquette who endeavours, by the wild tawdriness and laborious gaiety of her attire, to compensate for the loss of the natural charms of freshness, novelty, and youth.[3]

William Hazlitt also attacked the book in the *Edinburgh Review* (February 1815): "The difficulties in which she involves her heroines are indeed 'Female Difficulties;'—they are difficulties created out of nothing."[4] According to Hazlitt, Burney, like all women writers, possessed only limited abilities:

> The author of the present novel is . . . a very woman. . . . There is little in her works of passion or character, or even manners. . . .
>
> There is little other power in Miss Burney's novels, than that of immediate observation: her characters . . . are equally superficial and confined. The whole is a question of form. . . . It is this circumstance which takes away dignity and interest from her

3. Croker, review, 125–26. See also Margaret Anne Doody, *Frances Burney: The Life in the Works* (New Brunswick, N.J.: Rutgers University Press, 1988): "Croker attacks her gloatingly in specifically sexual terms; her books are merely a reflection of her body" (335); and Claudia L. Johnson, *Jane Austen: Women, Politics, and the Novel* (Chicago: University of Chicago Press, 1988): "By 1814 the climate had changed for women writers, and the novel [*The Wanderer*] was stridently denounced by J. W. Croker in 1815 as the work of a shriveled hag. Novel and novelist alike have grown too old to delight discriminating male readers. . . . Fiction by women must be fiction by young women—modest, delicate, wispy, delightful . . . " (xv).

4. William Hazlitt, review of *The Wanderer; or, Female Difficulties,* by Madame D'Arblay, *Edinburgh Review* 24 (February 1815): 337. For a detailed discussion of the early criticisms of *The Wanderer,* see Julia Epstein, *The Iron Pen: Frances Burney and the Politics of Women's Writing* (Madison: University of Wisconsin Press, 1989), 207–14. Epstein's comments on Hazlitt's review are particularly perceptive, as she argues, "Hazlitt was actually quite correct here, though what irritated him is precisely Burney's point . . . " (212).

> story and sentiments, and makes the one so teazing and tedious, and the other so insipid.[5]

Byron wrote to John Murray (24 July 1814) that he hated *The Wanderer* "and all the feminine trash of the last four months."[6] Lord Normanby commented in *Blackwood's Magazine* (January 1826), "Madame d'Arblay, in *The Wanderer,* has afforded convincing proof of the decay of her literary powers, at no time very varied or extensive."[7] Sir Walter Scott insisted that in *The Wanderer* "Madame D'Arbley [*sic*] has certainly made a miss. . . . "[8]

These critics—all men—were unanimous in damning *The Wanderer.* Many reviewers used the book as a means to attack women novelists, emphasizing Burney's "defects" as those common in "feminine trash." This obvious strain of antifeminism encourages the sympathetic reader to ignore the early reviews as misogynist,[9] especially since male disdain is balanced against female approval and support. The reputable historian of the novel, Anna Letitia Barbauld, suggested in a letter to Burney (6 July 1813) "that Burney print and copyright *The Wanderer* in America and offer[ed] her assistance."[10] Burney's friend, Mary Waddington, not only praised the book herself but also sent to Burney any favorable comments made by others.[11] This early private recognition of merit has only recently been substantiated by favorable attention in print: respected scholars such as Patricia Meyer Spacks, Kristina Straub, Margaret Anne Doody, and Julia Epstein have rediscovered Burney's final work.[12]

The criticisms of *The Wanderer* offered by the male reviewers cannot

5. Hazlitt, review, 336–37.

6. George Gordon, Lord Byron, *Letters and Journals,* ed. Leslie A. Marchand (Cambridge: Harvard University Press, 1975), 4:146.

7. Quoted in Grau, *Fanny Burney,* 135.

8. Sir Walter Scott, *The Letters of Sir Walter Scott,* ed. H.J.C. Grierson (London: Constable, 1932), 3:465.

9. See Doody: "They [the male critics] had axes to grind. Their axes were to be the sharper and more ruthless because the novelist explicitly developed questions of woman's rights and woman's wrongs" (*Frances Burney,* 333).

10. Grau, *Fanny Burney,* 138. See also *The Journals and Letters of Fanny Burney,* ed. Edward A. Bloom and Lillian D. Bloom (Oxford: Clarendon Press, 1978), 7:146n.

11. *Journals and Letters,* 7:258n., 360n.

12. See Patricia Meyer Spacks, *Imagining a Self: Autobiography and Novel in Eighteenth-Century England* (Cambridge: Harvard University Press, 1976); Kristina Straub, *Divided Fictions: Fanny Burney and Feminine Strategy* (Lexington: University Press of Kentucky, 1987); Doody, *Frances Burney;* and Epstein, *Iron Pen.*

fully be ignored, however. The word that appears most frequently is "tedious," and in many ways the book *is* tedious: Burney's novel is long, even by eighteenth-century standards. Its plot is highly repetitive, consisting of cyclical episodes in which Juliet fruitlessly struggles to find employment and Elinor unsuccessfully attempts to commit suicide. The characters are overdrawn—Juliet is too decorous, too gifted; Elinor is too outspoken, too irrational. The text is constructed around too many secrets and too many disguises—the reader does not learn until well into the fourth volume who Juliet is. The text is at once overly didactic and melodramatic: the rights of woman are openly canvassed while the wrongs of woman are exaggeratedly portrayed. The response produced by these excesses is frustration, since every employment proves abortive, every woman seems helpless, and every man appears to be an oppressor.[13] It is no wonder that male critics gave up on the work in disgust—its polemical tracts on women's rights and "female difficulties" were little different from the arguments found in more popular works such as Mary Wollstonecraft's *A Vindication of the Rights of Woman* (1792) and Mary Anne Radcliffe's *The Female Advocate; or, An Attempt to Recover the Rights of Women from Male Usurpation* (1799). The content of *The Wanderer* offered nothing to the reviewers to make up for the excesses of the form.

Why, then, does Burney clothe her ideas in such overly elaborate garb? If Inchbald's is an art of compression and subtlety, subversive in what it leaves unsaid, in its blanks, silences, and gaps, Burney's is an art of excess, subversive in its overabundance. Her text tends to "*undo* the effects of phallocentric discourse simply by *overdoing* them."[14] If, as Luce Irigaray posits, the feminine role is one of "mimicry"[15]—a woman playing out her culturally assigned role in order to expose the operative structures by which women are marginalized—then Burney overmimes, overacts. Burney writes on the subject that men expected women to write about, but she overwrites, revealing the strategies by which men suppress female dis-

13. The excesses of *The Wanderer* are akin to those of Mary Wollstonecraft's *Maria, or The Wrongs of Woman,* and the sensations produced by both books are similar. In the latter work, every woman is a victim and every man is a tyrant—the work piles episode upon episode to reveal women's oppression. The reader waits in vain for a compassionate male and an empowered female character.

14. Toril Moi, *Sexual/Textual Politics: Feminist Literary Theory* (London: Methuen, 1985), 140 (she is speaking about Luce Irigaray's *Speculum*).

15. Luce Irigaray, *This Sex Which Is Not One,* trans. Catherine Porter, with Carolyn Burke (Ithaca: Cornell University Press, 1985), 76.

course even as they allow writings about "female difficulties." In what follows, I examine the "excesses" of *The Wanderer* that pertain to its foremost female characters; my emphasis falls on the issue of naming and the insistence upon disguise.

I

> The heroine is occasionally gloomy, and seems "unsociable" in her very lack of that basic social sign, a name.
>
> —Margaret Anne Doody

> Even names are a means to confusing, not defining, identity. . . .
>
> —Kristina Straub

In *The Wanderer,* Burney creates a heroine who, orphaned, impoverished, and solitary, must find a way to maintain an honorable independence. Juliet is enjoined by her absent guardians to support herself: "That where occasion calls for female exertion, mental strength must combat bodily weakness; and intellectual vigour must supply the inherent deficiencies of personal courage; and that those, only, are fitted for the vicissitudes of human fortune, who, whether female or male, learn to suffice to themselves. Be this the motto of your story" (220).[16] The "motto" of Juliet's story is in fact quite different: no amount of exertion, intelligence, courage, or ability will allow an unprotected woman to "suffice to" herself. Burney runs through the catalog of occupations for gentlewomen—needleworker, governess, music instructor, public performer, lady's companion, milliner, mantua maker, and haberdasher—and reveals that each employment is nonlucrative, physically debilitating, mentally stifling, and, finally, out of reach for an unnamed and unknown woman.

Juliet's abortive attempts to achieve financial independence form the primary subject of Burney's text. Such an overt protest about the scarcity

16. Frances Burney, *The Wanderer; or, Female Difficulties* (1814), ed. Margaret Anne Doody, Robert L. Mack, and Peter Sabor (Oxford: Oxford University Press, 1991). Subsequent page citations appear in parentheses.

and unpleasantness of the few jobs open to women was, however, a well-worn subject by the time Burney came to it, having appeared in works by women from Mary Astell onward. Juliet's continual efforts to find employment are the first excesses of *The Wanderer*—Burney emphasizes the futility of the woman's struggle through labored repetition. Not only does Burney exhaustively rehearse an already threadbare topic, but she pushes the subject to its limit: the pattern of search, temporary success, and final failure that recurs throughout the text produces, through its lack of variety and hopeless closure, weariness and frustration. The pattern exposes the limitations of the woman's role through reenactment.[17]

The recurring pattern of *The Wanderer* is complicated, however. Juliet's movements from one futile search for an occupation to another are punctuated by a second woman's equally futile attempts at suicide. Burney's text offers a complex cycle in which Juliet's struggles to find a job are interrupted by Elinor Joddrel's outbursts of madness and threatened self-murder. Of all the secondary characters in the text, Elinor appears the most frequently and during the most crucial periods in the plot. Elinor's first attempt to kill herself finalizes Juliet's decision to leave Mrs. Maple and begin harp instruction (195); Elinor's second near-suicide prevents Juliet from performing the loathsome task of exhibiting herself at a public concert (360); her third appearance preserves Juliet from the scandal of being suspected of making a tryst with Sir Lyell (471); her final abortive effort at self-annihilation serves to bring Juliet and Harleigh together and precedes Juliet's brief reunion with Gabriella and flight from her brutal "husband" (576ff.); and Elinor's last appearance, in which she emerges to discuss the possibility of an afterlife (779), again reunites Juliet with Harleigh and begins the events that will solve all of Juliet's difficulties. The juxtapositions are too frequent to be accidental or trivial, and the differences of the two women too extreme to be ignored.

17. Two critics have seen the effect of repetition as one of being trapped in nightmare: in her article "A Wreath for Fanny Burney's Last Novel: *The Wanderer*'s Contribution to Women's Studies" (*Illinois Quarterly* 37 [Spring 1975]), Rose Marie Cutting comments, "The people who persecute Juliet change and the torments vary, but she meets so much cruelty throughout the novel that her experiences take on the repetitious, irrational and extreme quality of a nightmare" (55). Kristina Straub echoes Cutting: "In *The Wanderer,* the sexual vulnerability and economic powerlessness imposed on the heroine by a forced marriage take on the nightmare quality of recurrent horror as Juliet runs from them only to meet, again and again, the socially institutionalized fact of women's sexual and economic victimization" (*Divided Fictions,* 185).

Like Inchbald's *Simple Story,* Burney's *Wanderer* seems at first to be constructed around the binary opposition between the good woman and the bad woman.[18] Juliet is the timid, steady, virtuous woman who is rewarded with marriage; Elinor is the outspoken, unstable, sexually aware woman punished with spinsterhood. Harleigh emphasizes the contrast between them when he says,

> Her [Elinor's] spirit I admire; but where is the sweetness I could love? I respect her understanding; but where is the softness that should make it charm while it enlightens? I am grateful for her partiality; but where is the dignity that might ennoble it, or the

18. Many critics read the text as a sort of Hegelian dialectic: "Its [*The Wanderer*'s] principal theme was a conflict between the ladylike Juliet and Elinor, the anti-heroine, enthusiast for the Revolution and the rights of men and women alike"—Claire Tomalin, *The Life and Death of Mary Wollstonecraft* (New York: Harcourt Brace Jovanovich, 1974), 248; "But Burney develops the complexities of women's dilemma in a fascinating, if perhaps over-schematic, contrast between Juliet and a more militant feminist figure, Elinor Joddrel. These two represent opposing policies in women's struggle for an independent life and they turn the novel into a vivid and dramatic debate about strategy. . . . Certainly in *The Wanderer,* Elinor's directness does not achieve the positive results she hopes for and her fate embodies Burney's mistrust of outspokenness as set against the more reliable, if more insidious, survival techniques adopted by Juliet. For these two characters, united in their common understanding of female oppression, are conceived as opposites in terms of the tactics they employ and together they form an ironic enquiry into the acceptable face of feminism. . . . Juliet and Elinor form two sides of the feminist coin"—Judy Simons, *Fanny Burney* (Totowa, N.J.: Barnes & Noble, 1987), 107, 108, 113; and "The small boat making its dangerous escape to England has on board the two principal characters of the novel; these are the Wanderer herself (the heroine, Juliet) . . . and the anti-heroine, Elinor. . . . Elinor, of course, is not the heroine, but to call her the anti-heroine is misleading and wrong. The term suggests that she and Juliet (the heroine) are established in opposition as some sort of thesis and antithesis in the argument of the book; and there is much to suggest that this could have been Fanny Burney's intention"—D. D. Devlin, *The Novels and Journals of Fanny Burney* (New York: St. Martin's Press, 1987), 106, 108–9. The last formulation is, admittedly, somewhat cryptic. In her recently published *Woman as 'Nobody' and the Novels of Fanny Burney* (Gainesville: University Press of Florida, 1992), Joanne Cutting-Gray calls for the dismantling of this binary logic: "What constitutes female liberty is graphically contrasted in the characters of Juliet and Elinor and helps to explain why Juliet is so often seen as the passive sufferer and Elinor as the active revolutionary. . . . In order to see *The Wanderer* as other than 'female difficulties,' the antinomic thinking which privileges aggressive action and denigrates nonaction as passivity must be dismantled" (85). Cutting-Gray offers a provocative but, for me, not altogether persuasive analysis of "the power of Juliet's silence and inaction" (92).

> delicacy that might make it as refined as it is flattering? Where—where the soul's fascination, that grows out of the mingled excellencies, the blended harmonies, of the understanding with the heart and the manners?
>
> Vainly Ellis [Juliet] strove to appear unconscious of the comparison, and the application, which the eyes of Harleigh, yet more pointedly than his words, marked for herself in this speech.... (189)

Burney's narrative continuously holds the two women together and encourages comparison—Elinor herself sets her own passionate character against Juliet's "compound of cold caution, and selfish prudence" (181) and accuses Juliet of being one of the "tame animals of custom, wearied and wearying plodders on of beaten tracks" (586)—very unlike "the champion of her sex...shewing it the road...to a new walk in life" (165).

Elinor is outspoken and improper, "Lady Wronghead" as she dubs herself (90), while Juliet is the embodiment of female decorum. If Elinor is in some ways similar to Inchbald's Miss Milner, Juliet is the counterpart to Matilda and, like the earlier heroine, is brought up "in the school of refining adversity" (869). Also like Matilda, Juliet's chief desire is to be acknowledged as a daughter; her primary goal is to remain hidden until she can be received and owned by the family of her late father, Lord Granville.

Juliet, however, cannot remain hidden. Her need to find employment—a search for work that is not an end in itself but only a temporary measure to keep her alive while she waits to hear from her guardian—forces her to come forward and push herself into notice. This search, though, is not the main thing that makes other people pay attention to the wanderer. For all her timidness and propriety, Juliet attracts more notoriety than Elinor, in spite of Elinor's flamboyant near-suicides. The latter woman is observed with annoyance, amusement, or contempt, but the former is regarded with alarm: Juliet is in fact far more dangerous to society than Elinor, for she is outside the patriarchal system of exchange—not because she is suicidal, homicidal, or mad, but because she has no name.

Julia Epstein, in *The Iron Pen: Frances Burney and the Politics of Women's Writing,* points out that "a woman's name indicates not her identity *tout court,* but her social identity: it tells us...'to whom she most belongs,' by referring to her father or husband. To lack a name is to belong to no one. . . ."[19] Since she has no proper name, Juliet is not marked as any man's property. From the beginning of Burney's text until the end, everyone (including the reader, no doubt) repeats and echoes the same question:

> ". . . What is it, then, once for all, that you call yourself? . . ." [asked Mrs. Maple].
>
> "Yes, your name! your name!" repeated Elinor.
>
> "Your name! your name!" echoed Selina.
>
> "Your name! your name!" re-echoed Ireton.
>
> The spirits and courage of the stranger seemed now to forsake her; and, with a faultering voice, she answered, "Alas! I hardly know it myself!" (58)

The heroine's "birth, her name, her connexions, her actual situation, and her object in making the voyage [to England], resisted enquiry, eluded insinuation, and baffled conjecture" (41). Although Juliet's behavior is perfectly decorous and her breeding obviously genteel, as a woman unable to situate herself with reference to a father, brother, or husband Juliet cannot obtain any form of acceptance or credit, either social or financial. In a society based upon the needs, wishes, and laws of men, one in which women serve only as objects in transactions among men, a "loose woman"—one not claimed by any of the principal subjects—is a threat, as Irigaray writes:

> In what arena, then, is woman situated? Who or what is her "father"? What is her "proper name"? To whom does she belong? What "family" or "clientele" does she come from? If all this is not clearly settled, the only way to maintain the economy in place is by rejecting the feminine. Of course, commodities should never speak, and certainly should not go to market alone. For such actions turn out to be totally subversive to the economy of exchange among subjects.[20]

Because Juliet's proper name and family are not "clearly settled," she is rejected as an "outcast of society" (49) and is regarded with suspicion.

19. Epstein, *Iron Pen,* 178.
20. Irigaray, *This Sex,* 158.

Juliet is considered an adventuress, a fortune hunter, a toadeater, a cheat, and "an illegitimate stroller, who does not so much as know her own name" (86). A woman without a name cannot be innocent, as Mrs. Howel severely points out: "Innocent? . . . without a name, without a home, without a friend?—Innocent? . . . you will find, that people who enter houses by names not their own . . . will be considered only as swindlers; and as swindlers be disposed of as they deserve" (133).

The issue of names and naming is another excess of *The Wanderer.* Far from wanting to help her remain independent, every man in the text is eager to appropriate Juliet, to turn her into a commodity and absorb her into the patriarchal system of exchanges. Epstein's insistence that "to lack a name is to belong to no one, that is, to belong to oneself"[21] is only half-true for Juliet—belonging to no one, for a woman, is not equivalent to belonging to herself. Property cannot own itself; unowned commodities are quickly claimed. Because Juliet is nameless, she can be given a name. When she cannot tell her name and "dare not say who, nor what I am,—and hardly even know it myself!" (66), Juliet offers herself as a blank page that men can title as they please. As Burney writes of their repeated and ceaseless efforts to debauch Juliet, marry her, or otherwise own her, she reveals that her heroine's difficulties are created and then compounded by the very persons to whom Juliet must turn for assistance.

Juliet is endowed with various appellations throughout *The Wanderer* —the Fair Incognita, the Fair Enigma, the Fair Unknown, L. S., Miss Ellis, The Ellis, The Doll, Mademoiselle Juliette, *la belle, la sage petite Anglaise, le citoyenne Julie,* The Honourable Miss Granville, and finally Mrs. Harleigh—but only two names offer her any freedom from brutal treatment. The heroine's sole fixed name, her Christian name Juliet, offers some comfort when it comes from the lips of Gabriella. Her name functions as a sign of recognition between them and as a pledge of their future female community. However, the name "Juliet" is not assigned to Burney's heroine until the third volume, and then it is offered within a paragraph written in French

21. Epstein, *Iron Pen,* 178. Joanne Cutting-Gray, in *Woman as 'Nobody,'* offers an extended analysis of Juliet's namelessness. Like Epstein, however, she concludes: "Far from constituting a woman as a named, passive object, namelessness discloses her as a human agent. . . . Having the world to begin again enables Juliet to authenticate her identity as an ongoing possibility. . . . Accordingly, it is by means of an injunction against naming herself that she finds access to speech" (85, 101, 102). This insistence on the positive potentiality of namelessness strikes me as offering a rather rosy view of the predicament faced by Burney's heroine.

(387)—the delayed revelation and the distancing through foreign language highlight the problem of naming and identity: Juliet cannot identify herself and Gabriella also cannot identify her, for neither of them is able to bestow upon Juliet a surname to define her in relation to men.[22] Their female community lacks economic and societal power and is therefore impermanent.

Juliet does obtain one surname from women: the name of Ellis is bestowed upon Juliet by the marchioness, who chooses the letters "L. S." for their correspondence, and Miss Bydell, who mistakes those initials for a last name. Juliet is happy to take the name Ellis because

> the embarrassed avowal of Juliet . . . that she knew not, herself, what she ought to be called; stood, ever after, in the way of any regulation upon that difficult point. She had been glad, therefore, to subscribe to the blunder of Miss Bydell, which seemed, in some measure, retaining an appellation, at least a sound, designed for her by the Marchioness. . . . (821)

Like the other name offered by women, the name of Ellis cannot be retained either. This strikingly feminine last name—which suggests the French word for "she," *elle*—is exposed as a sham and discredited.[23]

Juliet requires a name given to her by a man. As long as she retains only women-given names, she is open to appropriation. When the hideous

22. "Under representation, women appear nameless not only in the traditional sense that they are named only by taking their husband's name, but also in that they have no authority to confer names, to employ the concept-invoking process that claims mastery over language"—Cutting-Gray, *Woman as 'Nobody,'* 82–83.

23. Doody sees the name "Ellis" as a linguistic connection between the primary female characters of the text: "The novel as a whole has at its symbolic heart a kind of tripartite female being composed of *El*inor—*El*lis-Juliet—Gabri*ella.* We can hear in their names the ring of *elle . . . elle.* Elle is" (*Frances Burney,* 331). The name "Ellis" is, however, an "unstable arbitrary composition of syllabic sounds . . . always ready to dissolve again into the strange initial letters 'L. S.'" (329). In those letters, Doody finds an echo of the British abbreviation for currency: "Until the 1970s, L. S. had for English people a basic meaning as the first two symbols of the signification of money: l.s.d. The heroine in her false riddling denomination represents a means of exchange—as indeed she does, for Ellis-Juliet is a token of currency between the bishop and the commissary. Women in our culture (and others) are a medium of exchange between men . . . " (329). Arrived at differently, Doody's conclusion is similar to my own.

Frenchman comes to claim her, Juliet cannot decide whether or not she is his wife:

> . . . when she . . . heard him called her husband! and saw herself considered as his wife! duty, for that horrible instant, seemed in his favour; and, had not Sir Jaspar summoned her by her maiden name [the Honourable Miss Granville], to attend her own nearest relations, all her resistance had been subdued, by an overwhelming dread that to resist might possibly be wrong. (844–45)

Although she said no word of assent during the mockery of a marriage ceremony, Juliet is uncertain whether or not she is the Frenchman's wife: lacking a last name, she can offer no defense against his efforts to own her. Sir Jaspar may rescue her because he offers her a title she hopes to receive from her father's heir; although it is a name that brings Juliet into vexed relationships with men, for "to have used the name of Granville, would have been courting danger and pursuit" (821), her father's name is preferable to the unspoken and unspeakable last name of the Frenchman.

Harleigh also invokes the name of Granville and stresses the uncertainty of names when he proposes marriage to Juliet:

> Will not Miss Granville be more gracious than Miss Ellis has been? Miss Granville can have no tie but what is voluntary: no hovering doubts, no chilling scruples, no fancied engagements—
>
> . . . Miss Granville is wholly independent; mistress of her heart, mistress of herself. . . . (860)

Miss Granville actually has more ties, involuntary but necessary, than Miss Ellis, for the name of the father binds Juliet to the authority of an uncle and a brother, while the name created from letters chosen for Juliet by the marchioness serves only as a pledge of friendship. Harleigh, of course, wishes to dispense with both names in order to replace them with his own: "If I solicit to hear your name—it is but with the hope . . . that you will suffer me to change it!" (593). When he succeeds in winning her consent to his proposal, Harleigh seizes all of Juliet's names and assumes ownership of the lot: "Loveliest Miss Ellis! most beloved Miss Granville! My own,—at length! at length! my own sweet Juliet!" (862). Juliet's namelessness allows Harleigh to name her—only the man's last name can be the last.

Elinor Joddrel seems to be exempt from the confusions of identity that

Juliet faces. Independently wealthy, loosed from many of the constraints imposed upon women, she seems formidable. Harleigh explains,

> . . . her peculiar character, her extraordinary principles, and the strange situation into which she has cast herself, give her, for the moment, advantages difficult, nay dangerous to combat. Unawed by religion, of which she is ignorant; unmoved by appearances, to which she is indifferent; she utters all that occurs to an imagination inflamed by passion . . . with a courage from which she has banished every species of restraint. . . . (590)

The "champion of her sex" appears to be a radical feminist who successfully frees herself from patriarchal domination. When Elinor is introduced, she is "laughing immoderately" (15) and, like Miss Milner, later reveals that "a spirit of ridicule . . . so largely pervades her whole character, as to burst forth through all her sufferings, to mix derision with all her sorrows. . . . Reason and argument appear to her but as marks for dashing eloquence or sportive mockery" (590). Immediately identified with the "excesses" of the French Revolution (18) and soon abandoning herself to an "excess" of love (169), Elinor seems to be a disruptive feminine force who, having liberated herself, will go on to subvert the patriarchal domination of others.[24] "Throwing off the trammels of unmeaning custom" (151), Elinor boldly asserts her rights and her desires while she laments the bondage of other members of her sex, especially Juliet, of whom she says, "you only fear to alarm, or offend the men—who would keep us from every office, but making puddings and pies for their own precious palates!" (399). Elinor continues,

> Oh woman! poor, subdued woman! thou art as dependant, mentally, upon the arbitrary customs of man, as man is, corporally, upon the established law of his country! . . .
>
> By the oppressions of their own statutes and institutions, they render us insignificant; and then speak of us as if we were so born! But what have we tried, in which we have been foiled? They dare not trust us with their own education, and their own opportuni-

24. For a discussion of Elinor as a "true feminist," see Rose Marie Cutting, "Defiant Women: The Growth of Feminism in Fanny Burney's Novels," *Studies in English Literature, 1500–1900* 17 (Summer 1977): 525–28.

> ties for distinction.... Woman is left out in the scales of human merit, only because they dare not weigh her! (399)

Elinor pities women who are not free because she believes herself to be autonomous. But even as she insists upon her independence—"I dare speak and act, as well as think and feel for myself!"—she proves herself imprisoned: "something within involuntarily, invincibly checked her" (154). From both within and without, Elinor's situation of apparent freedom and autonomy is actually just a more subtle form of oppression. Her position is very little different from Juliet's; her defiance of the patriarchal system fails almost before it begins.

Elinor's desire for Harleigh, like Miss Milner's desire for Dorriforth, is a desire for the forbidden: not only is Harleigh the elder brother of Elinor's fiancé, but "his pride is so scrupulous, and his scruples are so squeamish, that he would deem it a crime of the first magnitude" to even think of wanting his brother's betrothed (160). Harleigh is inaccessible to Elinor both by custom and by his own repugnance to women who deviate "from the long-beaten track of female timidity" (343). Elinor's pursuit of Harleigh, then, defies the latter's own strictures about female decorum and, in its opposition to customary roles, can be read as a bold assertion of female freedom: Elinor refuses to remain inactive and instead actively seeks the object of her desires.

As with Miss Milner's passion, however, Elinor Joddrel's love for Harleigh is inscribed within the patriarchal system she apparently defies. It is an Oedipal desire for the father/guardian who himself "has no desire for her."[25] Harleigh is not simply her fiancé's brother—he is the man sent to bring Elinor home from the Continent when the Reign of Terror endangers the lives of British travelers.[26] Harleigh is "to be her guide and her

25. Luce Irigaray, *Speculum of the Other Woman,* trans. Gillian C. Gill (Ithaca: Cornell University Press, 1985), 39.

26. Elinor has been traveling because (again like Miss Milner) her mental anguish over Harleigh has resulted in physical illness: "The conflict of her mind, during this doubting state, threatened to cast her into a consumption" (155). Not only does Elinor share Miss Milner's hysterical symptoms, she also responds to a letter from Harleigh with similar excessive pleasure. The episode of the letter in *A Simple Story* is, with some variations, reproduced in *The Wanderer:*

> At sight of the hand-writing of Harleigh, addressed to herself, every other feeling gave way to rapturous joy. She snatched the letter ... blew it all

guard" (155), a substitute for the father that Elinor does not have.[27] After Elinor declares her love for him, Harleigh refuses "to become her permanent guardian" (366)—the terms he uses again point to his role as that of father substitute. The relationship is never one of equals: Harleigh is Elinor's master, her sovereign, and finally her God. Her first letter to him portrays her as "enslaved" and obedient to his "tyranny" (189–90), while her final speeches show her attentive to his counsel as to words "dropt straight from heaven!" (796). Instead of defying patriarchy, Elinor's passion upholds and strengthens it by placing Harleigh in the position of supreme lawmaker.

Elinor's response to Harleigh's rejection is another indication that her desire is not the expression of female independence. Elinor sees only two alternatives for herself: "a wedding-garment . . . or . . . a shroud" (168). Relinquishing the position of vocal, single champion of her sex, Elinor insists upon choosing one of the two acceptable roles—wife or corpse—that men have allowed women to play for centuries. Not only does Elinor fail to admit other alternatives, she sets up her categories in conventional binary opposition: being a wife, she suggests, is the highest state of being, while becoming a corpse, given her insistence on total annihilation, is the lowest. The path Elinor treads and would have other women follow is not new at all.[28]

> around, as if to disperse the contagion of any foreign touch, and then, in a transport of delight, pressed it to her lips, to her heart, and again to her lips, with devouring kisses. She would not read it, she declared, till night: all she experienced of pleasure was too precious and too rare, not to be lengthened and enjoyed to its utmost possible extent; yet, nearly at the same moment, she broke the seal, and ordered every one to quit the room; that the air which would vibrate with words of Harleigh, should be uncontaminated by any breath but her own. . . . Eagerly, rapidly, and without taking breath till she came to the conclusion, she then read aloud. . . . (373)

Like the letters of Miss Woodley and Dorriforth, Harleigh's letter is not worth such expenditure of emotional energy.

27. Juliet McMaster notes this and writes, "In *The Wanderer,* the hero, Harleigh, is on one occasion referred to as 'Monsieur le Moniteur,' and he does become a spiritual guide to the secondary heroine, Elinor" ("The Silent Angel: Impediments to Female Expression in Frances Burney's Novels," *Studies in the Novel* 21 [Fall 1989]: 238).

28. Doody, who also views Elinor as a "mixed character" (*Frances Burney,* 339), elaborates, "Yet the female suicidal gesture, though it seems defiant, original, and liberating, is an obedience to social commands. . . . The customary command for woman

In "Ev'ry Woman Is at Heart a Rake," Patricia Meyer Spacks stresses that, in the eighteenth century, "women are doomed no matter what they do—particularly if they allow themselves feelings. . . . only by emotional repression can a woman survive successfully in a world which penalizes female expressiveness."[29] Burney's text emphasizes the dilemma: when Elinor angrily asks, on behalf of her sex, "must even her [woman's] heart be circumscribed by boundaries as narrow as her sphere of action in life? Must she be taught to subdue all its native emotions? To hide them as sin, and to deny them as shame?" (177), the answer implied is an emphatic "yes." While Elinor's ungoverned passions reduce her to notorious attempts at self-destruction and threaten her with incarceration for madness, "the perfect conduct, and icy coldness of Juliet, rescued her from all evil imputation" (455).[30] Juliet's frigidity saves her from one type of appropriation (mistress) so that she may be reserved for the other (wife). As the libertine Sir Lyell puts it, "I should have adored her . . . if I had not believed her a thing of alabaster" (444). Only by being a "composition of ice, of snow, of marble" (475) does Juliet escape such unworthy attentions and maintain her independent existence.

Through repression, Juliet survives; however, she pays an immense price. Although Elinor dubs her "icy Ellis" and insists that she who voluntarily suppresses desires must lack "spirit, sense, or soul" (477)—"all within was not chilled, however all without might seem cold" (336). Juliet feels, but smothers her feelings; she desires, but denies desire. When pressed by Harleigh to declare whether or not she has given her heart to another, Juliet answers, "I have no heart!—I must have none!" (341). Known to no one, Juliet finally seems scarcely to know herself.[31] She masks so seriously and so completely that the masquerade becomes her

is that she be unobtrusive, slender, and quiet. . . . There is no better way to be unobtrusive, slender, and mute than to be dead—which is perhaps woman's ideal condition. . . . In turning her sexual feeling and her anger against herself, Elinor is not helping other women but betraying them" (342–43).

29. Patricia Meyer Spacks, "Ev'ry Woman Is at Heart a Rake," *Eighteenth-Century Studies* 8 (Fall 1974): 43.

30. See Simons: ". . . Juliet's feminine pose of delicacy and restraint belies her inner courage and is in itself something of a decoy. The mask she wears at the beginning of the novel is more than just a narrative ploy but reflects the indispensability of disguise for women as a means of protection. Elinor's emotional honesty and her directness lead her to disaster, as Burney demonstrates that artifice is the only sure method of female survival" (*Fanny Burney,* 111).

31. In response to Mrs. Ireton's vindictive "who told you to go?" Juliet answers, "A person, Madam, who has not the honour to be known to you,—myself!" (526). Later,

reality. Her habits of concealment and repression having become customary, Juliet, when freed from her various entanglements, still avoids Harleigh even though she wants to marry him: "The immediate impulse of Juliet urged her to remonstrance, or flight; but it was the impulse of habit, not of reason; an instant, and a look of Harleigh, represented that the total change of her situation, authorized, on all sides, a total change of conduct" (860).

"My conduct must be liable to no inference of any sort," insists Juliet (594). But throughout the text her conduct is neutral and therefore liable to inferences of *every* sort. Juliet's seeming absence of desire makes her fascinating to the men around her—Sir Jaspar Herrington is not the only man to ask Juliet, "What is it you have about you that sets one's imagination so to work?" (435). It is not what Juliet has that fuels imagination and desire—it is what she lacks.

Woman's lack is the guarantee of man's possession, placing her as the "other" of and mirror for the masculine subject.[32] In *The Wanderer,* Juliet serves as a beautiful blankness to reflect the fantasies of the men who surround her. From the lowest class to the highest, men assume that they can appropriate Juliet to their own needs; she is for them an emptiness that can contain their dreams and wishes. Yokels in the woods, "each believing her to be alike at the service of either, or of both," argue about who will receive the first kiss (689); young farmer Gooch assumes that Juliet will be eager to accompany him to a party and perhaps to marry him if he chooses to ask her (412–20); Riley sees her as a diversion and hunts her as though she were an animal, obtaining "the cynical satisfaction, of having worried a timid deer from the field" (772); Ireton assumes Juliet is a promiscuous swindler and uses her to make "sneering calumnies, chiefly pointed at Harleigh," whom he envies (143, 509–10); Admiral Powel pleases himself with his own benevolence in aiding a fallen woman who has not "kept tight to her own duty, and taken a modest care of herself" (37); Sir Lyell views her as "easy prey" for his own licentious amusements and kidnaps her, so certain is he that she loves him (247, 458–59); and Sir Jaspar, finding her "so exquisite a piece of workmanship," proposes his ancient

Juliet wonders when her difficulties will ever end and asks, "when appear,—when alas!—even know what I am!" (673).

32. "... the *flat mirror*... may be used for the self-reflection of the masculine subject.... Now woman, starting with this flat mirror alone, can only come into being as the inverted other of the masculine subject (his *alter ego*), or as the place of emergence and veiling of the cause of his (phallic) desire, or again as lack, since her sex for the most part—and the only historically valorized part—is not subject to specularization"—Irigaray, *This Sex,* 129.

and decrepit self for her husband and, failing that, takes her to Stonehenge to satisfy "the wish next [his] . . . heart, the idea of being the object of some marvellous adventure" (506, 634, 767).

Minor male characters are not the only ones who wish to fix Juliet, to possess her, to objectify her, to use her. Harleigh and Lord Melbury, the heroes of *The Wanderer,* are little different from the other men: Lord Melbury's unknowingly incestuous proposition (139) and Harleigh's persistent pursuit both commodify Juliet. The virtual sameness of the many men in the text is yet another of Burney's "excesses."[33] Through Harleigh, in fact, the reader is offered a close look into the ways in which Juliet's neutrality fuels male fantasy. Harleigh supplies every gap in his knowledge with his own desires; he assumes that Juliet offers an empty page on which he may write his own description of her. Having no positive information, Harleigh imagines Juliet as fulfilling his own ideals:

> To him, her language, her air, and her manner, pervading every disadvantage of apparel, poverty, and subjection, had announced her, from the first, to have received the education, and to have lived the life of a gentlewoman. . . .
>
> . . . Harleigh grew every instant more enchanted. . . . (75, 100)

Elinor accuses him: "to what a chimera you have given your heart! to an existence unintelligible, a character unfathomable, a creature of imagination, though visible!" (181).[34] Juliet, as Harleigh knows her, *is* a creature of his

33. Doody notes, "Harleigh seems to participate in a general blight of males. . . . The male characters in *The Wanderer* are all weak men . . . " (*Frances Burney,* 344, 347). See also Straub: "Flawed male lovers and fathers provide the problematic context of male power and male impotence in which Burney's heroines attempt to act, to arrange their lives" (*Divided Fictions,* 210).

34. Elinor's obsession with Harleigh prevents her from truly befriending Juliet—this, perhaps more forcefully than anything else, indicates that Elinor's desire strengthens patriarchal oppression of women instead of circumventing it. Because she is jealous of Juliet, Elinor "never spoke one word" and "was just like a person dumb" when Juliet required someone to come to her defense with Mrs. Howel and the Granvilles (128–29; compare Elinor's behavior to Gabriella's, who quickly speaks to defend her friend from Sir Jaspar's suspicion that Juliet is illegitimate [640ff.]). To Harleigh, Elinor emphasizes Juliet's "double dealing, false appearances, and lurking disguise! without a family she dare claim, without a story she dare tell, without a name she dare avow!" (181), thereby attempting to cut off that source of succor. When Juliet, deprived of every other support, comes to Elinor for help, " . . . Elinor, with strong derision, called out,

own imagination: when he finds out that she is married, "a sudden sensation, kindred even to hatred, took possession of his feelings. Altered she appeared to him, and delusive" (730). Once Juliet seems to be the property of another, she has altered as far as Harleigh is concerned because she can no longer serve as the repository of his wishes.

Good men and bad men are conflated in Burney's text in order to emphasize the scope and force of patriarchal oppression: men from all classes and at least two nations are implicated. Thus, heroes and villains merge completely and are confused with each other at times. Harleigh is mistaken for Juliet's brutal French "husband" when he asks to come up to her flat: "Strong and palpable affright, now seized Ellis; am I—Oh heaven! —she murmured to herself, pursued?" (335). Later, when "a tall man, muffled up, whose air denoted him to be a gentleman" follows her to the cemetery, Juliet feels "terrour . . . [begin] to take possession of her mind. She had surely been deluded, and she was evidently followed. . . . the unprincipled Sir Lyell Sycamore alone occurred to her, as capable of so cruel a stratagem to enveigle her to a lonely spot" (575–76). The man who follows her is in fact Harleigh. A third time, Juliet finds herself "hurt and offended that, at such a juncture, Harleigh could break into her retreat" when he appears as a mysterious intruder in her rural seclusion (775). Finally, when a man "encircled her in his arms," Juliet assumes it to be the horrid Frenchman and "shrieked with sudden horrour and despair, strenuously striving to disengage herself; though persuaded that the only person who would dare thus to assail her, was him to whom she was intentionally resigning her destiny . . . " (847). This time the unknown assailant is Lord Melbury, whose manner with Juliet is not far different from that of his close friend Sir Lyell (147, 244). If Sir Lyell confined Juliet in a carriage to proposition her (458), Lord Melbury had trapped her in a parlour for the same purpose (139).

Good men are equivalent to bad because all approach Juliet in the same

---

'Debility and folly! Put aside your prejudices, and forget that you are a dawdling woman, to remember that you are an active human being, and your FEMALE DIFFICULTIES will vanish into the vapour of which they are formed' " (397). By refusing to recognize Juliet's very pressing pecuniary distresses, Elinor can avoid giving real assistance. In her hatred of her rival, Elinor smugly offers Juliet as a sacrifice to Mrs. Ireton's venom: " . . . Elinor conveyed her submissive and contemned, yet agonizingly envied rival, to Brighthelmstone" (475). By participating in female rivalry, Elinor misses an opportunity of forming a female community that would uphold the ideas about women's rights and women's freedom that she speaks about but fails to act upon.

way: Harleigh's pursuit is just as relentless as the Frenchman's and he is every bit as eager as Sir Lyell to lead her to a secluded spot, while Lord Melbury is as quick as her loathed intimate or the licentious nobleman to assail her physically. All men wish to possess her—it is Juliet's attitude toward each that separates them into heroes and villains. When Harleigh realizes that Juliet runs from his pursuit just as surely as she does from that of her "husband" and questions whether or not she puts both of them on a par, Juliet answers, "him I fly because I hate;—You . . . "—the blank is obviously meant to be filled by "because I love" (779). The two men are equated by the parallel construction, and only Juliet's response to each differentiates them. Regarded as a commodity by all, Juliet manages to obtain through her repression and restraint only the right to refuse one commodification in favor of another. She rejects the Frenchman's brutal appropriation in order to accept Harleigh's genteel one. To continue to fit herself to his desires, though, Juliet is compelled to maintain the rigid female decorum that Harleigh demands. At the end of Burney's *Wanderer,* Juliet remains in the masquerade of femininity.

II

> For the actress is herself an artist, the creator of herself—of her selves, rather. These are, suggestively, assumed, several, and temporary.
>
> —Rachel Brownstein

> . . . *The Wanderer* also address[es] the complex and contradictory position of the woman who seeks to control the way she is seen, the woman as manipulator of appearances, as the maker of her own identity—in short, of the woman as artist.
>
> —Kristina Straub

The rigid control Juliet puts upon her feelings and wishes separates her from Elinor; at another level, however, she is united to the latter "improper" woman. Juliet and Elinor both adopt a variety of disguises; the many roles each woman plays and the multiple transformations she undergoes are other significant "excesses" of Burney's *Wanderer.* Unlike Elinor, however, Juliet does not eagerly embrace the opportunity for theatrical display. The theater scene that initially brings the two women under comparison reflects, in miniature, the behavior that characterizes them throughout the novel, for while Elinor delights in staging a production of *The Provoked Husband,* Juliet must be forced to act her part (70 ff.).[35] The overabundance of disguises in *The Wanderer* emphasizes that, while Juliet and Elinor respond in opposite ways to the limitations of the female role, neither can escape it: masquerade is the condition of femininity. Just as Juliet's various metamorphoses highlight her passive receptiveness to male desire, so too Elinor's multiple roles reveal her lack of power and play into patriarchal politics.

Juliet represents the excess of the "good" woman, playing out and overplaying all the culturally sanctioned roles. Her many transformations are not conscious efforts to attract the male gaze like the masquerade costumes of Behn's Maria and Belvideera, Haywood's Dalinda and Philecta, or Inchbald's Miss Milner. Juliet's disguises are, in fact, an effort to "say nothing. Absolutely *nothing.* And in order to produce this nothing the woman uses her own body as disguise."[36] Juliet's body becomes, then, a tabula rasa upon which anything and everything can be written. Such nothingness, such sexual blankness, is the very definition of female decorum in the eighteenth century, the masquerade of femininity required by a society that assigns passivity to women, activity to men. Riley, when hunting for Juliet at the harp rehearsal, says that he must "see through a mask; for . . . if she be here, she must wear one" (252). He describes Juliet's real face as a mask and considers her disguised face to be real, thus blurring the distinction between reality and disguise. This collapse of distinction defines the masquerade that is femininity, as Stephen Heath, writing about "Joan Riviere and the Masquerade," points out: "Disguising herself as a castrated woman, the woman represents man's desire and finds her identity as, precisely, woman—genuine womanliness and the masquerade are the same thing, as Riviere insists. . . . "[37] Juliet's unwilling disguise leaves her

35. In her extended discussion of the meaning of Cibber's play in Burney's text, Straub notes that the theatrical "function[s] . . . as a sort of litmus test for characters' social and moral qualities. . . . [Juliet's] role is, literally, selfless in that she is not licensed to act out her desires, but rather serves others' needs" (*Divided Fictions,* 217–18).

36. Michèle Montrelay, "Inquiry into Femininity," trans. Parveen Adams, in *French Feminist Thought: A Reader,* ed. Toril Moi (Oxford: Basil Blackwell, 1987), 239.

37. Stephen Heath, "Joan Riviere and the Masquerade," in *Formations of Fantasy,* ed. Victor Burgin, James Donald, and Cora Kaplan (London: Methuen, 1986), 52.

in the same position as the earlier heroines' willing self-display: Juliet remains inscribed as the object of male scopic pleasure and masculine sexual enjoyment. Her transformations conform to the Irigarayan sense of masquerade as "what women do in order to recuperate some element of desire, to participate in man's desire, but at the price of renouncing their own. . . . [Women] 'appear' and circulate only when enveloped in the needs/desires/fantasies of . . . men."[38]

At the beginning of *The Wanderer,* the passengers on the boat from France gradually find out that their latest companion is a shabby, battered Creole:

> . . . the stranger, having taken off her gloves, to arrange an old shawl, in which she was wrapt, exhibited hands and arms of so dark a colour, that they might rather be styled black than brown.
>
> . . . a closer view of the little that was visible of the muffled up face . . . [showed] it to be of an equally dusky hue. . . .
>
> The wind just then blowing back the prominent borders of a French night-cap . . . displayed a large black patch, that covered half her left cheek, and a broad black ribbon, which bound a bandage of cloth over the right side of her forehead. (19–20)

This initial deception is the most dramatic of Juliet's disguises: bruised, beaten, and impoverished, Juliet is the embodiment of oppressed womanhood. She begins at the lowest rank of society as the poorest and most outcast of women. In this guise, she is of little interest to the men around her—Riley finds her fit to mock, while Harleigh and the admiral see her as suitable for pity. As an impoverished black woman, Juliet is an object of curiosity, subject to racism or benevolence; however, when her "skin changed from a tint nearly black, to the brightest, whitest, and most dazzling fairness . . . [and] the blackest, dirtiest, raggedest wretch . . . turned into an amazing beauty" (43), she becomes an object of obsessive erotic interest. Juliet reverses the male expectation that hideousness and grotesqueness lurk beneath the female mask.[39] In her disguise, what the men reject as vulgarity and deformity covers what they accept as gentility and

38. Irigaray, *This Sex,* 133–34.

39. Jonathan Swift's "Progress of Beauty" (1719) and "A Beautiful Young Nymph Going to Bed" (1731), along with Richard Steele's discussion of the Picts (women who paint) in *The Spectator,* no. 41 (17 April 1711), testify to male fears of what may appear beneath a woman's mask.

beauty. As Juliet gradually reveals her skills as a gifted harpist (75), fine needleworker (78), elegant scribe (83), graceful dancer (84), accomplished sketcher (88), and beautiful actress (94), she captivates the men and arouses envy in the women who surround her. In her jealousy, Elinor mocks Harleigh's concern with the "maimed and defaced Dulcinea" (50) and insists, quite rightly, that his romantic yearning to find a princess-in-disguise has now an object within which to locate itself:

> Oh, you must fall in love with her, I suppose, as a thing of course. . . .
>
> . . . you dream of nothing but that dismal Incognita. . . .
>
> . . . when you were in such a tindery fit as to be kindled by that dowdy, you could [not] have resisted being blown into flames at once by a creature such as this [beautiful mysterious charmer]. . . . (18, 49, 52)

Mrs. Ireton tauntingly asks Juliet if her "bandages and patches are to be converted into . . . the order of Maria Theresa? or of the Empress of all the Russias?" (44); Harleigh believes in the possibility of either and delights in the idea that all of Juliet's accomplishments can be called forth for his amusement.

Juliet's other transformations, though not so extreme as her rejection of "stained skin, and garb of poverty" (750) in favor of fair skin and the trappings of aristocracy, still cater to male desires. Juliet enacts an excessive number of disempowering roles: she poses as male manqué, "wrapt . . . in a man's great coat, [wearing] . . . a black wig, and a round hat" (747); she appears as a French milliner subject to "licentious" and improper male attentions (430, 449); and she dons the guise of a rural girl of light character (665–66). In every case, Juliet is mute and prey to physical assault; her identity is fragmented and her body fetishized. Ironically, it is Mrs. Ireton who draws attention to the distortion of the self involved in Juliet's various disguises:

> So you had disfigured yourself in that horrid manner, only to extort money[?] . . .
>
> . . . Will it be impertinent, too, if I enquire whether you always travel with that collection of bandages and patches? and of black and white outsides? or whether you sometimes change them for wooden legs and broken arms?

> . . . What business is it of mine to confine your genius to only one or two methods of maiming or defacing yourself? as if you did not find it more amusing to be one day lame, and another blind; and, to-day, it should seem, dumb? . . .
>
> . . . You have been bruised and beaten; and dirty and clean; and ragged and whole; and wounded and healed; and a European and a Creole, in less than a week. (45–46)

Although she is speaking of Juliet's first disguise as the "walnut-skinned gypsey" (52), Mrs. Ireton points out that being an "adept in metamorphoses" (46) involves self-disfigurement. What Mrs. Ireton fails to note is that the amusement of such "maiming and defacing" does not go to the one who becomes maimed and powerless: Juliet does not enjoy her own disguises—only those around her, particularly men, find pleasure in her numerous transformations.

Elinor's multiple roles provide a shadowy echo of Juliet's. As Epstein notes, "Elinor is Juliet's mirror image and alter-ego":[40] if Juliet overplays the roles of the "good" woman, Elinor appears too often in those of the "bad." Yet these two female characters do not stand in binary opposition: the parts that Elinor plays are finally just as culturally sanctioned as those of Juliet.

In *Ways of Seeing,* John Berger speaks of the means by which a woman is constrained by male-dominated society to "[turn] herself into an object—and most particularly an object of vision: a sight."[41] In *The Wanderer* Elinor Joddrel does just that: in her many suicide attempts, Elinor transforms herself into a spectacle for male voyeurism.[42] Even before she attempts to kill herself, Elinor begins to describe herself and her life using metaphors of acting and theatricality:

> . . . I regard and treat the whole of my race as the mere dramatis personae of a farce; of which I am myself, when performing with such fellow-actors, a principal buffoon. . . .

40. Epstein, *Iron Pen,* 186.

41. John Berger, *Ways of Seeing* (New York: Penguin Books, 1972), 47.

42. See Catherine Clément, "The Guilty One," in *The Newly Born Woman,* by Hélène Cixous and Catherine Clément, trans. Betsy Wing (Minneapolis: University of Minnesota Press, 1986): "These women [hysterics], to escape the misfortune of their economic and familial exploitation, chose to suffer spectacularly before an audience of men: it is an attack of spectacle, a crisis of suffering" (10).

> The second act of the comedy, tragedy, or farce, of my existence, is to be represented to-morrow. . . .
>
> . . . But let us not anticipate act the third. The second alone can decide, whether it will conclude the piece with an epithalamium—or a requiem!
>
> . . . And though I know not whether the catastrophe will be tragic or comic, I am prepared in my part for either. (153, 161–62, 157)

After her attempts at self-annihilation prove unsuccessful, Elinor goes on to ridicule herself using these same images:

> Away with this burlesque dumb shew! . . . No more of these farcical forms! . . .
>
> . . . You conclude that I only present myself a bowl and a dagger, like a Tragedy Queen, to have them dashed from my hands, that I may be ready for a similar exhibition another day? . . .
>
> . . . Yet I am not ignorant how tired you must be of those old thread-bare topics, bowls, daggers, poignards, and bodkins. . . . (377, 585, 596)

Throughout the latter portion of the text, Elinor comes to view herself solely as a spectacle and a sight—she finally offers herself to Juliet for exhibition, saying, "If I were poor myself, I would engage to acquire a large fortune, in less than a week, by advertising, at two-pence a head, a sight of the lady that stabbed herself" (400).

The self-consciousness of Elinor's theatricality separates her performances from those of Juliet. While Juliet unwillingly adopts the disguises men offer to her, Elinor "sees herself as empowered by feminine self-display" and eagerly chooses to act out roles.[43] Does this distinction between unwilling and willing exhibition correspond to the two notions of masquerade—submission to the dominant economy of male voyeurism and desire versus resistance to it—that I outlined in my discussion of Eliza Haywood's fiction? Is Elinor's masquerade in *The Wanderer* comparable to Fantomina's?

Mary Ann Doane's formulation in "Film and the Masquerade: Theorising the Female Spectator"—which posits that masquerade "is anti-hysterical

43. Straub, *Divided Fictions,* 218. See also Epstein: ". . . Elinor is a self-activating chameleon" (*Iron Pen,* 187).

for it works to effect a separation between the cause of desire and oneself. . . . By destabilising the image, the masquerade confounds this masculine structure of the look"[44]—seems to conform to Margaret Doody's analysis of Elinor. While admitting that Elinor is "a mixed character," Doody emphasizes the rebellious nature of her theatricality and focuses on the subversiveness of her self-willed masquerade:

> Elinor has a restless, self-conscious mind, quick to catch sight of her own exhibitionism at work, mocking herself with a Romantic irony that also mocks the world that mocks and judges. . . .
>
> In Elinor, Burney deliberately created a character who is strongly and consciously theatrical. . . .
>
> . . . she acts out theatrically roles which are socially proffered, and literalizes what is usually left metaphorical (girls may have wounded hearts, one would rather shoot oneself, love is a dagger to the breast). . . . If Elinor is an actress *en costume,* so, after all, is Juliet, who is decidedly in costume when we first see her, and whose whole progress through England is a sort of unwilling masquerade. Juliet adopts the roles of women who are socially lower and weaker than she "really" is (poor Creole, seamstress, teacher in a dame-school). Elinor adopts the male role, which is much stronger than her own, and then, almost in parody of Gabriella, the humble role of the mourning woman—woman in weakness and misery. . . . she wants to disturb the peace with shrieks and "fierce harangues." Eve in a veil (a veil that can become a shroud), she keeps trying to unveil the mystery of who or what woman can or may be.[45]

Elinor's theatrical exhibitions are *designed* to disrupt, but whether or not she *succeeds* in her efforts is another question. Doane's later assessment, "Masquerade Reconsidered: Further Thoughts on the Female Spectator," begins by asserting:

> There is a type of violence in my 1982 essay, "Film and the Masquerade: Theorizing the Female Spectator," which is a result of the attempt (which fails in many respects) to tear the con-

44. Mary Ann Doane, "Film and the Masquerade: Theorising the Female Spectator," *Screen* 23 (September–October 1982): 82.

45. Doody, *Frances Burney,* 339, 341.

> cept of masquerade out of its conventional context. Generally, masquerade is employed not to illuminate the agency usually associated with spectatorship, but to designate a mode of being for the other—hence, the sheer objectification or reification of representation. . . . Masquerade would hence appear to be the very antithesis of spectatorship/subjectivity. . . .
>
> . . . For Riviere, as well as for Lacan and Irigaray who take up the concept within their work, masquerade specifies a norm of femininity—not a way out, a "destabilization" of the image, as I argued. . . . But it is a curious norm, which indicates through its very contradictions the difficulty of *any* concept of femininity in a patriarchal society.[46]

In *The Wanderer* Elinor becomes the embodiment of the difficulties Doane speaks of. Although she attempts to constitute herself as a subject, there is no role open to her through which she can arrive at such a position. Unlike Haywood's *Fantomina,* Burney's text does not allow the gap between the constructed image and the female self necessary for subjectivity: Elinor plays out her roles in earnest, "for real," and fails to maintain the ironic distance from them that Haywood's character achieves. The guises Elinor adopts in themselves indicate her lack of power since, far from collapsing hierarchical categories and challenging the dominant ideology, they remain entirely within patriarchal norms.

Elinor is the spokesperson and enthusiast of the French Revolution, and thus becomes "a lady so expert in foreign politics, as to make an experiment, in her own proper person, of the new atheistical and suicidical doctrines, that those ingenious *gentlemen,* on t'other side the water, are now so busily preaching . . . " (371; italics mine). Not only does Elinor enact with her own body the doctrines of men, she herself becomes a man in her second suicide attempt:

> . . . the poor gentleman . . . was deaf and dumb. . . .
>
> . . . His dress and figure were equally remarkable. . . . The whole of his habiliment seemed of foreign manufacture; but his air had something in it that was wild, and uncouth; and his head was continually in motion.
>
> . . . [His face was] masked. . . . (356–58)

46. Mary Ann Doane, "Masquerade Reconsidered: Further Thoughts on the Female Spectator," *Discourse* 11 (Fall–Winter 1988–89): 42–43.

Deaf, mute, alien, uncouth, masked, castrated, impotent—Elinor, "dressed . . . grotesquely . . . in man's attire . . . in the character of a foreigner, who was deaf and dumb" (395), recalls Juliet's escape from France in a similar disguise. Such a costume is the portrait of the mutilated woman who attempts to hide her "lack" by masquerading as man: "the female can at least pretend that she is other. . . . The idea seems to be this: it is understandable that women would want to be men, for everyone wants to be elsewhere than in the feminine position."[47] Elinor's pose as male manqué, however, doubly places her in the role of the one without the phallus, or the one outside the dominant economy. The mask here paradoxically does not hide the lack that is the very nature of culturally constructed femininity but makes that lack all the more visible: as a woman, Elinor does not possess the phallus and, as a woman-disguised-as-a-man-without-the-phallus, she is doubly lacking. Elinor becomes, in Irigaray's terms, "mutilated, wounded, humiliated, overwhelmed by a feeling of inferiority that can never be 'cured.' In sum . . . castrated"; she would then express her guilt through her body, giving herself up "to be punished—by the accomplished fact of castration—without knowing what [she] . . . had done wrong" or what she was suffering from.[48] This is in fact what Elinor did when she "plunged a dagger into her breast" (359), punishing herself for her inability to win Harleigh's love.[49]

47. Doane, "Film and the Masquerade," 81. Doody's analysis is somewhat different: ". . . Elinor parodies the masculine role in taking it on. It is not maleness but masculine freedom, especially freedom of sexual choice, that she wants. . . . She gets momentary freedom in the gaudy masculine attire, but at the price of concealing her female self in appearing 'deaf and dumb' " (*Frances Burney,* 340).

48. Irigaray, *Speculum,* 88.

49. See Straub: "Elinor's self-mutilation gestures toward a psychological tendency often apparent in women's attempts at rebellion . . . the tendency of female rebellion unmediated by social consciousness to turn in on the rebel, to convert its own energy into a weapon against the rebellious woman herself. . . . Burney . . . [is explicit] about the social constraints on female behavior in romantic love that leave Elinor with no way out of the social system that forces her energy into self-destructive channels" (*Divided Fictions,* 188).

Although less overtly than Elinor, Juliet too exhibits female self-destructiveness. Instead of raging at the male-dominated society that has left her unprotected and rendered her unable to protect herself, instead of objecting to the violence practiced upon her, Juliet turns her anger inward and "upon more mature reflexion, she enquired by what right she expected kinder treatment" (72). At another juncture, reluctant to fault Harleigh for his relentless pursuit, Juliet takes the blame to herself:

Giving herself up to punishment is also what Elinor accomplishes in her enactment of the roles of the madwoman, one of the "undistinguished herd of common broken-hearted, broken-spirited, love-sick fanatics" (381), and the witch:

> The eyes of Elinor were wild and fierce, her complexion was livid, her countenance was become haggard; and, while she talked of triumph, and fancied it was what she felt, every feature exhibited the most tortured marks of impetuous sorrow, and ungoverned disappointment.
>
> . . . Elinor appeared in deep mourning; her long hair, wholly unornamented, hanging loosely down her shoulders. Her complexion was wan, her eyes were fierce rather than bright, and her air was wild and menacing. (172, 359)

> "You terrify me, Mr. Harleigh! Let me go!—instantly! instantly! —Would you make me hate—" She had begun with a precipitance nearly vehement; but stopt abruptly.
>
> "Hate me?" cried Harleigh, with a look appalled: "Good Heaven!"
>
> "Hate you?—No,—not you! . . . I did not say you!—"
>
> "Who, then? who then, should I make you hate?—Lord Melbury?—"
>
> "O no, never!—'tis impossible!—Let me be gone!—let me be gone!—"
>
> "Not till you tell me whom I should make you hate! I cannot part with you in this new ignorance! Clear, at least, this one little point. Whom should I make *hate you?* —"
>
> "Myself, Sir, myself!" cried she, trembling and struggling. "If you persist in thus punishing my not having fled from you, at once, as I would have fled from an enemy!" (619; italics mine)

Though most likely a printer's error, the transposition of "whom should I make you hate?" into "whom should I make hate you?" (a transposition that occurs both in the London 1814 edition and in the Oxford 1991 edition) is significant: women are not to hate but are only to be the objects of hatred. Women, in their powerlessness, do not turn violence against male oppressors; they poise weapons against only their own breasts. In her "Woman's Influence" (*Studies in the Novel* 11 [Spring 1979]), Paula Backscheider traces this phenomenon of female self-destructiveness through a number of eighteenth-century novels by women, and comments, "The gesture which began aimed at the male could in an instant be turned on the woman against herself. . . . The last step in human destructiveness is aggression turned against the self. Such an act expresses ultimate helplessness, self-loathing, and emphasizes the perceived threatening nature of the real object of hostility. In the final analysis, the heroine most often turns the violence against herself" (7, 17–18).

The "hagard [*sic*], yet piercing eyes" and "hollow voice" (471), along with the streaming hair, are attributes traditionally assigned to the sorceress. Both the hysteric and the sorceress are, in Catherine Clément's analysis, associated with the idea of woman as spectacle for men. These "deviants . . . all occupy challenging positions foreseen by the social bodies, challenging functions within the scope of all cultures. That doesn't change the structures, however. On the contrary, it makes them comfortable."[50] Elinor's metamorphoses into the witch and the madwoman fail to dismantle the established order of her society and, in fact, accomplish nothing except the endangerment of the little financial and physical independence she is allowed as an heiress of legal age. Elinor's physician threatens to "send for proper persons to controul and take care of her, as one unfit to be trusted to herself" (582). The structures of patriarchal society are equipped to deal with female deviants.[51] While the character fails in her defiance, however, the author succeeds in challenging: Burney's representation of Elinor exposes the methods used to silence women.

In her last failed effort to kill herself, Elinor literalizes the trope she had begun with—that of the "wedding-garment" or the "shroud" (168). In the church cemetery, Elinor appears as "a form in white; whose dress appeared to be made in the shape, and of the materials, used for our last mortal covering, a shroud" (579). At the same time, "a veil of the same stuff fell over the face of the figure" (579). Darting toward the church altar, Elinor embraces not a spouse but a "tablet of white stone, cut in the shape of a coffin," inscribed to serve as her gravestone (579). Marriage and death are repeatedly conflated in this scene, as Elinor cries, "Here stands the altar for the happy;—here, the tomb for the hopeless!" (580). Elinor is another Clarissa Harlowe, but Clarissa deranged, hurling the anger she feels at Harleigh back upon herself, like Clarissa turning the letter opener toward her own heart. Frustrated in her desire to be a bride—in her own words, a "poor wretch . . . [in] a fair way . . . to be soon denied every thing" (53)—Elinor will become a corpse, a wretch literally denied everything. Each role that Elinor takes on increases in helplessness and powerlessness, until finally she is the woman "buried alive" (583), the extreme of the

50. Catherine Clément, "Exchange," in *Newly Born Woman,* 155.

51. See Mary Russo, "Female Grotesques: Carnival and Theory," in *Feminist Studies/Critical Studies,* ed. Teresa de Lauretis (Bloomington: Indiana University Press, 1986): "Historically, Clément is right: hysterics and madwomen generally have ended up in the attic or in the asylum, their gestures of pain and defiance having served only to put them out of circulation" (222).

hysteric who hopes that her dead body will be a final appeal to the man she desires.[52]

That man, Harleigh, and the other men in the text do not take Elinor seriously. Many are witness to her suicidal spectacle and enjoy the show: ". . . the men, though all eagerly crowding to the spot of this tremendous event, [were] approaching rather as spectators of some public exhibition, than as actors in a scene of humanity" (359–60). Harleigh, "ashamed . . . at his own situation, thus publicly avowed as the object of this desperate act; earnestly wished to retreat from the gazers and remarkers, with whom he shared the notice and the wonder excited by Elinor" (361). Harleigh is angry to be included in Elinor's scopic objectification. He is further annoyed by Elinor's devotion when it forms an unpleasant impediment to his union with Juliet. In spite of the fact that Juliet's promise never to marry Harleigh seems to be the only thing keeping Elinor alive, Harleigh asks Juliet to "break a forced engagement made with a mad woman" (193) and queries,

> And can you suffer the wild flights of a revolutionary enthusiast, impelled by every extravagant new system of the moment; —however you may pity her feelings, respect her purity, and make allowance for her youth, to blight every fair prospect of a rational attachment? to supersede every right? and to annihilate all consideration, all humanity, but for herself? (204–5)

In his attempt to extinguish Juliet's feelings for Elinor, Harleigh reveals his own callousness toward the madwoman.

Other men, those not the subject of Elinor's displays, react more favorably. Dr. Naird, Elinor's physician, is amused by her adroitness in "turning the world upside down" (372). More significantly, Ireton—the "male jilt" (532), "a pitiful egotist, who seeks nothing but his own diversion" (164), and a man who develops a perverse passion for Elinor's fourteen-year-old sister, Selina[53]—admires Elinor and wishes her for himself. He insists,

52. Epstein comments on the excesses of this passage: "The dagger, the shroud, the gravestone: Elinor plays out the trappings of female Gothic. However, in so doing she lampoons the very conventions she defies by overplaying them" (*Iron Pen,* 188).

53. In describing their engagement, Burney clearly shows it to be the result of sexual perversion, for she stresses Selina's youth while hinting that only Ireton's money procures him his desire: "He then saw Selina, Elinor's younger sister, a wild little girl, only fourteen years of age, who was wholly unformed, but with whom he had become so desperately enamoured, that, when Mrs. Maple, knowing his character, and alarmed

> . . . I can never be happy without being adored. . . .
>
> "Yes, adored! loved to distraction! I must be idolized for myself, myself alone; yet publicly worshiped, that all mankind may see, —and envy,—the passion I have been able to inspire!" . . .
>
> "O that noble stroke! That inimitable girl! Happy, happy, Harleigh! . . . If I could meet with one who would take such a measure for my sake, and before such an assembly,—I really think I should worship her!"
>
> . . . [Elinor was] the only girl in the world who knew how to love, and what love meant. . . . (530, 531, 533, 534)

Ireton's approval of Elinor's suicide attempts is the strongest textual condemnation of them.[54] Far from challenging patriarchy, Elinor has become an object that exists only to put men into relationship with each other; her self-sacrifice marks and distinguishes the one, the man for whom she displays and destroys herself, in the eyes of many other men. Ireton would "worship" a woman who would consume herself spectacularly for him—"worship" is an appropriate word here, for if Elinor succeeded in self-murder, it would make no difference. She would not, in Ireton's scheme, be loved for herself but rather for what she accomplishes for him—making him envied by other men.

Men also derive pleasure from following Juliet's career. Riley articulates what the others think when he says,

> "What a rare hand you are, Demoiselle . . . at hocus pocus work! Who the deuce, with that Hebe face of yours, could have thought of your being a married woman! Why, when I saw you at that old

by his assiduities, cautioned him not to make a fool of her young niece, he abruptly demanded her in marriage. As he was very rich, Mrs. Maple had, of course, Elinor added, given her consent, desiring only that he would wait till Selina reached her fifteenth birth-day; and the little girl, when told of the plan, had considered it as a frolic, and danced with delight" (55).

54. Doody comments on Ireton's infatuation: "His wish for a woman to attempt suicide publicly for his sake is of course a form of woman-hating, and reminds us of the ironic consequences of Elinor's sensibilist romanticism. Her heroic demonstration might, in fact, be digested all too readily by a culture which believes that women should be submissive, wounded, and appropriated. . . . The admiration or, rather, fantasies of Ireton would be one of the most humiliating penalties Elinor could undergo for her action" (*Frances Burney,* 345).

> Bang'em's concert, at Brighthelmstone, I should have taken you for a boarding-school Miss. But you metamorphose yourself about so, one does not know which way to look for you. Ovid was a mere fool to you. . . . "
>
> "I have met with nothing like her . . . all the globe over. Neither juggler nor conjuror is a match for her. She can make herself as ugly as a witch, and as handsome as an angel. . . . Now she turns herself into a vagrant, not worth sixpence; and now, into a fine player and singer that ravishes all ears, and might make, if it suited her fancy, a thousand pounds at her benefit: and now, again, as you see, you can't tell whether she's a house-maid, or a country girl! yet a devilish fine creature, faith! as fine a creature as ever I beheld. . . . Look but what a beautiful head of hair she's displaying to us now! . . . But I won't swear that she does not change it, in a minute or two, for a skull-cap! She's a droll girl, faith! I like her prodigiously!" (771)

A princess-in-disguise for Harleigh, Juliet becomes Mrs. Betty, "a young nursery-maid" (759), for Sir Jaspar. Unlike Haywood's Fantomina and Glicera, who both delight in deceptions that serve their own desires, Juliet is encouraged to satisfy the fancies of men, making "all disguise . . . disgusting to her" (773). Juliet's masquerade forces her into powerlessness because she is made to enact roles that men thrust upon her and wish to watch her perform. Juliet, like Elinor, becomes a spectacle: like Elinor's role of male manqué, Juliet's masks ironically serve to expose, objectify, and imprison her. Juliet is a caged bird: "the besiegers [Ireton and the Miss Crawleys] of the cage perceived that the bird was flown" (512), "the bird he [Lord Denmeath] so much wished to sing to him was flown" (630), "you [Juliet and Gabriella] should coo together in the same cage" (640)—the trope, after Sterne's *Sentimental Journey* (1768), resonates with ideas of spectacle, entrapment, and oppression. Juliet is also compared to a zoo animal, "stared at like a wild beast" (54) and surveyed with curiosity (79). These images emphasize that Juliet's namelessness, apparent lack of wishes and feelings, and multiple transformations reduce her to being an unwilling repository of others' desires, not her own.

It is fitting, then, that *The Wanderer* concludes with Juliet's overt reabsorption into the patriarchal system of exchange. Only thus can the male desire to appropriate her be fully satisfied. At the end of Burney's novel, Juliet openly becomes what men have been trying to make her all along—an object of their transactions. Transactions among men for Juliet occur throughout the text: Ireton wagers that Riley will not be able to recognize her at the harp concert, and Sir Lyell vies with Mr. Tedman to escort her home (252–55); Sir Lyell, young Gooch, Mr. Stubbs, Mr. Scope, and Mr. Tedman compete for her attention and company after church (268–71); and Sir Lyell and Sir Jaspar, "two Baronets mutually struck by her superiour air and manner . . . each, though equally desirous to follow her, involuntarily standing still, to wait the motions of the other; and thence to judge of his pretensions to her favour," rival each other openly on her behalf (442). In each case the desires of the men are the important factors, while Juliet's wishes remain unstated or ignored.

The Wanderer closes with the most important transactions. Juliet has "played to perfection the role of femininity in all its bourgeois perversity"[55] and, as a reward, becomes the property of the aristocratic Harleigh instead of the savage French citizen. Everything that Juliet has been missing—a father, a name, a stable identity, an income—is provided for her, but provided in ironic overabundance. At the end of Burney's text, the penniless, nameless orphan bereft of protectors is overwhelmed with fathers and guardians, with names, and with riches. Juliet's difficulties are indeed only "FEMALE DIFFICULTIES" (275, 397, 873) because men, who established them, can just as easily dispel them.

Juliet's problems seem "extraordinary, . . . sad and difficult":

> Entitled to an ample fortune, yet pennyless; indebted for her sole preservation from insult and from famine, to pecuniary obligations from accidental acquaintances. . . . pursued, with documents of legal right, by one whom she shuddered to behold . . . ; unacknowledged,—perhaps disowned by her family; and, though born to a noble and yet untouched fortune, consigned to disguise, to debt, to indigence, and to flight! (816)

These difficulties all stem from agreements between men. Lord Denmeath, "who disputed, or denied" Juliet's relation to his family, unites with the

55. "Even if someday she plays to perfection the role of femininity in all its bourgeois perversity, it will in no way fill, will only deck with nothingness, this fault, this lack, of a specific specular economy and of a possible representation of her value, *for her and by her,* which could bring her into the system of exchange as something other than 'object' "—Irigaray, *Speculum,* 114.

French commissary to make Juliet "an alien" to her own country (752). "In actual communication and league with her persecutor" (757), Lord Denmeath's offer of Juliet's portion to the Frenchman fuels that greedy man's desire to drag her back to France. The commissary's threats to kill Juliet's guardian, the bishop, complicate the matter and enjoin the secrecy that hinders Juliet's ability to protect herself (740, 746, 750).

If the problems come from men, so do the solutions. Juliet's appeals to men raise their interest and finally secure her an overwhelming number of guardians and protectors. Her early patron, Admiral Powel, turns out to be Juliet's uncle. His sexism—"a woman is but a woman; which a a [*sic*] man, as her native superiour, ought always to keep in mind"[56] and "though he might be but a rogue, a husband's a husband; and I don't much uphold a wife's not thinking of that; for, if a woman may mutiny against her husband, there's an end of all discipline" (856)—seems appropriately ironic, since the admiral is the man who proves Juliet's paternity. "The discovery of an uncle, a protector, in so excellent a man as the Admiral, offered a prospect of solid comfort" (846), but the appearance of a second guardian, the man whom Juliet refers to as "My guardian! my preserver! my more than father!" (857), brings joy in spite of the fact that this guardian, the bishop, has required far more protection than he has bestowed and has almost occasioned Juliet lifelong misery. The unwilling Lord Denmeath, who relents under the pressure of the others, completes the trio of relations. Every branch of patriarchal authority is represented in this triumvirate—military, religious, and civil. The admiral, in his toast to Juliet, emphasizes this fact:

> . . . I shall make bold to propose a second bumper, to the happy espousals of the Honourable Miss Granville; who, you are to know, is my niece; with a very honest gentleman, who is at my elbow; and who had the kindness to take a liking to her before he knew that she had a Lord on one side, and, moreover, an Admiral on t'other for her relations; nor yet that she would have been a lady in her own right, if her father had not taken the long journey before her grandfather. (868)

To the many protectors who rush in after Juliet has ceased to need them (her French "husband" has already been executed) are added a husband,

56. I repeat the fortuitous printer's error in the original edition of *The Wanderer* ([London: Longman, Hurst, Rees, Orme, and Brown, 1814], 5:294).

Harleigh, and a brother, Lord Melbury. These last two emphasize how simple it is for one man to barter with another to determine the fate of a woman. Money can easily be substituted for the woman in the exchange, thereby reducing all of Juliet's problems to a very direct and straightforward business transaction. When Lord Melbury claims that he can set Juliet "completely at liberty," she thinks such a thing impossible; but he explains, "Not at all! 'tis the easiest thing in the world! only hear me. That wretch who claims you, shall have the portion he demands; the six thousand pounds; immediately upon signing your release, sending over the promissory-note of Lord Denmeath, and delivering your noble Bishop into the hands of the person who shall carry over the money . . . " (849). Burney emphasizes that Juliet's "generous brother . . . alone could realize such a project" (850)—money is a thing women have no control over.[57]

Patriarchal society failed to aid Juliet when she was alone and in need, but it will shower her with an overabundance when she has plenty. The ending of Burney's text seems ironic. As Terry Castle writes of *Cecilia,* "the turn is too arbitrary and false—too numbingly a piece of literature. . . . "[58] After all of Juliet's struggles to obtain a mere subsistence, now she is to have thirty thousand pounds settled on her from the Melbury estate (849), a generous marriage settlement from Harleigh (864–65), and an inheritance from the admiral (865). Burney stresses that all of this occurs as transactions among men: when Admiral Powel, Lord Denmeath, Lord Melbury, and Harleigh gather to determine the various financial arrangements, the narrator insists that "nothing, when once 'tis understood, is so quickly settled as business" (867).

As she is overwhelmed with protectors and settlements, Juliet is also to have an overabundance of names. At the end of *The Wanderer,* Juliet abandons her woman-bestowed title of "Ellis" to be named and defined wholly in terms of her relationships to men—uncles, husband, brother,

57. For an extended discussion of women and money in Burney's novels, see Edward W. Copeland, "Money in the Novels of Fanny Burney," *Studies in the Novel* 8 (Spring 1976): 24–37. Of *The Wanderer,* Copeland states, "The question is a real one: how to avoid want and penury, but Madame d'Arblay cannot find any way out of the situation for her heroine except by the good fortune of proving her birth and locating her a wealthy suitor. . . . The real difficulties of a female, at least those of the middle-class woman, are unsolvable . . . " (35).

58. Terry Castle, *Masquerade and Civilization: The Carnivalesque in Eighteenth-Century English Culture and Fiction* (Stanford, Calif.: Stanford University Press, 1986), 283.

and the absent but oft-mentioned father. She is again entirely an object of male transactions:

> The impatient Harleigh besought Lord Melbury to be his agent, with the guardian and the uncle of his lovely sister. Lord Melbury joyfully complied. The affair, however momentous, was neither long nor difficult to arrange. The Bishop felt an implicit trust in the known judgment and tried discretion of his ward; and the Admiral held that a female, as the weaker vessel, could never properly, nor even honourably, make the voyage of life, but under the safe convoy of a good husband. (864)

Juliet is Melbury's sister, the bishop's ward, the admiral's niece, and Harleigh's wife[59]—it is not surprising that Juliet's final identifying tag is "mother," and of a boy-child, "a new heir" (871). Juliet's name, always uncertain, is finally lost in marriage and in her ties to male authority. Burney seems to question the structures of patriarchal society by overwhelming her heroine with guardians, riches, and names; she nevertheless satisfies the expectations of novel readers by offering them a marriage ending. The conventional close is made unconventional, however, through overabundance: "Here, and thus felicitously, ended, with the acknowledgement of her name, and her family, the DIFFICULTIES of the WANDERER . . . " (873).[60]

59. Burney repeatedly emphasizes Juliet's ties to patriarchy at the end of the text. Lady Aurora leaves Juliet to banquet alone with her male kindred: " . . . the Admiral insisted that Juliet should preside at his hospitable board; where, seated between her revered Bishop and beloved brother, and facing her generous uncle, and the man of her heart, she did the honours of the table . . . " (867).

60. See Straub: " . . . the romance plot that finally resolves the heroine['s] problems in the happily-ever-after of married love also exposes the contradictory nature of this resolution . . . " (*Divided Fictions,* 185); Spacks: "Given the detailed realizations along the way of what the female plight means, the happy ending of *The Wanderer* and the novel's artifices of plot and character seem to comprise a bitter mockery, so inadequate are artifices of plot to solve the problems here richly exposed" (*Imagining a Self,* 188); and Castle: "The special poignancy of Burney's fiction is that she half-recognizes how much women give up in marriage, yet feels obliged to preserve the traditional plot of female destiny" (*Masquerade and Civilization,* 285). See also Katharine M. Rogers's recent *Frances Burney: The World of 'Female Difficulties'* (New York: Harvester Wheatsheaf, 1990): "The fairy-tale ending is effective in *The Wanderer,* for it contrasts so glaringly with the grim realism used to detail Juliet's practical problems in making her living that it seems intended to draw attention to them rather than to offer a pretended solution . . . " (151).

If Juliet's restraint and perfect enactment of the role of femininity secure her a traditional place in patriarchal society, Elinor's transgressions against the codes of female behavior obtain for her an equally conventional position. As Cixous writes, even if woman "transgresses, her word almost always falls on the deaf, masculine ear, which can only hear language that speaks in the masculine."[61] Madwomen and simpletons (like Flora, the silly, ignorant shopgirl who openly claims Sir Lyell as her "lover" [438]), unlike proper women, are allowed to express sexual desire because they are "above, or below, whatever argument, or reason can offer" (589–90). Not speaking "reasonably" (that is, not speaking "in the masculine"), these women are not feared because they are not heard.

Thus, Elinor, who in departing from the path of female decorum seems to be so different from Juliet, is actually just as enmeshed in the snares of patriarchal expectations as is the passive, proper heroine.[62] Elinor, in her own words, "strayed from the beaten road, only to discover that all others are pathless" (873). She fails to escape from the male-dominated system because she simply reverses it: she removes herself from the role of the proper woman only to enact that of the improper woman. This simple reversal does nothing to transform the patriarchal system itself, and thus Elinor has little choice at the end of the text but to return to another traditional role—that of spinster.[63] The analysis of Elinor's situation that Burney offers (tellingly through the voice of the arch-patriarch, Harleigh) anticipates the work of Luce Irigaray. Burney writes,

> . . . [Elinor may] return to her friends, contented to exist by the general laws of established society; which, though they may be ameliorated, changed, or reformed, by experience, wisely reflecting upon the past; by observation, keenly marking the present; or by genius, creatively anticipating the future, can never be wholly reversed, without risking a rebound that simply restores them to their original condition.

61. Hélène Cixous, "Sorties," in *Newly Born Woman,* 92.

62. "Elinor is caught in a no-win situation in that neither breaking nor playing within the rules seems to change the essential nature of the game in which male power and female powerlessness are acknowledged in every move"—Straub, *Divided Fictions,* 188.

63. "At the end of the novel when Juliet is happily freed from her hateful marriage and united with Harleigh, Elinor must return to conventional female behavior—not because it is desirable, but because she has no choice . . . "—ibid.

> . . . When Elinor . . . sees the fallacy of her new system; when she finds how vainly she would tread down the barriers of custom and experience . . . she will return to the habits of society and common life, as one awakening from a dream in which she has acted some strange and improbable part. (206–7, 863)

Burney's sense that reversal cannot disrupt is repeated more than a hundred and fifty years later in Irigaray's *This Sex Which Is Not One:*

> But if their [women's] aim were simply to reverse the order of things, even supposing this to be possible, history would repeat itself in the long run, would revert to sameness: to phallocratism. It would leave room neither for women's sexuality, nor for women's imaginary, nor for women's language to take (their) place. . . .
>
> It clearly cannot be a matter of substituting feminine power for masculine power. Because this reversal would still be caught up in the economy of the same, in the same economy—in which, of course, what I am trying to designate as "feminine" would not emerge. There would be a phallic "seizure of power."[64]

The case of Elinor, Burney's "excessive" feminist, tells us something about radical women writers of the period. Just as male characters in *The Wanderer* allow Elinor to assert her rights and desires as a spectacle and a sight, an object not to be taken seriously, so male critics grudgingly allowed women to write about "women's rights" in essays and novels that were also treated as oddities. No doubt this is why critics pounced on the details of Wollstonecraft's life (published by her husband) to spectacularize the content of her books. The initially favorable reception of *A Vindication of the Rights of Woman* was replaced by outrage when Godwin's *Memoirs* "disclosed details about her sexual improprieties and suicide attempts."[65]

64. Irigaray, *This Sex,* 33, 129–30.

65. Johnson, *Jane Austen,* xxiii, 15. For an extended discussion of the impact of Godwin's *Memoirs,* see R. M. Janes, "On the Reception of Mary Wollstonecraft's *A Vindication of the Rights of Woman,*" *Journal of the History of Ideas* 39 (April–June 1978): 293–302. Janes notes, "The furious clamorings of 1798 quite overwhelmed the calm approbation of 1792 in both intensity and duration. . . . For those opposed to her politics, the *Memoirs* and *Maria* served up a delicious evidence of the consequences of Jacobin principles in action. . . . Providing a vulnerable combination of sexual and political error, Wollstonecraft became the symbolic center for attacks on radical female writers" (293, 298, 300).

Burney's overwriting of Elinor—an excess that produced angry responses from critics like Croker, who called her "monstrous"[66]—raises larger questions about eighteenth- and nineteenth-century female discourse in general.

Both the primary female character, Juliet, and the secondary one, Elinor, fail to escape the masquerade of femininity.[67] Through her excesses, however, Burney exposes the structures of patriarchy that cause the oppression suffered by her characters. Burney mimes—and "the mimetic role itself is complex, for it presupposes that one can lend oneself to everything, if not to everyone. That one can *copy* anything at all, anyone at all, can receive all impressions. . . ."[68] Burney does lend herself to everything in *The Wanderer.* The excesses at the close of Burney's novel look back to the excesses throughout it—to the extremes of characterization and plot and to the many repetitions that parody in order to subvert.

66. Croker, review, 129.

67. See Straub: "Although Elinor is left odd woman out at the end of the novel, while Juliet is restored to the domestic safety of conjugal love, the parallel between the two women's experience beyond the boundaries of conventional middle-class female behavior casts some doubt on whose is the special case—the defeated Elinor's or the rewarded Juliet's. Leaving the beaten path of courtship, love, and marriage, the institutions that subordinate women to male control in the patriarchal family, is not a real option for either Juliet or Elinor" (*Divided Fictions,* 189).

68. Irigaray, *This Sex,* 151.

Conclusion

> . . . a device of *making-strange* would seem to be the key strategy by means of which the discourse of the woman subverts and dislocates the dominant discourse of the man and patriarchal ideology in general.
>
> —Claire Johnston, in *Feminism and Film Theory,* ed. Constance Penley

Providing a satisfactory closure to a study of the relationship of masquerade to female identity is difficult at best. Cultural constraints make it impossible for a woman to achieve a full "identity"; whatever identity she can negotiate is always in a complex and complicitous relationship to the identity (identities) her society constructs for her. Hence, critics have found it difficult to "read" eighteenth-century women authors' lives. Does one, for example, emphasize Aphra Behn's economic, social, and sexual freedom or her conservative Royalist politics? How does one reconcile Elizabeth Inchbald's association with late-century radicals such as William Godwin and Mary Wollstonecraft to her irreproachable life and allegiance to Catholicism? In attempting to highlight Frances Burney's feminism, how should one grapple with the contrary evidence offered by her diaries and letters?

If the historical "facts" of women's lives pose problems to interpretation, women's fictions do so to an even greater extent. Women's texts, as Claire Johnston points out in the passage quoted above, "make strange"—they repeat, represent, and expose the conflicts and contradictions inherent in patriarchal ideological systems. To articulate the ways in which female writings render the dominant discourse strange, the feminist critic is forced to analyze the places where the feminine speaks—the gaps and fissures of the text; its elisions, ellipses, and excesses; its overabundances and incoherencies. Such a criticism, one that looks into the mute crevices of texts, is necessary but also necessarily tentative.

A case in point of the difficulties faced by the feminist critic is the question of how to approach the writings of Maria Edgeworth. Her novel *Belinda* (1801) contains one of the few masquerade scenes to be found in a nineteenth-century work and is worthy of examination. However, critical debate over the extent to which Edgeworth's father influenced or even composed her writing has rendered her a problematic figure for feminist scholarship. An early biographer, Helen Zimmern, concluded that "... Mr. Edgeworth's literary tinkering of his daughter's works was far from being to their advantage.... It was Mr. Edgeworth, too, who wrote and interpolated the worthless, and highflown Virginia episode.... "[1] A later critic, Elizabeth Harden, echoes Zimmern, although she blames the daughter rather than the father for the lack of literary taste:

> There seems to be little doubt that Mr. Edgeworth ruined the plot of *Belinda*.... In the case of *Belinda* we have internal evidence which suggests that [Mr.] Edgeworth's advice was destructive to his daughter's art.... [Mr.] Edgeworth's moral and philosophical influence on his daughter was profound ... and it is responsible for the pedagogical basis of the majority of the works. If censure is merited, we are more accurate in condemning Miss Edgeworth for her implicit faith in her father's precepts and teachings, for her unquestioning confidence in his abilities as a critic, than in ridiculing Mr. Edgeworth.... [2]

1. Helen Zimmern, *Maria Edgeworth* (1883), quoted in Marilyn Butler's *Maria Edgeworth: A Literary Biography* (Oxford: Clarendon Press, 1972), 283.

2. O. Elizabeth McWhorter Harden, *Maria Edgeworth's Art of Prose Fiction* (The Hague: Mouton, 1971), 104.

By contrast, Edgeworth's most recent biographer, Marilyn Butler, attempts to lay to rest stories of Richard Lovell Edgeworth's unfortunate interference; she writes that

> Miss Zimmern's influential assertion rests . . . on no authority except her own. . . .
>
> . . . we are left with no evidence that Edgeworth decisively changed the course of the novels when he saw the sketches. . . .
>
> Once the legend about *Belinda* is cleared out of the way, there is very little to support the traditional view of [Mr.] Edgeworth's part in the novels. The whole conception that he either inserted passages conveying his views, or sought in general to influence the novels so that they did convey his opinions, is based on the hostile nineteenth-century reading of his character and of his relationship with Maria. . . . it was much more common for him to take the subordinate position of supplier of detail, or the still less exalted role of proof-reader.[3]

In *Their Fathers' Daughters,* Elizabeth Kowaleski-Wallace argues that, despite Butler's evidence to the contrary, it is difficult for feminist critics to read Richard Edgeworth's paternal influence as disinterested or benevolent.[4] Kowaleski-Wallace portrays the relationship as a case of the daughter's "seduction" by the father:

> Paradoxically, the most powerful kind of patriarchal control is one that is least coercive, one that, in making the daughter so dependent on her father's love and esteem, makes her least likely to view him critically. . . . the most powerful kind of patriarchal control is precisely a *seduction.* In addition, that a literary daughter like Edgeworth should become the mouthpiece of her father indicates the thoroughness of her investment in his discourse. Privileging his voice in her texts, time and again, she speaks for him and through him to argue for the benevolent effects of patriarchal training. If the gesture temporarily empowers her by

3. Butler, *Maria Edgeworth,* 284–85.

4. Elizabeth Kowaleski-Wallace, *Their Fathers' Daughters: Hannah More, Maria Edgeworth, and Patriarchal Complicity* (New York: Oxford University Press, 1991), 95.

> lending her paternal authority, it can also disquiet us: at what price does this kind of empowerment occur?[5]

The difficulty of interpreting Edgeworth's life spills over into difficulties in assessing her fictions; biographical details obstruct any clear political placement of Edgeworth's novels. Despite the problems, however, *Belinda*'s representation of female masquerade remains interesting through its emphasis on the relationship of the eponymous heroine with the faulty but dazzling Lady Delacour.

Belinda develops many of the same themes as Burney's *Wanderer.*[6] Like the later novel, Edgeworth's fiction insists that there is no place for woman outside traditional domesticity. Belinda, an even more impossibly perfect heroine than Burney's Juliet, has far fewer difficulties in finding the safe haven of a husband's home. In an often-quoted passage, Edgeworth herself lamented Belinda's stiff rectitude: "I really was so provoked with the cold tameness of that stick or stone Belinda that I could have torn the pages to pieces. . . . "[7] The wooden immobility of Edgeworth's central character does render *Belinda* less complex and less absorbing than Burney's final novel. On the other hand, a brief exploration of the guises in which womanhood appears in this text, of the ways in which gender is constructed in *Belinda,* is necessary to an understanding of how and why masquerade disappears from the woman's novel in the nineteenth century.

Unlike Juliet, Belinda learns vicariously rather than firsthand of the dangers that beset a woman who pushes herself forward in the world. She watches and analyzes the behavior of her older companion, Lady Delacour, who "assumes the character of Mistress of the Revels in public, masquerades as the comic muse at a ball, affects theatrical behavior toward her husband, and treats her acquaintances as *dramatis personae.*"[8] A forerunner of Burney's theatrical Elinor, Lady Delacour is a complex and mixed figure. Witty, vivacious, energetic, and often warm-hearted, she is at the

5. Ibid., 97.

6. While Butler indicates that Edgeworth was familiar with Burney's novels (*Maria Edgeworth,* 308), there is no record of Burney's having read *Belinda.* Burney may have done so, however, for she did read Edgeworth's later work, *Patronage* (1814) (see *The Journals and Letters of Fanny Burney,* ed. Warren Derry [Oxford: Clarendon Press, 1982], 9:451–52).

7. Maria Edgeworth to Mrs. Ruxton (26 December 1809), quoted in Butler, *Maria Edgeworth,* 494.

8. Harden, *Maria Edgeworth's Art of Prose Fiction,* 104.

same time insensitive, jealous, and self-destructive. Given the prudence and prudery of Belinda, however, Lady Delacour's faults are easy to overlook; several critics have found her the most fascinating character in Edgeworth's work.[9]

Although the masquerade scene itself in *Belinda* is little more than a somewhat anachronistic set piece, the novel's depiction of the masked assembly bears important similarities to the more extended treatments of female disguise in previous fictions by women. As in the earlier works I have discussed at length, female masquerade in this later woman's fiction becomes emblematic not of female freedom and desire, but of limitation and oppression. Although they flirt with the idea of entering the ball in characters opposed to those of their everyday lives, Belinda and Lady Delacour end up masquerading essentially as themselves. As the silent, serious tragic muse, Belinda is surrounded by a group of young men who (mistaking her for Lady Delacour) entertain themselves by mocking all the marriage-hunting nieces of Mrs. Stanhope, Belinda included. Tauntingly, they refer to the young woman as an overadvertised piece of merchandise, one hard to sell on the marriage market:

> As for this Belinda Portman, 'twas a good hit to send her to Lady Delacour's; but, I take it she hangs upon hand; for last winter, when I was at Bath, she was hawked about every where.... You heard of nothing, wherever you went, but of Belinda Portman, and Belinda Portman's accomplishments: Belinda Portman, and her accomplishments, I'll swear, were as well advertised as Packwood's razor strops. (17–18)[10]

9. In *Maria Edgeworth's Art of Prose Fiction,* Elizabeth Harden insists, "Lady Delacour's jealousy of Belinda is the chief interest of the narrative . . . " (84). Elsewhere she writes, ". . . the novel succeeds because of Lady Delacour, the only character whose thoughts and actions are consistently dramatized in the course of the action. Her personality combines intellectual and intuitive brilliance in such a way that no other character (and no reader) is untouched by her" (*Maria Edgeworth* [Boston: Twayne, 1984], 56). Marilyn Butler notes that Lady Delacour is "by far the best-remembered character in the novel" (*Maria Edgeworth,* 311). John Newcomer finds "the entire creation of Lady Delacour . . . a major achievement" (*Maria Edgeworth* [Lewisburg, Pa.: Bucknell University Press, 1973], 54). Colin B. and Jo Atkinson add that "Lady Delacour grew somewhat beyond the author's control into a charming woman and a sympathetic character" ("Maria Edgeworth, *Belinda,* and Women's Rights," *Éire-Ireland* 19 [Winter 1984]: 94).

10. Maria Edgeworth, *Belinda* (1801) (London: Pandora Press, 1986).

A second speaker emphasizes that this last of the Stanhope nieces is available for purchase by the highest bidder, but cautions that "girls brought to the hammer this way don't go off well" (18). In the eyes of all the men who enclose her and prevent her departure, Belinda is a commodity. The only advantage to her masquerade is that it allows Belinda to learn about the slight regard men have for her, and for women in general. Belinda appears to gain little from her newly acquired knowledge, however: she maintains her belief in domestic felicity and eventually marries one of the speakers.

There is a seamless continuity between masquerade and women's reality in *Belinda.* If Belinda remains untransformed by her costume, Lady Delacour, as the comic muse, merely sustains the disguise that she practices in her life. Believing herself dying of breast cancer, Lady Delacour insists upon showing the world a mask of gaeity: "Abroad, and at home, Lady Delacour was two different persons. Abroad she appeared all life, spirit, and good humour—at home, listless, fretful, and melancholy; she seemed like a spoiled actress off the stage, over-stimulated by applause, and exhausted by the exertions of supporting a fictitious character" (4–5). The best advice that Lady Delacour can offer to Belinda is to keep up a good show, even in misery: ". . . dry up your tears, *keep on your mask. . . .* Show them you've no feeling," she insists, "and they'll acknowledge you for a woman of fashion" (20–21). Although Edgeworth takes pains to rehabilitate Lady Delacour and transform her from a society belle into a model wife and mother, it is impossible to see Lady Delacour as doing anything other than acting a part. She moves from impressing the fickle beau monde to pleasing an unloved husband—in either case, it is difficult to say what Lady Delacour's own desires are and how they are satisfied.

Such submersion of female desire remains a pressing theme of nineteenth-century women's fictions. Another late masquerade work, Mary Brunton's *Discipline* (1814), repeats but simplifies Inchbald's treatment of the subject. Like Miss Milner, Ellen Percy defies the wishes of her mentor/lover by attending a masquerade ball. This act of the headstrong heroine, combined with her flirtation with the frivolous Lord Frederick (also the name of the rival suitor in *A Simple Story*), nearly causes her to lose her more sedate lover until a series of catastrophes "reforms" her into a sober woman. Brunton, however, ends her tale with Miss Percy's marriage and, unlike Inchbald, implies that the heroine's union will produce lasting happiness. Like the rehabilitation of Edgeworth's Lady Delacour, the transformation of Ellen Percy highlights an ideological contradiction at the heart of the domestic novel: at the same time that the events of plot delineate the ways in which women are compelled and trained to accommodate themselves to domestic roles, the narrative also insists that these roles of wife and mother are "natural" and inherent to womanhood. In other words, the novel finds its existence in the very *unnaturalness* of woman's *natural* function.[11]

Discipline is told from the first-person perspective of the "reformed" Ellen Percy. Because she consistently refers to her former willful self in negative terms, the reader is never allowed to find the faulty heroine engaging, as was possible with Miss Milner. Ellen's narrative perspective, however, reveals the subtleties of patriarchal coercion, the direct and indirect pressures that are brought to bear to force women into compliance with their conventional roles. Since the older Ellen Percy has entirely imbibed the Christian principles of her strict, serious husband, her viewpoint unself-consciously reflects the methods by which she was brought to embrace the attributes and values that would ensure his pleasure, not her own.

It is the immature, headstrong Ellen Percy who attends the masquerade in the costume of "the fair Fatima" (68),[12] a scanty Turkish dress intended (like the attire of Defoe's Roxana) to draw the male gaze to her fine features and cleanly shaped limbs. When the costume arrives, Ellen practices "before a looking-glass the attitudes most favourable to the display of . . . [her] dress and figure" (83). She promises herself extreme pleasure from the masquerade but, instead, finds herself "bewildered by the confusion of the scene, and the grotesque figures of the masks" (89). Ending in "weariness and disgust" (90) like Miss Milner, Ellen finds the masked assembly a disappointment:

> . . . my pastime very poorly compensated the concealment, anxiety, and remorse which it had already cost me. . . . The whole

11. A discussion of this paradox is central to Kowaleski-Wallace's reading of *Belinda:* ". . . taste for domestic pleasures—although *natural*—must be *taught* to those who fail to recognize them. . . . The ascendency of the ideal new-style patriarchal family depends, in other words, on the important negation or absence of all other competing modes of social life. . . . In *Belinda* the 'not spoken of'—or, rather, what the novel takes pains *not* to articulate—is the way in which human desires, female desires in particular, do not always accommodate themselves to the exigencies of domestic life" (*Their Fathers' Daughters,* 122–23).

12. Mary Brunton, *Discipline* (1814) (London: Pandora Press, 1986).

> entertainment . . . amounted to nothing more than looking at a multitude of motley habits, for the most part mean, tawdry, and unbecoming; and listening to disjointed dialogues, consisting of dull questions and unmeaning answers, thinly bestrown with constrained witticisms, and puns half a century old. (90)

In this text, the masquerade is again not the arena for feminine *jouissance.* Lord Frederick, who sent Ellen the tickets for the ball, controls her participation at the event and uses it for his own purposes. Appearing as the Grand Signior, Lord Frederick dominates the fair Fatima completely. After pouring her a large glass of champagne to dull her senses, he leads her to an unoccupied room where he attempts to persuade her to elope with him. Although she refuses, Lord Frederick pursues his plans, having invited Ellen to the masquerade for the express purpose of luring her into the carriage that waits to take them to Scotland. Only the warning of a mysterious black domino, the proxy of Ellen's grave suitor, Mr. Maitland, foils Lord Frederick's schemes.

Caught between the unscrupulous force of one suitor and the scrupulous surveillance of the other, Ellen Percy is little more than a puppet to male whims. She is incited to partake of pleasures that satisfy the desires of the men around her but offer little joy for herself. If Lord Frederick holds out the promise of masquerade titillation, Mr. Maitland offers the comforts of protection from harm. Although he does not attend the masquerade himself, he sends a worthy friend to act as an "inspector" (95), "guardian" (97), and "protector" (99). In either case, the woman is the object of the male gaze—an obsessive, predatory, sexual gaze in the first instance, a watchful, critical, monitoring gaze in the second.

In losing her fortune and finding herself abandoned by the avaricious Lord Frederick, Ellen is forced to see her second suitor as preferable to her first. Her inability to support herself comfortably after her father's death seems to have a strong bearing on her decision to adopt more traditional values. Unable to sustain a stable life outside the home, subject to pecuniary distresses and even to confinement in a madhouse (286ff.), Ellen hungers for the safety of domestic life. Instructed, like Inchbald's and Burney's heroines, in the "school of adversity," she comes to laud domestic pleasures over fashionable ones: ". . . intemperate pleasure is not more fatal to the understanding than to the heart. It is not more adverse to the 'spirit of a sound mind,' than to the 'spirit of love.' Social pleasures, call we them! Let the name no more be prostituted to that which is poison to every social feeling" (86). Ellen ends by living with Maitland on an isolated Scottish estate, Glen Eredine, a refuge remote from London high-life where she describes herself as "a humbled creature, thankful to find, in his [her husband's] sound mind and steady principle, a support for her acknowledged weakness" (374). Whether Ellen's metamorphosis represents a Christian conversion or a broken spirit is difficult to determine. Even more than Edgeworth's *Belinda,* Brunton's *Discipline* uses masquerade to construct a limited and limiting vision of the domestic ideal.

There is no doubt that eighteenth-century male writers shared Henry Fielding's fears that the masquerade would breed "another Amazonian race,"[13] empowering women and destroying male prerogative. Joseph Addison's *Spectator,* no. 8 (9 March 1711), reprints a letter from "one of the Directors of the Society for the Reformation of Manners" that complains of the fraternity's inability to police the "promiscuous Multitude" at "this libidinous Assembly" of the "Midnight Masque" (1:35–37).[14] The writer is particularly concerned that the freedom of conversation and movement allowed to women is "wonderfully contriv'd for the Advancement of Cuckoldom" (1:37). A second letter, this "written by some young Templer," appears in the same paper (1:37). In his epistle, the young man bemoans his mistaking a prostitute for a peeress. Admitting that his own desires transformed a cloud into a Juno (1:38), he nevertheless blames the woman for the escapade: ". . . I am not the first Cully whom she has pass'd her self upon for a Countess" (1:38). Fearing that masquerade allowed women to usurp privileges that they marked as their own, especially those of sexual choice, men equated female disguise with male victimization.

The texts by women that I have examined, spanning the period from the Restoration to the early nineteenth century, belie the male writers' views. In women's fictions, female masquerade remains at best double-sided and problematic. In only two works is masquerade an empowering defiance of the dominant norms for female behavior. A forthright acknowledgment of the underlying terms of heterosexuality and a distancing of the heroine from both her self-constructed image and the man attracted to that image allow Haywood's Fair Incognita of *Fantomina* and her Glicera

13. Henry Fielding, *The Masquerade, a Poem. Inscribed to C—T H—D—G—R.* (London: J. Roberts and A. Dodd, 1728), l. 130.

14. Joseph Addison and Richard Steele, *The Spectator,* ed. Donald F. Bond (Oxford: Clarendon Press, 1965).

of *The City Jilt* to subvert and deconstruct entrapping binary schemes. Only these heroines—who attempt to separate themselves from the representations of womanhood they consciously construct, who refuse to resolve the ambiguities of their disguises, and who thereby distance themselves from the men attracted to the masquerade display—escape unharmed.

More often, however, masquerade appears in women's writing as a disempowering capitulation to patriarchal strictures that posit female subordination. Disguise donned "for real," costume intended to direct the male gaze toward what the female identifies as her genuine self—either for illicit union, as with Maria in Aphra Behn's *Dumb Virgin* and Dalinda and Philecta in Eliza Haywood's *Masqueraders,* or for marriage, as with Miss Milner in Elizabeth Inchbald's *Simple Story* and Ellen Percy in Mary Brunton's *Discipline*—serves only to objectify women and lock them into the system of exchanges controlled by men. Maria Edgeworth's Belinda and Lady Delacour are also heroines who, by taking seriously the costumes they adopt, are immersed within the patriarchal economy.

Not even a willing, self-acknowledged masquerade, like Elinor's in *The Wanderer,* offers a way out of the dilemma of femininity within patriarchy—the difficulty of women's reduction to functioning as the mirror-double of men. Although frequently theorized as sexually enabling, transvestism or role-reversal proves insufficient to the task of challenging accepted hierarchies for the heroines of Mary Davys's *Accomplished Rake* and Frances Burney's *Wanderer.* In Maria Edgeworth's *Belinda* as well, transvestism reduces a woman to the status of spectacle and "freak":[15] the cross-dressed Revolutionary radical in that text, Mrs. Freke, is caught in a "mantrap" and is thoroughly punished for her usurpation of male prerogatives. Ineffectual and ridiculed as she swaggers about supporting "the character of a young rake" (38), Harriot Freke is doubly male manqué when she steps into a spring-trap and "the beauty of her legs" is spoiled to the extent that "she would never more be able to appear to advantage in man's apparel" (284).

Adoption of male roles and rights, then, neither dismantles patriarchal hierarchies nor deconstructs oppressive binary logic. At most, transvestite masquerade offers a temporary escape. The central insight that emerges

15. Colin and Jo Atkinson, in their extensive discussion of Mrs. Freke, remind us that "the word 'freak' in the sense of monstrosity or abnormality is a much later meaning, and in 1800 the word was used as a synonym for a caper, a capricious humor or whim" ("Women's Rights," 100).

from my work, then, on distinguishing subversive from coercive masquerade is not role-reversal but, instead, distance: distance between the woman's self and her representation, distance between the woman's desire and the man's. In Irigarayan terms, mimicry or the distancing of the woman from the feminine representation and from the male spectator who gazes upon it alone produces the gap necessary for subjectivity.

In nineteenth-century writing by women, such distancing through masquerade could no longer be envisioned. Terry Castle argues in *Masquerade and Civilization* that masquerade disappeared from the English novel in part because nineteenth-century writers could offer "a less mediated and increasingly self-conscious presentation of subversive desire":

> . . . the radical legacy of the late eighteenth century . . . may have rendered the subversive appeals of the masquerade unnecessary. Stylized reversals of class and gender may have seemed less suggestive once such reversals became a possibility in everyday life. . . .
>
> . . . For the nineteenth-century novelist, unlike his or her eighteenth-century counterpart, transgression no longer has the shape of a discontinuous or naïve diversion. It has become in some sense the central, self-conscious concern of the fictional enterprise itself.[16]

Castle's reading implies that the constraints imposed on women's lives lessened—that everyday life partook of festive misrule. The nineteenth-century works by women that I have examined—Edgeworth's *Belinda,* Burney's *Wanderer,* and Brunton's *Discipline*—suggest that masquerade did, in effect, become the condition of femininity. Far from a carnivalesque "world upside-down," however, later women novelists depict masquerade as the "world rightside-up," as women's repression of desire and their role-playing to conform to a repressive domestic ideal. The costs of female masquerade, not the advantages, are emphasized by women writers.

Taken as a whole, women's masquerade texts both construct and deconstruct conventional roles for women. Early female authors, by portraying female economic and sexual victimization, by exiling their heroines or submerging them in marriage, helped to form and define the

16. Terry Castle, *Masquerade and Civilization: The Carnivalesque in Eighteenth-Century English Culture and Fiction* (Stanford, Calif.: Stanford University Press, 1986), 343, 328–29, 344.

codes and institutions of society that persist into the present. At the same time, they questioned the foundation of those systems, exposed their injustices and violence, and emphasized that the "domestic woman" was a culturally produced category. Like successful masquerade heroines, the texts I have examined maintain complex attitudes toward their own representations.

Bibliography

Abel, Elizabeth, ed. *Writing and Sexual Difference.* Chicago: University of Chicago Press, 1982.

Addison, Joseph, and Richard Steele. *The Spectator.* 5 vols. Ed. Donald F. Bond. Oxford: Clarendon Press, 1965.

Althusser, Louis. *Lenin and Philosophy and Other Essays.* Trans. Ben Brewster. New York: Monthly Review Press, 1971.

Armstrong, Nancy. *Desire and Domestic Fiction: A Political History of the Novel.* New York: Oxford University Press, 1987.

Atkinson, Colin B., and Jo Atkinson. "Maria Edgeworth, *Belinda,* and Women's Rights." *Éire-Ireland* 19 (Winter 1984): 94–118.

Auerbach, Nina. *Communities of Women: An Idea in Fiction.* Cambridge: Harvard University Press, 1978.

Austen, Jane. *Northanger Abbey, Lady Susan, The Watsons, and Sanditon.* Ed. John Davie. Oxford: Oxford University Press, 1990.

Bachelard, Gaston. *The Poetics of Space.* Trans. Maria Jolas. New York: Orion Press, 1964.

Backscheider, Paula R. "Woman's Influence." *Studies in the Novel* 11 (Spring 1979): 3–22.

———. "Women Writers and the Chains of Identification." *Studies in the Novel* 19 (Fall 1987): 245–62.

Bakhtin, Mikhail. *Rabelais and His World.* Trans. Helene Iswolsky. Bloomington: Indiana University Press, 1984.

Barker, Jane. *Love Intrigues: Or, The History of the Amours of Bosvil and Galesia.* London: E. Curll and C. Crownfield, 1713.

Barthel, Manfred. *The Jesuits: History and Legend of the Society of Jesus.* New York: William Morrow, 1984.

Beauvoir, Simone de. *The Second Sex.* Trans. and ed. H. M. Parshley. New York: Alfred A. Knopf, 1952. Reprint. New York: Vintage Books, 1974.

Behn, Aphra. *Oroonoko and Other Prose Narratives.* Ed. Montague Summers. New York: Benjamin Blom, 1967.

Bender, John. *Imagining the Penitentiary: Fiction and the Architecture of Mind in Eighteenth-Century England.* Chicago: University of Chicago Press, 1987.

Benstock, Shari, ed. *Feminist Issues in Literary Scholarship.* Bloomington: Indiana University Press, 1987.

Berger, John. *Ways of Seeing.* New York: Penguin Books, 1972.

Blondel, Madeleine. *Images de la femme dans le roman anglais de 1740 à 1771.* 2 vols. Paris: H. Champion, 1976.

Bloom, Edward A., and Lillian D. Bloom. "Fanny Burney's Novels: The Retreat from Wonder." *Novel* 12 (Spring 1979): 215–35.

Boaden, James. *Memoirs of Mrs. Inchbald.* 2 vols. London: Richard Bentley, 1833.

Brooks, Peter. *Reading for the Plot: Design and Intention in Narrative.* New York: Alfred A. Knopf, 1984.

Browne, Alice. *The Eighteenth-Century Feminist Mind.* Detroit: Wayne State University Press, 1987.

Brownstein, Rachel M. *Becoming a Heroine: Reading About Women in Novels.* New York: Viking Press, 1982.

Brunton, Mary. *Discipline.* 1814. Reprint. London: Pandora Press, 1986.

———. *Self-Control.* 1810/11. Reprint. London: Pandora Press, 1986.

Burgin, Victor, James Donald, and Cora Kaplan, eds. *Formations of Fantasy.* London: Methuen, 1986.

Burney, Frances. *Cecilia; or, Memoirs of an Heiress.* 1782. Reprint. New York: Penguin Books, 1986.

———. *Evelina, or The History of a Young Lady's Entrance into the World.* 1778. Reprint. Ed. Edward A. Bloom, with Lillian D. Bloom. Oxford: Oxford University Press, 1968.

———. *The Journals and Letters of Fanny Burney.* Vol. 7. Ed. Edward A. Bloom and Lillian D. Bloom. Oxford: Clarendon Press, 1978.

———. *The Journals and Letters of Fanny Burney.* Vol. 9. Ed. Warren Derry. Oxford: Clarendon Press, 1982.

———. *The Wanderer; or, Female Difficulties.* 5 vols. London: Longman, Hurst, Rees, Orme, and Brown, 1814.

———. *The Wanderer; or, Female Difficulties.* 1814. Reprint. Ed. Margaret Anne Doody, Robert L. Mack, and Peter Sabor. Oxford: Oxford University Press, 1991.

Butler, Marilyn. *Maria Edgeworth: A Literary Biography.* Oxford: Clarendon Press, 1972.

Byron, George Gordon, Lord. *Letters and Journals.* 12 vols. Ed. Leslie A. Marchand. Cambridge: Harvard University Press, 1973–81.

Campbell, D. Grant. "Fashionable Suicide: Conspicuous Consumption and the Collapse of Credit in Frances Burney's *Cecilia.*" *Studies in Eighteenth-Century Culture* 20 (1989): 131–45.

Carver, Larry. "Aphra Behn: The Poet's Heart in a Woman's Body." *Papers on Language and Literature* 14 (Fall 1978): 414–24.

Castle, Terry. *Masquerade and Civilization: The Carnivalesque in Eighteenth-Century English Culture and Fiction.* Stanford, Calif.: Stanford University Press, 1986.

Chodorow, Nancy. *The Reproduction of Mothering: Psychoanalysis and the Sociology of Gender.* Berkeley and Los Angeles: University of California Press, 1978.

Cixous, Hélène, and Catherine Clément. *The Newly Born Woman.* Trans. Betsy Wing. Minneapolis: University of Minnesota Press, 1986.

Copeland, Edward W. "Money in the Novels of Fanny Burney." *Studies in the Novel* 8 (Spring 1976): 24–37.

Craft, Catherine A. "Reworking Male Models: Aphra Behn's *Fair Vow-Breaker,* Eliza Haywood's *Fantomina,* and Charlotte Lennox's *Female Quixote.*" *Modern Language Review* 86 (October 1991): 821–38.

Croker, John Wilson. Rev. of *The Wanderer; or, Female Difficulties,* by Madame D'Arblay. *Quarterly Review* 11 (April 1814): 123–30.

Culler, Jonathan. *The Pursuit of Signs: Semiotics, Literature, Deconstruction.* Ithaca: Cornell University Press, 1981.

Cutting, Rose Marie. "Defiant Women: The Growth of Feminism in Fanny Burney's Novels." *Studies in English Literature, 1500–1900* 17 (Summer 1977): 519–30.

———. "A Wreath for Fanny Burney's Last Novel: *The Wanderer*'s Contribution to Women's Studies." *Illinois Quarterly* 37 (Spring 1975): 45–64.

Cutting-Gray, Joanne. *Woman as 'Nobody' and the Novels of Fanny Burney.* Gainesville: University Press of Florida, 1992.

Daugherty, Tracy Edgar. *Narrative Techniques in the Novels of Fanny Burney.* New York: Peter Lang, 1989.

Davis, Lennard J. *Factual Fictions: The Origins of the English Novel.* New York: Columbia University Press, 1983.

Davis, Natalie Zemon. "Women on Top." In *Society and Culture in Early Modern France,* 124–51. Stanford, Calif.: Stanford University Press, 1975.

Davis, Robert Con, ed. *Contemporary Literary Criticism: Modernism Through Post-Structuralism.* New York: Longman, 1986.

Day, Robert Adams. *Told in Letters: Epistolary Fiction Before Richardson.* Ann Arbor: University of Michigan Press, 1966.

de Lauretis, Teresa. *Alice Doesn't: Feminism, Semiotics, Cinema.* Bloomington: Indiana University Press, 1984.

———, ed. *Feminist Studies/Critical Studies.* Bloomington: Indiana University Press, 1986.

———. *Technologies of Gender: Essays on Theory, Film, and Fiction.* Bloomington: Indiana University Press, 1987.

Devlin, D. D. *The Novels and Journals of Fanny Burney.* New York: St. Martin's Press, 1987.

Doane, Mary Ann. *The Desire to Desire: The Woman's Film of the 1940s.* Bloomington: Indiana University Press, 1987.

———. "Film and the Masquerade: Theorising the Female Spectator." *Screen* 23 (September–October 1982): 74–87.

———. "Masquerade Reconsidered: Further Thoughts on the Female Spectator." *Discourse* 11 (Fall–Winter 1988–89): 42–54.

Doane, Mary Ann, Patricia Mellencamp, and Linda Williams, eds. *Re-Vision:*

Essays in Feminist Film Criticism. Frederick, Md.: University Publications of America, 1984.

Donovan, Josephine. "Women and the Rise of the Novel: A Feminist-Marxist Theory." *Signs* 16 (Spring 1991): 441–62.

Doody, Margaret Anne. *Frances Burney: The Life in the Works.* New Brunswick, N.J.: Rutgers University Press, 1988.

Eagleton, Mary, ed. *Feminist Literary Theory: A Reader.* Oxford: Basil Blackwell, 1986.

Eagleton, Terry. *Literary Theory: An Introduction.* Minneapolis: University of Minnesota Press, 1983.

Edgeworth, Maria. *Belinda.* 1801. Reprint. London: Pandora Press, 1986.

Epstein, Julia. *The Iron Pen: Frances Burney and the Politics of Women's Writing.* Madison: University of Wisconsin Press, 1989.

Epstein, Julia, and Kristina Straub, eds. *Body Guards: The Cultural Politics of Gender Ambiguity.* New York: Routledge, 1991.

Evans, Caroline, and Minna Thornton. "Fashion, Representation, Femininity." *Feminist Review* 38 (Summer 1991): 48–66.

———. *Women and Fashion: A New Look.* London: Quartet Books, 1989.

Faller, Lincoln. *Turned to Account: The Forms and Functions of Criminal Biography in Late Seventeenth- and Early Eighteenth-Century England.* Cambridge: Cambridge University Press, 1987.

Felman, Shoshana. "Women and Madness: The Critical Phallacy." *Diacritics* 5 (Winter 1975): 2–10.

Fetterley, Judith. *The Resisting Reader: A Feminist Approach to American Fiction.* Bloomington: Indiana University Press, 1978.

Fielding, Henry. *The Masquerade, A Poem. Inscribed to C——T H—D—G—R.* London: J. Roberts and A. Dodd, 1728.

Flynn, Elizabeth A., and Patrocinio P. Schweickart, eds. *Gender and Reading: Essays on Readers, Texts, and Contexts.* Baltimore: Johns Hopkins University Press, 1986.

Foucault, Michel. *Discipline and Punish: The Birth of the Prison.* Trans. Alan Sheridan. New York: Vintage Books, 1979.

———. *The History of Sexuality, Volume 1: An Introduction.* Trans. Robert Hurley. New York: Vintage Books, 1978.

———. *The Use of Pleasure: Volume 2 of the History of Sexuality.* Trans. Robert Hurley. New York: Vintage Books, 1985.

Frank, Marcie. "The Camera and the Speculum: David Cronenberg's *Dead Ringers.*" *PMLA* 106 (May 1991): 459–70.

Fraser, Antonia. *The Weaker Vessel.* New York: Alfred A. Knopf, 1984.

Freud, Sigmund. "Beyond the Pleasure Principle," "Female Sexuality," "Femininity," "On Narcissism: An Introduction," "Some Psychical Consequences of the Anatomical Distinction Between the Sexes," "The Psychogenesis of a Case of Homosexuality in a Woman," and "The 'Uncanny.'" In *The Standard Edition of the Complete Psychological Works of Sigmund Freud.* Trans. and ed. James Strachey, in collaboration with Anna Freud. 24 vols. London: Hogarth Press, 1953–74.

———. *Dora: An Analysis of a Case of Hysteria.* Ed. Philip Rieff. New York: Macmillan, 1963.

———. *The Future of an Illusion.* Trans. and ed. James Strachey. New York: W. W. Norton, 1961.

———. *A General Selection from the Works of Sigmund Freud.* Ed. John Rickman. New York: Liveright, 1957.

———. *The Interpretation of Dreams.* Trans. and ed. James Strachey. New York: Avon Books, 1965.

———. *Studies in Parapsychology.* Ed. Philip Rieff. New York: Macmillan, 1963.

———. *Three Case Histories.* Ed. Philip Rieff. New York: Macmillan, 1963.

Freud, Sigmund, and Joseph Breuer. *Studies on Hysteria.* Trans. and ed. James Strachey, in collaboration with Anna Freud. 1955. Reprint. New York: Basic Books, n.d.

Friedberg, Anne. "*Les Flâneurs du Mal(l):* Cinema and the Postmodern Condition." *PMLA* 106 (May 1991): 419–31.

Fritz, Paul, and Richard Morton, eds. *Woman in the Eighteenth Century and Other Essays.* Toronto: Samuel Stevens Hakkert, 1976.

Gallagher, Catherine. "Who Was That Masked Woman? The Prostitute and the Playwright in the Comedies of Aphra Behn." *Women's Studies* 15 (1988): 23–42.

Gallop, Jane. *The Daughter's Seduction: Feminism and Psychoanalysis.* Ithaca: Cornell University Press, 1982.

Gardiner, Judith Kegan. "Aphra Behn: Sexuality and Self-Respect." *Women's Studies* 7, nos. 1–2 (1980): 67–78.

Garner, Shirley Nelson, Claire Kahane, and Madelon Sprengnether, eds. *The (M)other Tongue: Essays in Feminist Psychoanalytic Interpretation.* Ithaca: Cornell University Press, 1985.

George, M. Dorothy, ed. *England in Johnson's Day.* 1928. Reprint. Freeport, N.Y.: Books for Libraries Press, 1972.

Gilbert, Sandra M., and Susan Gubar. *The Madwoman in the Attic: The Woman Writer and the Nineteenth-Century Literary Imagination.* New Haven: Yale University Press, 1979.

Goreau, Angeline. *Reconstructing Aphra: A Social Biography of Aphra Behn.* New York: Dial Press, 1980.

Grau, Joseph A. *Fanny Burney: An Annotated Bibliography.* New York: Garland, 1981.

Green, Katherine Sobba. *The Courtship Novel, 1740–1820: A Feminized Genre.* Lexington: University Press of Kentucky, 1991.

Greene, Gayle, and Coppelia Kahn, eds. *Making a Difference: Feminist Literary Criticism.* London: Methuen, 1985.

Harden, Elizabeth. *Maria Edgeworth.* Boston: Twayne, 1984.

Harden, O. Elizabeth McWhorter. *Maria Edgeworth's Art of Prose Fiction.* The Hague: Mouton, 1971.

Hays, Mary. *Memoirs of Emma Courtney.* 1796. Reprint. London: Pandora Press, 1987.

Haywood, Eliza. *The British Recluse: or, The Secret History of Cleomira, Suppos'd Dead.* London: D. Browne, W. Chetwood, and S. Chapman, 1722.
———. *The City Jilt; or, The Alderman Turn'd Beau.* 2d ed. London: J. Roberts, 1726.
———. *Four Novels of Eliza Haywood.* Ed. Mary Anne Schofield. Delmar, N.Y.: Scholars' Facsimiles & Reprints, 1983.
———. *The History of Miss Betsy Thoughtless.* 1751. Reprint. London: Pandora Press, 1986.
———. *Masquerade Novels of Eliza Haywood.* Ed. Mary Anne Schofield. Delmar, N.Y.: Scholars' Facsimiles & Reprints, 1986.
Hazlitt, William. Rev. of *The Wanderer; or, Female Difficulties,* by Madame D'Arblay. *Edinburgh Review* 24 (February 1815): 320–38.
Heath, Stephen. "Difference." *Screen* 19 (Fall 1978): 50–112.
———. *Questions of Cinema.* Bloomington: Indiana University Press, 1981.
Hunter, J. Paul. *Before Novels: The Cultural Contexts of Eighteenth-Century English Fiction.* New York: W. W. Norton, 1990.
———. "Canon of Generations, Generation of Canons." *Modern Language Studies* 18 (Winter 1988): 38–46.
Inchbald, Elizabeth. *A Simple Story.* 1791. Reprint. Ed. J. M. S. Tompkins. Oxford: Oxford University Press, 1967; reissue, new introduction by Jane Spencer, 1988.
Irigaray, Luce. *Speculum of the Other Woman.* Trans. Gillian C. Gill. Ithaca: Cornell University Press, 1985.
———. *This Sex Which Is Not One.* Trans. Catherine Porter, with Carolyn Burke. Ithaca: Cornell University Press, 1985.
Jacobus, Mary. *Reading Woman: Essays in Feminist Criticism.* New York: Columbia University Press, 1986.
Janes, R. M. "On the Reception of Mary Wollstonecraft's *A Vindication of the Rights of Woman.*" *Journal of the History of Ideas* 39 (April–June 1978): 293–302.
Jardine, Alice A. *Gynesis: Configurations of Woman and Modernity.* Ithaca: Cornell University Press, 1985.
Johnson, Claudia L. *Jane Austen: Women, Politics, and the Novel.* Chicago: University of Chicago Press, 1988.
Kelly, Gary. *The English Jacobin Novel, 1780–1805.* Oxford: Clarendon Press, 1976.
Kern, Jean B. "Mrs. Mary Davys as Novelist of Manners." *Essays in Literature* 10 (Spring 1983): 29–38.
Kowaleski-Wallace, Elizabeth. *Their Fathers' Daughters: Hannah More, Maria Edgeworth, and Patriarchal Complicity.* New York: Oxford University Press, 1991.
Kristeva, Julia. *The Kristeva Reader.* Ed. Toril Moi. Oxford: Basil Blackwell, 1986.
Lacan, Jacques. *Écrits: A Selection.* Trans. Alan Sheridan. New York: W. W. Norton, 1977.
———. *Feminine Sexuality: Jacques Lacan and the "école freudienne."* Ed. Juliet Mitchell and Jacqueline Rose. Trans. Jacqueline Rose. New York: W. W. Norton, New York: Pantheon Books, 1985.

Langdell, Cheri Davis. "Aphra Behn and Sexual Politics: A Dramatist's Discourse with Her Audience." In *Drama, Sex and Politics,* 109–28. Cambridge: Cambridge University Press, 1985.

Lederer, Wolfgang. *The Fear of Women.* New York: Grune & Stratton, 1968.

Lennox, Charlotte. *The Female Quixote, or The Adventures of Arabella.* 1752. Reprint. London: Pandora Press, 1986.

Linville, Susan E. "Retrieving History: Margarethe von Trotta's *Marianne and Juliane.*" *PMLA* 106 (May 1991): 446–58.

London, Bette. *The Appropriated Voice: Narrative Authority in Conrad, Forster, and Woolf.* Ann Arbor: University of Michigan Press, 1990.

Lubbock, Percy. *The Craft of Fiction.* 1921. Reprint. New York: Viking Press, 1964.

Manvell, Roger. *Elizabeth Inchbald: A Biographical Study.* Lanham, Md.: University Press of America, 1987.

Marks, Elaine, and Isabelle de Courtivron, eds. *New French Feminisms: An Anthology.* New York: Schocken Books, 1981.

Mathew, David. *Catholicism in England: The Portrait of a Minority: Its Culture and Tradition.* 2d ed. London: Eyre & Spottiswoode, 1948.

McBurney, William H., ed. *Four Before Richardson: Selected English Novels, 1720–1727.* Lincoln: University of Nebraska Press, 1963.

McKeon, Michael. *The Origins of the English Novel, 1600–1740.* Baltimore: Johns Hopkins University Press, 1987.

McMaster, Juliet. "The Silent Angel: Impediments to Female Expression in Frances Burney's Novels." *Studies in the Novel* 21 (Fall 1989): 235–52.

Mews, Hazel. *Frail Vessels: Woman's Role in Women's Novels from Fanny Burney to George Eliot.* London: Athlone Press, 1969.

Miller, Nancy K. "The Exquisite Cadavers: Women in Eighteenth-Century Fiction." *Diacritics* 5 (Winter 1975): 37–43.

———, ed. *The Poetics of Gender.* New York: Columbia University Press, 1986.

———. *Subject to Change: Reading Feminist Writing.* New York: Columbia University Press, 1988.

———. "The Text's Heroine: A Feminist Critic and Her Fictions." *Diacritics* 12 (Summer 1982): 48–53.

Millett, Kate. *Sexual Politics.* New York: Ballantine Books, 1978.

Moers, Ellen. *Literary Women.* New York: Doubleday, 1976.

Moi, Toril. *Feminist Theory and Simone de Beauvoir.* Oxford: Basil Blackwell, 1990.

———, ed. *French Feminist Thought: A Reader.* Oxford: Basil Blackwell, 1987.

———. *Sexual/Textual Politics: Feminist Literary Theory.* London: Methuen, 1985.

Mulvey, Laura. "Visual Pleasure and Narrative Cinema." *Screen* 16 (Autumn 1975): 6–18.

Newcomer, John. *Maria Edgeworth.* Lewisburg, Pa.: Bucknell University Press, 1973.

Newton, Judith L. *Women, Power, and Subversion: Social Strategies in British Fiction, 1778–1860.* Athens: University of Georgia Press, 1981.

Newton, Judith, and Deborah Rosenfelt, eds. *Feminist Criticism and Social Change: Sex, Class, and Race in Literature and Culture.* New York: Methuen, 1985.

Nussbaum, Felicity A. *The Autobiographical Subject: Gender and Ideology in Eighteenth-Century England.* Baltimore: Johns Hopkins University Press, 1989.

———. *The Brink of All We Hate: English Satires on Women, 1660–1750.* Lexington: University Press of Kentucky, 1984.

Nussbaum, Felicity, and Laura Brown, eds. *The New Eighteenth Century: Theory, Politics, English Literature.* New York: Methuen, 1987.

O'Donnell, Mary Ann. *Aphra Behn: An Annotated Bibliography of Primary and Secondary Sources.* New York: Garland, 1986.

Patterson, Emily. "Elizabeth Inchbald's Treatment of the Family and Pilgrimage in *A Simple Story.*" *Etudes Anglaise* 29 (1976): 196–98.

Paulson, Ronald. *Satire and the Novel in Eighteenth-Century England.* New Haven: Yale University Press, 1967.

Pearson, Jacqueline. *The Prostituted Muse: Images of Women and Women Dramatists, 1642–1737.* New York: St. Martin's Press, 1988.

Penley, Constance, ed. *Feminism and Film Theory.* New York: Routledge, London: BFI, 1988.

Perry, Ruth. *Women, Letters, and the Novel.* New York: AMS Press, 1980.

Richetti, John J. *Popular Fiction Before Richardson: Narrative Patterns, 1700–1739.* Oxford: Clarendon Press, 1969.

———. "Voice and Gender in Eighteenth-Century Fiction: Haywood to Burney." *Studies in the Novel* 19 (Fall 1987): 263–72.

Rogers, Katharine M., ed. *Before Their Time: Six Women Writers of the Eighteenth Century.* New York: Frederick Ungar, 1979.

———. *Feminism in Eighteenth-Century England.* Urbana: University of Illinois Press, 1982.

———. *Frances Burney: The World of 'Female Difficulties.'* New York: Harvester Wheatsheaf, 1990.

———. "Inhibitions on Eighteenth-Century Women Novelists: Elizabeth Inchbald and Charlotte Smith." *Eighteenth-Century Studies* 11 (Fall 1977): 63–78.

Rogers, Katharine M., and William McCarthy, eds. *Anthology of Early Women Writers: British Literary Women from Aphra Behn to Maria Edgeworth, 1660–1800.* New York: Meridian, 1987.

Rousseau, G. S., and Roy Porter, eds. *Sexual Underworlds of the Enlightenment.* Chapel Hill: University of North Carolina Press, 1988.

Salvaggio, Ruth. *Enlightened Absence: Neoclassical Configurations of the Feminine.* Urbana: University of Illinois Press, 1988.

Schofield, Mary Anne. *Eliza Haywood.* Boston: Twayne, 1985.

———. "Expose of the Popular Heroine: The Female Protagonists of Eliza Haywood." *Studies in Eighteenth-Century Culture* 12 (1983): 93–103.

———. *Masking and Unmasking the Female Mind: Disguising Romances in Feminine Fiction, 1713–1799.* Newark: University of Delaware Press, 1990.

———. *Quiet Rebellion: The Fictional Heroines of Eliza Fowler Haywood.* Washington, D.C.: University Press of America, 1982.

Schofield, Mary Anne, and Cecilia Macheski, eds. *Fetter'd or Free? British Women Novelists, 1670–1815.* Athens: Ohio University Press, 1986.

Scott, Sir Walter. *The Letters of Sir Walter Scott.* 12 vols. Ed. H. J. C. Grierson. London: Constable, 1932–37.

Sedgwick, Eve Kosofsky. *Between Men: English Literature and Male Homosocial Desire.* New York: Columbia University Press, 1985.

———. *The Coherence of Gothic Conventions.* New York: Methuen, 1980.

Sheridan, Frances. *Memoirs of Miss Sidney Bidulph.* 1761. Reprint. London: Pandora Press, 1987.

Showalter, Elaine. *A Literature of Their Own: British Women Novelists from Brontë to Lessing.* Princeton: Princeton University Press, 1977.

———, ed. *The New Feminist Criticism: Essays on Women, Literature, and Theory.* New York: Pantheon Books, 1985.

———, ed. *Speaking of Gender.* New York: Routledge, 1989.

Silverman, Kaja. *The Acoustic Mirror: The Female Voice in Psychoanalysis and Cinema.* Bloomington: Indiana University Press, 1988.

Simons, Judy. *Fanny Burney.* Totowa, N.J.: Barnes & Noble, 1987.

Smith, Charlotte. *Emmeline, The Orphan of the Castle.* 1788. Reprint. London: Pandora Press, 1988.

———. *The Old Manor House.* 1794. Reprint. London: Pandora Press, 1987.

Spacks, Patricia Meyer. *The Adolescent Idea: Myths of Youth and the Adult Imagination.* New York: Basic Books, 1981.

———. *Desire and Truth: Functions of Plot in Eighteenth-Century English Novels.* Chicago: University of Chicago Press, 1990.

———. "Ev'ry Woman Is at Heart a Rake." *Eighteenth-Century Studies* 8 (Fall 1974): 27–46.

———. *The Female Imagination.* New York: Alfred A. Knopf, 1975.

———. "Forgotten Genres." *Modern Language Studies* 18 (Winter 1988): 47–57.

———. *Imagining a Self: Autobiography and Novel in Eighteenth-Century England.* Cambridge: Harvard University Press, 1976.

Spencer, Jane. *The Rise of the Woman Novelist: From Aphra Behn to Jane Austen.* Oxford: Basil Blackwell, 1986.

Spender, Dale, ed. *Living by the Pen: Early British Women Writers.* New York: Teachers College Press, 1992.

Staten, Henry. *Wittgenstein and Derrida.* Lincoln: University of Nebraska Press, 1984.

Staves, Susan. "British Seduced Maidens." *Eighteenth-Century Studies* 14 (Winter 1980/81): 109–34.

———. *Married Women's Separate Property in England, 1660–1833.* Cambridge: Harvard University Press, 1990.

Steeves, Edna. "Pre-Feminism in Some Eighteenth-Century Novels." *Texas Quarterly* 16 (Autumn 1973): 48–57.

Stone, Lawrence. *The Family, Sex, and Marriage in England, 1500–1800.* New York: Harper & Row, 1977.

Straub, Kristina. *Divided Fictions: Fanny Burney and Feminine Strategy.* Lexington: University Press of Kentucky, 1987.

Suleiman, Susan R., and Inge Crosman, eds. *The Reader in the Text: Essays on Audience and Interpretation.* Princeton: Princeton University Press, 1980.

Todd, Janet. *Feminist Literary History.* New York: Routledge, 1988.

———, ed. *Men by Women.* New York: Holmes & Meier, 1981.

———. *The Sign of Angellica: Women, Writing and Fiction, 1660–1800.* New York: Columbia University Press, 1989.

———. *Women's Friendship in Literature.* New York: Columbia University Press, 1980.

Tomalin, Claire. *The Life and Death of Mary Wollstonecraft.* New York: Harcourt Brace Jovanovich, 1974.

Tompkins, J.M.S. *The Popular Novel in England, 1770–1800.* London: Constable, 1932. Reprint. Lincoln: University of Nebraska Press, 1961.

Van Ghent, Dorothy. *The English Novel: Form and Function.* New York: Holt, Rinehart, 1953.

Warner, William Beatty. "Social Power and the Eighteenth-Century Novel: Foucault and Transparent Literary History." *Eighteenth-Century Fiction* 3 (April 1991): 185–203.

Watt, Ian. *The Rise of the Novel: Studies in Defoe, Richardson and Fielding.* Berkeley and Los Angeles: University of California Press, 1957.

White, Eugene. *Fanny Burney, Novelist: A Study in Technique.* Hamden, Conn.: Shoestring Press, 1960.

Williams, Merryn. *Women in the English Novel, 1800–1900.* New York: St. Martin's Press, 1984.

Williamson, Marilyn L. *Raising Their Voices: British Women Writers, 1650–1750.* Detroit: Wayne State University Press, 1990.

Wollstonecraft, Mary. *Maria, or The Wrongs of Woman.* 1798. Reprint. Ed. Moira Ferguson. New York: W. W. Norton, 1975.

Woodward, Kathleen. "Youthfulness as a Masquerade." *Discourse* 11 (Fall–Winter 1988–89): 119–42.

Woolf, Virginia. *A Room of One's Own.* New York: Harcourt Brace Jovanovich, 1929.

———. *Three Guineas.* New York: Harcourt Brace Jovanovich, 1938.

Index

About Chinese Women, 15n.34, 108n.46
Accomplished Rake; or, Modern Fine Gentleman, The, 6, 172; female victimization in, 23–25, 34–50; plot outline of, 37–40; role reversal in, 65; sexual "fires" in, 48
Addison, Joseph, 79, 171
Adventures of David Simple, The, 13
aggression, of feminine heroines, 10–11
anti-masquerade writers, 1–3, 171–73
approach-avoidance behavior, in *A Simple Story,* 110–12
Atkinson, Colin and Jo, 172n.15
Austen, Jane, 15–16

Backscheider, Paula R., 20n.47, 80n.9, 151n.49
Bakhtin, Mikhail, 2
Ballaster, Ros, 10n.22
banishment, of female, in *Fantomina,* 67–68, 72–73
Barbauld, Anna Letitia, 125
Barker, Jane, 11
Bataille, Georges, 86n.19
Behn, Aphra: *The Dumb Virgin,* 23–35; *The Fair Jilt,* 10–11; female sexuality discussed by, 6–8; fetishism and, 31–34; *The History of the Nun; or, The Fair Vow-Breaker,* 10–11; incest as theme of, 32–34; Inchbald compared with, 87–88; male hero as predator for, 8–9; masquerade scene in, 31–32; *The Nun; or, The Perjur'd Beauty,* 9; Oedipal conflict as theme of, 6, 28–34; victimization of female and, 23–35, 172. See also *The Dumb Virgin*
Belinda, 164–68, 172–73
Berger, John, 146
binary opposition: in *Fantomina,* 64–65; patriarchal systems and, 78–82, 171–72; in *The Wanderer,* 129–30
Blackwood's Magazine, 125
British Recluse, The, 9, 11
Brontë, Charlotte, 99–100
Brooke, Frances, 12
Brown, Laura, 6
Browne, Alice, 79
Brunton, Mary: *Discipline,* 168–71; *Self-Control,* 12
Burney, Frances (Madame d'Arblay), 3–4, 17–19; *Camilla,* 88; *Cecilia,* 3–4; critical failure of *The Wanderer* of, 123–26; *Evelina,* 17–18, 88–89; excessive techniques of, in *The Wanderer,* 127–62; familiarity with Edgeworth's work, 166–67; lover-mentor device used by, 88–89; "modest femininity," ideology of, 7–8. See also *The Wanderer*
Butler, Marilyn, 165
Byron, Lord (George Gordon), 125

Camilla, 88
carnival. *See* masquerade
carnivalesque, the. *See* Bakhtin, Mikhail
Castle, Terry: *Cecilia* discussed by, 3–4, 158; cultural history of masquerade, treatment of, 2–6; disappearance of masquerade as literary device, description of, 173; female cross-dressing at masquerades, theories of, 43–44;

on masquerade as resistance to patriarchy, 24–25, 52–53; *A Simple Story* discussed by, 75–77, 87. See also *Masquerade and Civilization*
castration complex: in *The Dumb Virgin,* 28–34; Lacanian theory of, 26–27; role of, in *The Accomplished Rake,* 41–42; in *A Simple Story,* 104–6; in *The Wanderer,* 143–44. *See also* feminization of heroes; self-destructive behavior
Catholic Church: patriarchal system and, 82; tolerance of masquerade in, 2n.3. *See also* Jesuits; priesthood
Catholic Relief Acts, 84
Cecilia, 3–4
chastity, as motif in *A Simple Story,* 84–86
City Jilt; or, The Alderman Turn'd Beau, The, 10–11, 68–73
Cixous, Hélène: on female sexuality, 35–36; patriarchal systems discussed by, 78
Clarissa, 21, 152
class structure: masquerade as threat to, 2; sexuality and, 47n.45, 62n.21
Clément, Catherine, 35–36, 82–83, 146n.42, 152
commodification of women: as device in Burney's *The Wanderer,* 155–60; in Haywood's work, 69–73; in Inchbald's *A Simple Story,* 88–103
compression technique, in *A Simple Story,* 6
Croker, John Wilson, 123–24, 162
cross-dressing. *See* transvestism
Cutting-Gray, Joanne, 129n.18, 132n.21, 133n.22

Davis, Lennard, 50, 55n.12
Davys, Mary: *The Accomplished Rake,* 6, 172; doubling technique used by, 37–40; female sexuality discussed by, 6–8; female victimization discussed by, 23–25, 34–50; incest as theme of, 37–40, 46–50; lover-mentor as device used by, 88–89; male hero as predator for, 9–10; Oedipal conflict as theme of, 35–50; *The Reform'd Coquet,* 88; role reversal in, 65; sexual "fires" in, 48; transvestism as device of, 42–47. See also *The Accomplished Rake*
" 'Descending Angels': Salubrious Sluts and Pretty Prostitutes in Haywood's Fiction," 70–71
Desire and Truth: Functions of Plot in Eighteenth-Century English Novels, 8, 14n.33, 76n.3
Desire to Desire: The Woman's Film of the 1940s, The, 61n.16
Discipline, 168–71
Doane, Mary Ann: on the effects of mimicry, 61n.16; on the filmic aspects of masquerade, 28n.15, 29n.19, 60–61; on masquerade as compensation, 54–55; on masquerade as survival tool, 147–49; on the mother's role in the family, 29; on phallocentrism, 25, 27; on role reversal, 65–66
Doody, Margaret Anne, 133n.23, 137n.28; analysis of *The Wanderer* by, 125, 140n.33, 148, 150n.47, 154n.54
Dumb Virgin; or, The Force of Imagination, The: female victimization in, 23–35, 172; masquerade scene in, 31–32; Oedipal conflict in, 6, 28–34; plot outline of, 28–30; psychological reading of, 28–34; *A Simple Story* compared with, 87–88

Edgeworth, Maria: *Belinda,* 164–68, 172–73; father's influence on, 164–65; letter to Inchbald by, 78n.4
Edgeworth, Richard Lovell, 164–65
Edinburgh Review, 124–25
education, as reaffirmation of patriarchal system, 116–17
Eighteenth-Century Feminist Mind, The, 79
Eloisa to Abelard, 104
Emmeline, The Orphan of the Castle, 20–21
empowerment of women: in *The City Jilt,* 68–73; in *Fantomina,* 61–68; female sexuality and, 88n.22; masquerade as device for, 3–4; role reversal ineffective for, 160–62; in *A Simple Story,* 76n.3. *See also* female sexuality; patriarchal system
Epstein, Julia, 124n.4, 125, 130–32
Etherege, George, 67n.30
Evans, Caroline, 27–28, 71n.37
Evelina, 17–18, 88–89
"Ev'ry Woman Is at Heart a Rake," 24, 78–79, 138

Fair Jilt, The, 10–11
Fair Vow-Breaker, The. See *History of the Nun*
Fantomina: or, Love in a Maze, 10–11, 53; banishment of female in, 67–68, 72–73; binary opposition in, 64–65; empowerment as theme in, 61–68; female friendship in, 72–73; fetishism in, 66–67; patriarchal system threatened in, 65–68; *A Simple Story* compared with, 87–88

fashion, eighteenth-century masquerade and, 71n.37
"Fashion, Representation, Femininity," 71n.37
father-daughter relationships: examples of, in late eighteenth-century literature, 14–21; femininity and, 6; nineteenth-century women writers and, 164–66; in *A Simple Story*, 76–121. *See also* law of the father; Oedipal conflict; patriarchal system
father-son relationships, *A Simple Story* and, 112–15
Felman, Shoshana, 27, 28n.15
Female Advocate; or, An Attempt to Recover the Rights of Women from Male Usurpation, The, 126
"Female Grotesques: Carnival and Theory," 152n.51
Female Quixote, The, 13
"female rakes," as compensation for predatory males, 10–11, 13n.31
female sexuality: characterization of Elinor, in *The Wanderer*, 135–42; in *The City Jilt*, 69–73; class structure and, 47n.45, 62n.21; depicted as submission, 14; as device in *Belinda*, 164–68; in *The Dumb Virgin*, 6–8, 32–36; empowerment and, 88n.22; equated with male sexuality, 10; in *Fantomina*, 62–68; Freud on, 41–42; high cost of, 24; Irigaray's discussion of, 35–36, 44n.42, 45–46, 54, 88n.22; masquerade and, 8, 24, 44–45, 54–59, 63–68; moralization/sentimentalization of, 11–12; in Restoration and early eighteenth-century fiction, 9–11; sexual blankness, in *The Wanderer*, 138–41, 143–44
femininity: masquerade as condition of, 51–73, 61n.17, 87–88, 142–62; as mirror of masculinity, 21–22
feminization of heroes, 12–13; examples of, 15–16, 19–21; Rushbrook in *A Simple Story*, 118–20
fetishism: in *The Dumb Virgin*, 31–34; in *Fantomina*, 66–67; in *The Masqueraders*, 55–56, 58; in *A Simple Story*, 107–10
Fielding, Henry, 1–3, 171–73
Fielding, Sarah, 13
"Film and the Masquerade: Theorising the Female Spectator," 60, 147–48
financial independence, Juliet's search for, in *The Wanderer*, 127–30
Freud, Sigmund, 107–8; on female sexuality, 41–42; *"fort-da"* play, 107n.43
Gardiner, Judith Kegan, 34
gender formation, parent/child relationships and, 6
Godwin, William, 161, 163
Griffith, Elizabeth, 12
guardian/ward relationships, 76–121. *See also* patriarchal system

Harden, Elizabeth, 164, 167n.9
Hays, Mary, 16–17, 77
Haywood, Eliza: *The British Recluse*, 9, 11; *The City Jilt*, 10–11, 68–73; equation of male-female sexuality by, 10; *Fantomina*, 61–73; female sexuality discussed by, 7–8; *The History of Miss Betsy Thoughtless*, 13n.31; male hero as predator for, 9; masquerade of femininity and, 51–73; masquerade as submission for, 55–59; *The Masqueraders*, 10, 53, 55–59, 68, 87–88, 172. *See also* specific works
Hazlitt, William, 124–25
Heath, Stephen, 62n.19, 66–67, 143
Hegelian dialectic, in *The Wanderer*, 129n.18
Heidegger, John James ("Count"), 2
heroes, conflation of good/bad, in *The Wanderer*, 140–42. *See also* feminization of heroes
heterosexuality: as commodity exchange in *The City Jilt*, 69–73; masquerade and, 44–45
History of Emily Montague, The, 12
History of Miss Betsy Thoughtless, The, 13n.31
History of the Nun; or, The Fair Vow-Breaker, The, 10–11
homosocial relationships, 44–45, 69
Hunter, J. Paul, 8
hysteria, in *A Simple Story*, 115–16; in *The Wanderer*, 150–52

ideology, in novels, 55n.12
incest: in *The Accomplished Rake*, 37–40, 46–50; castration complex and, 26–27; in *The Dumb Virgin*, 32–34; in *A Simple Story*, 89; in *The Wanderer*, 140
Inchbald, Elizabeth: Catholicism of, 84; modest femininity, ideology of, 7–8; *A Simple Story*, 75–121; use of textual silence by, 77–78. See also *A Simple Story*
International Journal of Psychoanalysis, The, 51
Irigaray, Luce: on the "blanks" in discourse, 77; construction of femininity described by, 25, 29, 156n.55; female sexuality discussed by, 35–36, 54, 88n.22; on heterosexuality, 44n.42, 45–46, 69; on hysteria, 115–16; mimicry, con-

cept of, 60–61; mirror motif discussed by, 46n.44, 90–92; obsession with pain critiqued by, 103n.37; Oedipal conflict discussed by, 17–18, 114n.54, 118; patriarchal system described by, 113; on role reversal and women's seizure of power, 82, 161; women as commodities for, 90, 93–96. *See also* specific works
Iron Pen: Frances Burney and the Politics of Women's Writing, The, 130–31
Italian, The, 77

Jesuits (Society of Jesus), 84–86, 92
Johnston, Claire, 163–64
jouissance, 15, 39–40, 108n.46, 170

Kelly, Gary, 111n.52
Kowaleski-Wallace, Elizabeth, 165–66, 169n.11
Kristeva, Julia, 14–15, 108n.46

Lacan, Jacques, 14n.33, 53, 110n.51; mirror stage and castration complex, theories of, 25–28, 90
Lady Julia Mandeville, 12
Lady Juliana Harley, 12
language, lost access to, in *A Simple Story,* 99–103, 105–8, 115–16
laughter as threat to patriarchal system: in French feminist theory, 36; in *A Simple Story,* 81–83, 85–86; in *The Wanderer,* 135
law, as love, male domination and, 14–15, 103–21
law of the father: in *The Accomplished Rake,* 46–47; in *The Dumb Virgin,* 32–34; in late eighteenth-century literature, 14–21; in *A Simple Story,* 103–21; theories regarding, 14–15, 26. *See also* father-daughter relationships; patriarchal system
Lennox, Charlotte, 13
lesbianism, gesture toward, in *The City Jilt,* 72–73
letters: in *A Simple Story,* 99–100, 136n.26; in *The Wanderer,* 136n.26
Love Intrigues: Or, The History of the Amours of Bosvil and Galesia, 11
love plot: in *A Simple Story,* 83, 102–3; in women's fiction, 10–11
lover-mentor, as device in *A Simple Story,* 88–103
Luke, Jennifer, 62n.21

male critics, criticism of women writers by, 123–26
male impersonation. *See* transvestism
male sexuality: as domination, feminine subversion of, 23n.1; manipulation of, in *The City Jilt,* 69–73; as preference for law over love, 14–15, 103–21
male writers, fear of masquerade among, 1–3, 171–73
Man of Mode, The, 67n.30
Manvell, Roger, 84
Maria, or The Wrongs of Woman, 11, 77, 79–80, 101n.35, 126n.13
market imagery, women as commodities and, 69–72, 93–98, 155–59
marriage paradigm: in *The Accomplished Rake,* 48–50; in *A Simple Story,* 94–98, 101–3
masked assembly. *See* masquerade
Masking and Unmasking the Female Mind: Disguising Romances in Feminine Fiction, 4–5
masquerade: in *The Accomplished Rake,* 42–50; as arena for female loss, 56–57; in *Belinda,* 166–68; competing theories of, 51–55, 60–61; cultural history of, 1–7; decline in use of, in nineteenth-century fiction, 173; in *Discipline,* 168–71; in *The Dumb Virgin,* 31–34; female vs. male, 4–5; femininity as, 51–73; filmic aspects of, 60–61; freedoms offered by, 1–3, 24–25; ideological symbolism of, 57–58; psychological double-sidedness of, 6, 53, 171–73; religious symbolism in, 59; in *A Simple Story,* 87–88; as subversion, 2–3; as survival tool, in *The Wanderer,* 138–62
Masquerade and Civilization: The Carnivalesque in Eighteenth-Century English Culture and Fiction: Cecilia discussed in, 3–4; cultural history of masquerade in, 2–6; female sexual freedom and masquerade discussed in, 2–3, 24–25; masquerade as resistance to patriarchy in, 52–53; *A Simple Story* discussed in, 75–76
Masquerade, A Poem. Inscribed to C—T H—D—G—R, The, 1–2
"Masquerade Reconsidered: Further Thoughts on the Female Spectator," 66n.27, 148–49
Masqueraders: or, Fatal Curiosity, The, 53, 55–59, 68, 172; equation of male-female sexuality in, 10; *A Simple Story* compared with, 87–88
McMaster, Juliet, 137n.27

Memoirs of Emma Courtney, 16–17, 77
Memoirs of Miss Sidney Bidulph, 19–21
Men by Women, 12
Miller, Nancy K., 21
mimicry, 60–61, 171–73; in *Fantomina,* 63–68; in *The Wanderer,* 6, 126
mirror as literary device: in *The Dumb Virgin,* 28–34; in *A Simple Story,* 88–103; in *The Wanderer,* 139–41, 146–62
mirror stage, Lacanian theory of, 26, 90
Montrelay, Michèle, 66n.29
More, Hannah, 116–17
mother: in *Fantomina,* 72; in *A Simple Story,* 77, 101–3, 107–21; and son, relationships with, 6, 29–30, 35–40, 46–50
Mysteries of Udolpho, 77

names and naming, as an issue in *The Wanderer,* 127–42, 158–60
New Eighteenth Century: Theory, Politics, English Literature, The, 6
nightmare of repetition, in *The Wanderer,* 128n.17
Normanby, Lord, 125
Northanger Abbey, 15–16
Nun; or, The Perjur'd Beauty, The, 9
Nussbaum, Felicity A., 6, 44, 50n.51

occupations for women, limitations of, 127–28
Oedipal conflict: in *The Accomplished Rake,* 35–50; in *The Dumb Virgin,* 6, 28–34; in father-daughter relationships, 14–21; Lacanian treatment of, 26–27; in *A Simple Story,* 107–21; in *The Wanderer,* 136–37
Old Manor House, The, 12–13

pain, obsession with, 103n.37
passive behavior, in late eighteenth-century heroines, 11–12
patriarchal system: challenge to, in *Discipline,* 169–71; challenges to, in *The Wanderer,* 130–42, 154–62; conformity to, by women novelists, 21–22, 55, 173–74; depicted in *The City Jilt,* 68–73; disruption of, and capitulation to, in *A Simple Story,* 76–121; father-daughter relationships and, 20–21; in late eighteenth-century women's novels, 14–15; male relations in, 105–7; masquerade as resistance to, 52–53; masquerade as threat to, 2–3, 171; military, religious, and civil triumvirate, in *The Wanderer,* 157; reaffirmation of, in Davys's and Behn's novels, 23–25, 49–50; threat to, in *Fantomina,* 60–68
phallocentrism: in *The Accomplished Rake,* 35–50; in *The Dumb Virgin,* 28–34; of Lacanian theory, 27–28; in *A Simple Story,* 105–10
Pope, Alexander, 104
possession, of women, as paradigm in *The Wanderer,* 139–42. *See also* commodification of women
priesthood, role of, in *A Simple Story,* 83–86
primal scene, role of, in *The Accomplished Rake,* 38–40
prostitution, in *The City Jilt,* 70–71
Provoked Husband, The, 143
psychoanalytic theory: gender identity and, 6–7; phallocentrism of, 27–28
punk fashion, eighteenth-century masquerade and, 71n.37

Quarterly Review, 123–24

Rabelais and His World, 2
Radcliffe, Ann, 14n.33, 77
Radcliffe, Mary Anne, 126
rape, seduction as, 59
Reform'd Coquet, The, 88
repetition, as device in *The Wanderer,* 128
Richardson, Samuel, 8, 21
Rise of the Woman Novelist: From Aphra Behn to Jane Austen, The, 7–8, 86n.19, 88–89
Riviere, Joan, 51, 54, 62nn.19–20, 66
Rogers, Katharine M., 12–13, 80n.9, 159n.60; on women's education, 117n.56
role reversal: in *Fantomina,* 65–66; female characters' aggression as, 10–11; in *The Wanderer,* 160–62
Roman Catholicism. *See* Catholic Church
romantic love, in *The Accomplished Rake,* 48–50
Russo, Mary, 152n.51

Schofield, Mary Anne, 4–5; analysis of *The Accomplished Rake,* 48n.47; analysis of *Fantomina,* 67nn.30–31; on *The City Jilt,* 70–71; on ideological symbolism of masquerade, 57n.13
scopophilia. *See* spectatorship; voyeurism
Scott, Sir Walter, 125
Self-Control, 12

self-destructive behavior, 20n.47; as motif in *The Wanderer,* 145–47, 149–60
Sentimental Journey, A, 155
sexual blankness, in *The Wanderer,* 138–41, 143–44
sexual perversion, in *The Wanderer,* 153–54
sexuality, class structure and, 47n.45, 62n.21. *See also* female sexuality; male sexuality
Sheridan, Frances, 19–21
sibling rivalry, in *The Dumb Virgin,* 32–34
Sign of Angellica, The, 8
Silverman, Kaja, 25, 31–32, 100–101
Simons, Judy, 129n.18
Simple Story, A, 75–121, 172; Catholicism in, 83–86; discontinuity of text in, 96n.30; fainting scene in, 110–12; familial conflicts in, 14–18; father/daughter union explored in, 6, 107–21; irony in, 98; lover-mentor device in, 88–103; structural symmetry of, 103n.38
sleepiness, as literary device, 58n.14
Smith, Charlotte, 12–13, 20–21
"Sorties: Out and Out: Attacks/Ways Out/ Forays," 78
Spacks, Patricia Meyer, 76n.3; on female sexuality, 8, 24, 138; patriarchal systems discussed by, 14n.33, 78–79; on *A Simple Story,* 111n.52; on *The Wanderer,* 125
spectacle, woman as, 172–73; in *Cecilia,* 3–4; in *Fantomina,* 61–62; in *The Masqueraders,* 55–56; in *The Wanderer,* 146–47, 152–53
Spectator, The, 79, 144n.39, 171
spectatorship, 55–57. *See also* voyeurism
Speculum of the Other Woman, 91–92
Spencer, Jane, 7–8; on feminization of heroes, 12; on mother-daughter relationships, 14n.33; on reform of heroine by lover-mentor, 88–89; on use of textual silence, 78n.4; on women's education, 117n.56
Steele, Richard, 144n.39
Sterne, Laurence, 155
Straub, Kristina, 125, 143n.35, 159n.60, 160nn.62–63
submission of women, masquerade as device for, 3–4, 54–59; in *A Simple Story,* 87–88
subversion, masquerade as, of patriarchy, 2–3; in *Fantomina,* 60–68
suicide, as literary device in *The Wanderer,* 128–29, 137, 146–54
Summers, Montague, 28

textual silence, in Inchbald's work, 77–78
Their Fathers' Daughters, 165–66, 169n.11
This Sex Which Is Not One, 35n.29
Thornton, Minna, 27–28, 71n.37
Todd, Janet, 8, 12
Tomalin, Claire, 129n.18
transvestism, 42–47, 53, 106, 149–50, 172–73

uncanny, the, 41–42

Villette, 99–100
Vindication of the Rights of Woman, A, 126, 161–62
virtue, women as standard of, 11–12, 78–81
voyeurism: in *The Accomplished Rake,* 38–40; in *Cecilia,* 3–4; in *Fantomina,* 66–67; masquerade and, 52–53, 60; in *The Masqueraders,* 55–56, 58; in *The Wanderer,* 146–47, 153

Waddington, Mary, 125
Wanderer; or, Female Difficulties, The: characterization of Elinor in, 130, 134–42, 146–62; critical failure of, 123–26; excessive techniques in, 127–62; fairy-tale ending of, 158–60; father-daughter relationships in, 17–19; feminization of heroes in, 19n.45; masquerade as survival tool in, 138–62; names and naming as issue in, 127–42, 158–60; sexual and class distinctions in, 62n.21; transvestism in, 172–73
Ways of Seeing, 146
West, Jane, 116
Williamson, Marilyn L., 34n.27
witch metaphor, in *The Wanderer,* 151–53
Wollstonecraft, Mary: *Maria, or The Wrongs of Woman,* 11, 77, 79–80, 101n.35, 126n.13; *A Vindication of the Rights of Woman,* 126, 161–62
"Woman's Influence," 20n.47
"Women on the Market," 93–94
women's fiction, mid-eighteenth-century shift in, 7–22
"World Upside-Down," 2–3, 173–74

Zimmern, Helen, 164